WEDDINGS

Southern Style

WEDDINGS

Southern Style

Beverly Reese Church

Text by Lisa Ruffin Harrison

Principal Photography

by Fran Brennan

Abbeville Press Publishers
New York London Paris

Editor: Jacqueline Decter
Project Coordinator: Amanda Adams
Designer: Molly Shields
Computer Consultant: Laura Lindgren
Copy Chief: Robin James
Copy Editor: Amy Handy
Production Supervisor: Hope Koturo

First edition

Illustrations on pages 223, 224, and 228
by Hélène Maumy Florescu.

Library of Congress Cataloging-in-
Publication Data

Church, Beverly Reese.
Weddings southern style/by Beverly
Reese Church; text by Lisa Ruffin
Harrison; principal photography by Fran
Brennan.
     p.   cm.
Includes bibliographical references
(p.   ) and index.
ISBN 1-55859-290-3
1. Weddings—Southern States—
Planning. I. Church, Beverly Reese. II.
Title.
HQ745.H23 1992   92-34905
395'.22—dc20   CIP

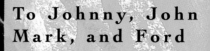

To Johnny, John Mark, and Ford

Jacket front: This bride and her children attendants are dressed in Pat Kerr designs.

Jacket back: Top row, left: Flower arrangements should always be in keeping with the ceremony site (see p. 136). Top row, center: Caterers prefer to use the local seasonal bounty for wedding fare. Top row, right: At this reception in the Texas Hill Country, wedding cake, coffee, and champagne were served in a rustic setting (see p. 200). Middle row, left: Clear tents trimmed with tiny lights created a dreamy atmosphere at this rehearsal dinner in Tulsa (see p. 70). Middle row, center: In keeping with this Mobile bride's vintage dress, her children attendants carried old-fashioned wedding hoops (see p. 42). Middle row, right: Some ideas for decorating rehearsal dinner tables: a hand-painted tablecloth, napkin rings featuring framed pictures of the bride and groom as children, and favor boxes filled with chocolates (see p. 88). Bottom row, left: A bottle of champagne decorated with flowers and an antique silver chalice combine to make a romantic wedding gift (see p. 93). Bottom row, center: For a formal engagement party at home, greet guests with champagne on a colorfully decorated table (see p. 31). Bottom row, right: During a reception at Evelynton Plantation in Virginia, children were entertained by the donkeys that roam the grounds (see p. 39).

Half-title page: Two of the children attendants at a plantation wedding near Mobile.

Frontispiece: The south lawn at Longue Vue, a historic house on the outskirts of New Orleans, provided a graceful setting for this rehearsal dinner. SCHERMAN

Copyright page: Oak Alley, a plantation in Louisiana, is a favorite site for Southern weddings. CHENN

Contents

A History of
Southern Weddings

"Always Ask Me Twice..."

*T*he South has always been a country within a country, with no passport required save good manners and a ready smile. Even now, nearly half a century after the great watering down that followed World War II and 125 years after the divisiveness of the Civil War, there is still a Southern vernacular, a bone-deep ethic that has somehow eluded the homogenizing effects of television, inexpensive travel, and corporate transfers.

Opposite: Stanton Hall, an antebellum plantation in Natchez, Mississippi, is now the site of many weddings. SCHEMMEL

Right: Weddings offer a chance to use family heirlooms that have been passed down from generation to generation. You might save the blooms from all the wedding party flowers and make your own potpourri. SALL

Some things have changed, to be sure, but the change has taken its time. For whatever reason, the South has been in no hurry to be assimilated. It frankly likes its separateness; it always has. And nowhere is that separateness, that distinctive essence, so resonant as in the weddings of the South.

As the fulfillment of a dream—the daydreams of a little girl, the aspirations of a young man, the well-meaning wishes parents have for their children—the wedding is perhaps the single most telling institution of a culture. Like birth and death, the wedding is a rite of passage that comes complete with its own alphabet of traditions and historical associations. And yet, at the same time it offers two people a blank slate on which they can make their own distinctive marks. Those scribblings, at times hesitant and waffling, at times quite emphatic, ultimately become a portrait, not only of a bride and groom, but also of a society and its times.

Those times may have changed a good deal since the days when Southern belles held sway, but as the expression goes, *plus ça change, plus ça reste la même chose.* I doubt there are many young Southern girls who still adhere to the antebellum etiquette of turning down proposals at least twice. But old habits die hard; marriage proposals may be less coyly dealt with nowadays, yet the peculiar Southern

9

Maria Ward Skelton Williams Sheerin in her wedding dress of satin and lace, 1920s. The horseshoe on the mantel symbolizes good luck.

tendency to say no one or two times before finally acquiescing is still very much around. I can't help thinking of Maria Ward Skelton Williams Sheerin—a notable Virginian who married in Richmond in the 1920s. She used to make fun of Southern coquetry. But in the next breath, she would insist, "Always ask me twice. No matter what it's for . . . even if it's just for a glass of sherry."

First and Foremost: Family and Friends

It would be a little too academic to try and neatly categorize what today's Southern weddings are all about; they are as varied as Southern people and their personal styles. Yet they still carry around an amazing amount of baggage from their colonial beginnings: a romanticization of the bride, strong religious underpinnings, no lack of theater in staging the reception, and old-world hospitality that seizes the occasion to celebrate not only the union of the bride and groom but also the homecoming of family and good friends. There is a frank acknowledgment in Southern weddings—from the announcement of the engagement to the tossing of the bouquet—that the whole affair is indeed a big event, a joyous occasion for good friends and family, always lots of family.

When a Southern family announces the engagement of a daughter, the wheels of community and extended family begin to turn. Engagement rituals and wedding traditions deeply entrenched in Southern history are rediscovered and reinvented, giving the occasion its own special character and scope. Whether it's held in an exclusive club in Atlanta, on a sprawling Texas ranch, in the mountains of North Carolina, on a historic Virginia plantation, or on the Florida seashore, the event is invariably marked by genuine familial affection, generous hospitality, customs, and traditions that reflect a Southern state of mind. Even the most superficial look at the social footprints of our ancestors offers up evidence as to why Southern weddings still bear their distinctive marks.

From Colonist to Cavalier to Confederate

From the moment Jamestown was established in 1607, two principal elements wedged control over the complexion of the South: it was rural, and it was English. For three hundred years, the South remained principally an agricultural belt; fertile, river-nourished lands, heavily timbered forests, and a temperate climate that ensured long growing seasons all combined in an irresistible lure for Englishmen seeking more favorable economic opportunities.

The tobacco and rice plantations—and later, cotton and sugar—that sprang up in this environment would become the cornerstone of the Southern states' economy. Wealthy planters ruled their vast, self-supporting acreage as latter-day feudal lords. The most prominent plantations fronted on the river, and had their own wharfs for direct import and export. Since, in effect, the plantation

The Wedding *by Clementine Hunter, 1955.*

was its own commercial marketplace, there was no particular need for trading centers. And without the township mentality that grew up in the North, Southerners really had no choice but to look inward, to the household and the family, for social definition.

Mail-Order Brides

The New England of the seventeenth century, with its own geography and climate, and its Puritan roots, urbanized and industrialized quickly. It was populated by a massive immigration of nuclear families from all over Europe. But in the rural colonial South, the feudal life of the plantation attracted single men. Southern society began with a ratio of six men to every woman. There was such a scarcity of women in those early decades that they were actually imported.

The struggle of the early colonial period fostered a tradition of early marriages for women, who often wed before their sixteenth birthday. Further, disease, immature child-bearing and labor-intensive lifestyles took a far grimmer toll in the South than in the Northern colonies. As one early

writer put it, "The reaper was forever busy trying to separate husband and wife," and succeeded so regularly that second and third marriages were very much the order of the day. The resulting extended families gave the populations of the South a distinctive skew, often littering the wedding ceremony with multiple mothers and fathers, stepsisters and -brothers—not unlike the familial landscape of today, although today's complicated family configuration is more often the result of divorce than of death.

Etiquette and Ethic: A Burgeoning Southern Style

Weddings in the early seventeenth century were rather plain, but as the century progressed and slipped into the next, the sexual populations evened out, and customs of courtship and marriage settled into distinctly Southern patterns. The Anglican character of the Southern colonies had much to do with the shaping of their

pastimes and diversions. Although a Scotch-Irish presence colored the Western frontier fringe, and the French and Spanish influences in Louisiana forged their own identity, most of the eighteenth-century South spoke with a distinctly English accent—and an upper class accent at that. It's true that after the British Civil War, many Cavaliers, having Royalist rather than Parliamentary sympathies, did indeed come to the newly settled South to make a new life, but whether the majority of Southern planters were as blue-blooded as they themselves thought is an issue that is hotly debated even today. Given their own perception, however, it's not surprising that the beau ideal of most Southerners was indeed the landed gentry back home; modified by slavery, the English class system was adopted whole hog, and along with it, the genteel lifestyle of the country squire.

Without the cultural opportunities of Northern cities, Southern colonists had to rely on visiting, dinner parties, hunts and splendid balls to amuse themselves. Dropping by was not a practical option because of the distances between plantations, so it was sensible for guests to plan on staying several days or weeks when attending an event. But, always anxious for an opportunity to enliven her lonely, often burdensome existence, the plantation mistress was ready to

Opposite: Fleet wedding, 1747. English pageantry was in evidence even at these unsavory marriages. But Southerners aspired to more aristocratic English traditions.

Below: The wedding dress featured in Godey's Lady's Book and Magazine, *December 1874.*

receive guests at any moment, even without an invitation. The element of Cavalier blood, whether real or imagined, the pleasant climate and abundant food, and, of course, the institution of slave labor all combined to create a sense of unbounded hospitality that was lacking in the North, with its restaurants and theater and opera.

Wedding Belles

Instinctive occasionalists, Southerners managed to wrest some measure of merriment even from funerals, so it's little wonder their weddings were practically unrestrained. In densely populated cities such as Boston, Philadelphia, or New York, the social calendar was likely to be crammed with important dates, but in the agrarian South, a wedding was more often than not the social event of the season. Far more was made of the event than in Puritan New England, where the marriage ceremony was a quiet affair. It is said that

An Event to Be Remembered

And, apropos of weddings, an old-fashioned Virginia wedding was an event to be remembered. The preparations usually commenced some time before with saving eggs, butter, chickens, etc.; after which ensued the liveliest egg-beating, butter-creaming, raisin-stoning, sugar-pounding, cake-icing, salad-chopping, coconut-grating, lemon-squeezing, egg-frothing, wafer-making, pastry-baking, jelly-straining, paper-cutting, silver-cleaning, floor-rubbing, dress-making, hair-curling, lace-washing, ruffle-crimping, tarlatan-smoothing, trunk-moving—guests arriving, servants running, girls laughing!

Imagine all this going on simultaneously for several successive days and nights, and you have an idea of "preparations" for an old-fashioned Virginia wedding.

—from *A Girl's Life in Virginia Before the War* by Letitia M. Burwell, 1895

after the ceremony, manor houses fairly rocked with merrymaking that often went on for days; after all, guests had negotiated several days' traveling by carriage or boat just to be there, and were in no hurry to cut the reveling short. And typically, eighteenth-century Southerners still trained their eyes on England, where the long wedding celebration reached its culmination. One recorded marriage among British aristocracy is said to have spun out for a solid month of fishing and hunting, fireworks, gaming, and feasting on a Bacchanalian scale.

Cornucopic presentations of food and drink were followed by endless rounds of dancing, and special effects were not unusual; perhaps because they were so rarely treated to the spectacle of urban theater, Southerners learned to create their own. It is said that at one wedding party servants actually gathered spiders and released them to spin webs all over the yard; then, just prior to the party, they sprinkled them with gold dust, creating a spectacular gilded canopy for bride and groom.

Since land ownership was the primary means of wealth and political influence, the dynasty syndrome was intrinsic to the South. Marriage among

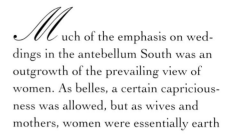

Flightiness and flirtations were checked at the altar in exchange for a life marked by virtue, modesty, piety, and, above all, devotion to family.

cousins may have been prevalent because of the sparse rural populations, but it was also a convenient means to a bigger bottom line. Keeping it all in the family was a way of life. And although belles generally preferred to choose the mate of their dreams, marriages were frequently arranged.

From Maiden to Mistress

*M*uch of the emphasis on weddings in the antebellum South was an outgrowth of the prevailing view of women. As belles, a certain capriciousness was allowed, but as wives and mothers, women were essentially earth

angels: pious, pure, and very much on a pedestal.

The pinnacle of a woman's life was her marriage and motherhood, with dim prospects at best for old maids. Young girls looked forward to being belles, one of the few windows of real freedom they would enjoy during their lifetimes. With spinsterhood staring them in the face by age twenty, maidens were often little more than misses when they married, taking on a lot of responsibility and sheer physical labor that history books have buried in their haste to perpetuate the myth of the Southern belle. While her husband may indeed have supervised the cash crop on the plantation, the mistress was the domestic engineer, managing all food and clothing pro-

duction for family and slaves, the dairy, garden, and smokehouse (complete with hog slaughtering and dressing), the relentless chore of soap and candlemaking, and, of course, child rearing. It has often been noted by calculating historians that Southern white women were in fact the slaves of slavery.

While the close of the Civil War marked the crumbling of the planter's way of life, it did not radically alter the traditional roles of wife and mother. Certainly, the suffragettes marched into the new century, and World War II catapulted women into the work force, but it was only a decade later that independence for Southern women seemed once again a spectral dream, as stereotypical 1950s role

Above: Marriage of a soldier at Vicksburg, performed by Chaplain Warren of the Freedmen's Bureau, 1866.

Left: A wedding couple, drawn by Alan Rodolph Waud, 1871.

models separated the genders with definitive parameters.

On the brink of the twenty-first century, the ideals of Southern women have gone through the ringer, particularly as regards unfashionable concepts like submissiveness. And yet certain characteristics—familial devotion, driving capability, old-fashioned good manners, and an inability not to be hospitable—still persist. Not sur-

Southern Wedding Customs: Then and Now

Racing for the bottle In Virginia's Shenandoah Valley during colonial times, wedding ceremonies were often performed at the minister's house rather than in church. After the ceremony, the wedding party made its way to the bride's house for the reception. About a mile away from their destination, the groomsmen let loose with a chorus of shouts signaling a race for

This lush garland of smilax, English ivy, flowers, and French ribbon decorating a bridal bed is an updated version of the ciel de lit, *or bridal canopy. Especially popular in the New Orleans area, the* ciel de lit *offered a touch of glamour to newlyweds, who rarely took a proper honeymoon.*

the bottle, at which all the young men in the party took off at full gallop for the bride's front door. The winner was awarded a choice bottle of whiskey and was charged with the responsibility of racing it back to the rest of the bridal party, still en route. Opening the bottle, he offered it first to the bride and groom, and finally to the rest of the company with a round of toasts.

Update: The best man might produce a special bottle of champagne trimmed with tiny satin ribbons and fresh flowers, and a fabulous set of flutes. Offer it immediately following the ceremony to bride, groom, and wedding party. The maid of honor can see to it that the kitchen staff washes the glasses and saves them for bride and groom as a memento.

Shivaree Practiced most often on the frontier, rather than in more established areas, the shivaree, or charivari, found friends of the bride and groom feting them long after they'd left the reception for the privacy of the honeymoon quarters, usually their own house. Raucous song and dance continued until the newlyweds invited the revelers in for refreshments. Failure to show hospitality might have resulted in a dunking in the local creek. In Kentucky and Tennessee, guests went so far as to kidnap the bride and groom until they offered food, beverage, and even money to their captors. Update: Give newlyweds a decent

interval for settling in after they return from their honeymoon; then organize a party and bring it to them.

Pounding Newlyweds often were unable to enjoy a honeymoon, but were assimilated immediately into the community. One of the first neighborhood gatherings was a pounding, in which family and friends brought furniture and food to help the new couple set up housekeeping.

Update: Take a camera to the wedding and snap your own candids. The photographer inevitably misses something, so drop off your own stills at the newlyweds' house after the wedding; they'll be eternally grateful to have some less structured souvenirs of the occasion.

Infaire In the Tidewater Virginia area, parents of the groom often hosted an infaire the day after the wedding. Usually it was an elaborate dinner to which the whole community was often invited.

Update: Instead of letting parents pick up any more tabs, the newlyweds might invite them over—along with any other family members who have been particularly helpful during the wedding planning—for a no-holds-barred thank-you dinner party, perhaps showing off new place settings for the first time.

prisingly, today's Southern women exercise a good deal more control over their own lives than did their ancestors. While marriage and motherhood are watershed events for them, they are not the only paths to self-definition. For one thing, they are no longer children when they marry; often they wear another ten or twenty years' experience under their belts, having been self-sufficient long before they're engaged. More often than not, they plan the details of their own weddings while juggling career and civic responsibilities. Self-confidence gives them edge enough to be able to look levelly at tradition, as a kind of quirky but immensely appealing iconography; the past, for them, is no longer a yoke, but an open door of opportunity for personal expression, for scooping up the most meaningful traditions and ignoring those that have become obsolete.

An 1835 New Orleans Wedding
Virginie Hermann and Joseph Landreaux

This account of the Hermann and Landreaux wedding is based on Creole wedding customs of the period, and we have made several suppositions in order to provide a more complete narrative.

Although much of the rest of the South remained rural into the mid-1800s, New Orleans had become a busy, sophisticated town, a melting pot of French, Spanish, African, and American cultures. The Vieux Carré, known as the French Quarter, was in full bloom. Graceful houses with wrought-iron balconies and lush gardens perched on bustling though unpaved streets, and steamboats churned down the mighty Mississippi, within sight of buildings erected decades earlier. At night, the city glittered with elaborate balls, theater, and opera. The theater was the site of many fledgling romances among the upper class, and it is likely that Virginie Hermann, the daughter of a prominent banker and merchant, first encountered Joseph Landreaux outside her family's elaborate theater box.

After some months of carefully chaperoned courtship, Virginie and Joseph became engaged. The dowry—no doubt an attractive one consisting of a large sum of cash, bedroom furniture, handmade linens, an extensive trousseau, and silver—was negotiated by the two fathers. With dowry and marriage contract satisfactorily resolved, the couple embarked on an exhaustive visit to every relative on both sides to announce the wedding plans and extend invitations.

As a matter of tradition, a few days prior to the wedding, the couple separated until the wedding; Virginie was expected to remain sequestered at home for the three days prior to the ceremony.

Detail of a reproduction of Virginie Hermann's wedding cake.

❧

Although most Southern weddings were held at home, Mrs. Hermann was devoutly Catholic, so Virginie and Joseph's nuptial mass took place at historic St. Louis Cathedral on a Wednesday. Weekday weddings were the rule in nineteenth-century Southern circles. Saturday was uncomfortably close to the Sabbath, and Friday was hangman's day; a schedule of executions was thought, not unexpectedly, to cast an unpleasant pall over the proceedings.

After the ceremony, guests returned by carriage to the Hermann

Virginie Hermann's silk moiré wedding dress with leg-of-mutton sleeves and appliquéd lace was the latest fashion statement from Paris. Her accessories included satin pumps and a lace veil. Her corbeille de noce, the traditional wedding basket, is filled with fan, brooch, lace handkerchief, and gloves and decorated with fresh flowers.

❧

house, which had one of the few stables in the French Quarter. A lavish banquet awaited them in the elegant dining room. Underneath crystal candlelit chandeliers, guests circulated among tables laden with assorted food and wine. Mrs. Hermann and her servants had spent months preparing the special menu: assorted breads, roasted meats and game, assorted sweets, ices and jellies, and, of course, the wedding cake. Wines were selected from Mr. Hermann's vast collection, numbering more than a thousand bottles.

Decorum required the bride to retire from her reception after an hour, so once dancing began, Virginie was led to the bridal chamber by her mother. Mrs. Hermann helped her daughter out of her wedding gown and into a lacy nightgown and peignoir, tied her hair back with a ribbon, and gave her a tearful embrace. Virginie's mammy had already tucked a bit of red cloth under the nuptial mattress to attract the *miche agoussou*, the Creole demon of love.

Instead of taking a lengthy European honeymoon, New Orleans newlyweds remained under the parental roof for five days. They were expected to stay confined in their bedroom with meals ferried in and out by servants. Traditionally, the bridal bed was festooned with an elaborate *ciel de lit*. This exquisite canopy was ordinarily made of pale blue silk trimmed with lace and accented with pink beribboned cherubs, to create an atmosphere of "eternal love, blue horizons, and rosy dreams."

A 1990
New Orleans
Wedding

*T*here were heavy rain clouds on the horizon on April 27, the day of Cindy Brennan's wedding, and by 3:00 p.m.—just a few hours before the ceremony—it was still raining steadily and dully. Everybody was at a loss—from Gordon Morey, who had figured on six and a half hours to do the flowers, to a very concerned mother of the bride. Suddenly, at 4:00 P.M., as if somebody had just put his foot down and refused to tolerate it, the skies cleared.

As the sun was setting on the Crescent City that Friday evening, six hundred friends and relatives gathered at majestic Holy Name Catholic

Church to watch Cindy and her fiancé, William Edward Davis III, get married.

Like most contemporary brides, Cindy made most of the wedding plans herself, with input from her mother on traditional elements. And like the best Southern weddings, this one fit the bride and groom like a good pair of gloves; every element made sense in the most personal way, from the host of prewedding parties to the distinctive choice of food and setting to the bride's absolute refusal to throw her bouquet and disappear at somebody else's idea of a dignified hour.

The Brennan family has been synonymous with New Orleans for decades. Cindy, who owns and runs the famed restaurant Mr. B's with her brother, Ralph, grew up surrounded by that special thing called restaurant kitchen camaraderie, and it was perhaps the same feeling of team effort, of one big happy family pulling together with a single goal, that put the finishing touches on her storybook wedding.

Like a lot of couples, Cindy and Eddie were tempted to have a small wedding, but with family considerations, they gave up on the idea, and wound up sending out about 425 invitations. Once they caved in to the numbers, they decided to do it up right and make a weekend of it. "Eddie and I wanted to really enjoy it and be with all our friends and fami-

ly." They both worked until two days before the wedding, when finally they embarked on a round of parties. Since they'd had trouble lining up the church for Saturday night, they opted for a Friday night wedding with full intentions of hanging around until Sunday to make the most of friends and family in town for the occasion.

Above: Cindy, who grew up surrounded by restaurant kitchen camaraderie, poses with her second family. GREVY

Left: Jackson Square. The skies cleared for Cindy and Eddie's wedding. SCHERMAN

Opposite: Gordon Morey wove dogwood, lilacs, peonies, and lilies through the fence in front of St. Louis Cathedral. SCHERMAN

The two families became acquainted at a small gathering at the Brennans' on Wednesday night. As they looked at the array of wedding presents, they got to know each other and talked excitedly about the events of the weekend to come.

The next day, relatives held a luncheon at Commander's Palace for Cindy's close friends and out-of-town guests. Since Cindy was in her thirties when she was married, she had felt uncomfortable about having lots of bridesmaids. "It just seemed ridiculous at my age, "she said. "I have one sister, so I just decided to stop there." As an opportunity to get together with old friends before the event, the luncheon was, she felt, more suitable than a traditional bridesmaids luncheon.

The rehearsal dinner was held on Thursday evening at Longue Vue, an historic house on the outskirts of New Orleans. "Eddie fell in love with it," Cindy said, "because when you drive up to it, with all those oak trees, it reminds you of Natchez [Mississippi], where he's from." A fine New Orleans jazz band provided music, and food came courtesy of Mr. B's. Staffers, most of whom had watched Cindy grow up, worked the party with seamless efficiency, dispatching flutes of champagne and butlered hors d'oeuvres to some two hundred guests. A toothsome buffet supper followed, featuring a lavish presentation of New Orleans's famous seafood dishes, all

seasoned with the avant-garde flair for which Mr. B's has developed a reputation. Afterward, an assortment of Cindy and Eddie's friends met them at the Bombay Club for easy jazz and great reminiscing that went on until 2:00 A.M.

Holy Name was a monument to simple elegance for the ceremony; pots of Easter lilies were already there, and the uncontrived addition of dogwood,

peonies, and myrtle branches set off the candlelit aisle to perfection. Cindy appeared a vision in silk and tulle, accented by pearls and iridescents.

The Brennans have given so much of themselves to the city of New Orleans that it seemed the perfect completion of the circle when Cindy and Eddie chose historic Jackson Square as the site of their reception. Ordinarily, it is locked at night, but the

Above: Before the rehearsal dinner, waiters passed an array of New Orleans specialities, including fried oysters and coconut shrimp with a honey mustard sauce. SCHERMAN

Right: The bride and groom cutting the cake. Cindy tried on dozens of dresses before she found this one of silk and tulle at House of Broel in New Orleans. The veil, 124 inches from top of the head to bottom of the dress, was crowned by three panels of illusion. GREVY

heart of the French Quarter during Jazz Fest so perfectly paraphrased Cindy and Eddie's lifestyle that it was worth getting all the permits, bringing in electricity, water, and even police to patrol on horseback.

Rain threw setup plans into total disarray, leaving only two hours to get three tents up (including the tent for the temporary kitchen!), arrange flowers, trim the tents and tables with yards of tulle, set up buffet tables, and decorate the cake. Somehow most of it was accomplished, and what wasn't, nobody noticed anyway.

After the ceremony, Cindy and Eddie stepped out of their limousine and made their way through Jackson Square with the cathedral lit up spectacularly in front of them and the sounds of Jimmy Maxwell's twelve-piece orchestra filling the air. Immediately, they were engulfed by the crowd in an unmistakable outpouring of affection.

The buffet dinner, a four-course New Orleans feast, was served at 10 p.m., the cake cut around 11:30. By midnight, festivities wound down, and bride and groom in full wedding regalia reconvened with friends and family at Napoleon House, a venerable institution in the Quarter, for another several hours of celebrating before they were picked up by their limousine.

A final party, hosted by Cindy's aunts and uncles, was held Saturday night at the Brennans' home. In a casual departure from the earlier festivities, the garden was decked out in black, white, and red balloons, and the pool covered with a dance floor.

Under a canopy of tiny tree lights, family, friends, and out-of-town guests danced to good jazz and dined on red beans and rice and other regional favorites catered by Commander's Palace.

On Sunday morning, Cindy and Eddie departed for a European wedding trip.

Above: Cindy's restaurant, Mr. B's, prepared succulent oysters from the Gulf of Mexico in a special pirogue, or boat. They were served with a spicy tomato cocktail sauce. SCHERMAN

Left: Gordon Morey used simple arrangements of cut flowers for the tables at the rehearsal dinner. SCHERMAN

The Planning

Breaking the News, Breaking New Ground

*E*ven today, there's an indefinable sweetness that permeates courtship and engagement in the South, a kind of naive, almost folkloric remnant of a bygone era. True enough, the art of wooing—in both North and South—has changed considerably in the course of the last hundred years: automobiles, coeducation, telephones, and the tendency to marry at an older age have all had a critically liberating effect on romancing. Now, even the most remote pockets of the South have

Opposite: Are you sentimental, traditional, or avant-garde? What type of wedding will you have? Talk to your mother about her own wedding day; she's likely to have some great memories. GAY

Right: A porch swing, a bottle of champagne, and a ring. Can wedding bells be far behind?

probably seen the last of chaperoned parlor dates.

And yet, the South has clung stubbornly to certain traces of its early traditions. Sororities and fraternities, still an integral part of Southern university social life, continue to preserve and perpetuate the sexual segregation so intrinsic to the colonial and antebellum South. Traditional dating rituals persist in that environment, re-creating the comparatively strict moral code and lack of privacy that dogged Southern couples of a few centuries ago. And even outside the pervasive Greek system, updated echoes of the Southern belle ethic still hang on, in courting attitudes and etiquette that are simply not present on Northern college campuses. While the quaint concepts of going steady and getting pinned or lavaliered may be the stuff of social history books, and despite relaxed attitudes about cohabitation, an engagement is still a matter of palpitating excitement in the South.

On Bended Knee

*W*hile Northern couples were allowed to spend time alone, Southern protocol in the eighteenth and nineteenth centuries dictated that unmarried couples were never to be left to their own devices. What little social contact Southern couples may have had was strictly chaperoned. There is an amusing anecdote about a disgruntled planter who complained that "his

Above: Thomas Bates proposed to Cindy Lee of Greensboro in the most elevating of places.
BROWN

Right: The front porch is so important to Southern culture and rituals, especially courtship.

indeed they would be turned down. Southern belles were notoriously fickle, their coquettish behavior a kind of feminine muscle flexing before leaving the sponsorship of father for that of husband. They routinely played havoc with their suitors, as if to enjoy their brief dominion over the opposite sex. Virginian Maria Mayo, for example, finally married Winfield Scott in 1817, after having allegedly turned down a hundred proposals. And there are some recorded instances of lawsuits pressed—usually without success—by scorned suitors whose proposals were accepted and then reneged on when more tempting offers came along.

In the colonial South, proposals were formal and rather tricky. In theory young men and women were free to select the mates of their choice, but parents applied considerable pressure through the use of dowries and estates. So customarily, when a young man decided to ask for his sweetheart's hand, he went not to her but to his own father. Providing he approved the choice, his father then contacted the girl's father to make him aware of his son's intentions and of the particular estate he planned to settle on him. The girl's father would then reply and, if granting his consent, would detail a summary of her dowry. Finally, with these financial matters out of the way, the young man was turned loose to try his luck.

wife never took his arm till she took it to be led to church on her wedding day; and that he never had an opportunity of kissing her but twice while he was addressing her (they were six months engaged!) and in both cases by means of a stratagem he resorted to of drugging a peach with laudanum which he gave to the attending servant and thereby put her into a sound sleep."

With so few opportunities for intimacy, it's a wonder eighteenth- and nineteenth-century Southern men ever got around to proposing. And when finally they did, odds were very good

Historically, when it came to proposals, Southern women were at something of a disadvantage in that propriety would not allow them to ask the question themselves. They were, however, perfectly within their rights to engineer the situation to their best interests. The eighteenth-century proposal of Betsy Hansford has often been cited as an example of just how manipulative Southern women could be while remaining "passive." It is said that, in desperation, an unsuccessful suitor turned to Betsy's minister, the Reverend John Camm—who had baptized Betsy in his early days in the parish—in hopes that his influence might sway her emphatic refusal.

Camm counseled with her tirelessly, quoting the Scriptures and reminding her of her moral duty to marry and bear children. All of this to no avail, however. Finally, as he made ready to quit the scene in failure, she submitted that he would find in 2 Samuel xii 7 the precise reason she continued to put off the pitiful beau. On his return home, Camm checked the reference only to find the significant phrase "thou art the man." Astonished, but evidently not displeased, he married her himself, as a social item in Williamsburg's *Virginia Gazette* records for posterity.

Proposals, like everything else, have swung back and forth on a pen-

dulum of fashion. Dowries and estates transacted by fathers were fine for the days when women went from one completely dependent state to another; but now, when more often than not both women and men build careers and some degree of independence before they marry, they usually settle their own finances, often with prenuptial agreements. In today's scenario, women are just as likely to pop the question as men are, although most Southern women report an admittedly romantic longing to be proposed to. And while most of them consider the old-fashioned bended-knee business obsolete and even a little embarrassing, they overwhelmingly lean toward other traditional trappings, such as a prior audience between father and fiancé.

Proposals, then, tend to reflect both the groom- and bride-to-be. In today's atmosphere of more relaxed sexual freedoms, when couples often live together for some time before even considering marriage, a proposal may be as offhand as a young man's looking distractedly up from the Sunday paper and saying, "Let's shoot for October . . ." Other fellows may ruminate for weeks, planning the perfect occasion and setting, considering the ideal turn of a phrase. Sometimes the mere surprise of a ring is all the theater necessary to couch the question with aplomb.

Next of Kin

*I*n the South, family has always been a source of strength. Up to and long after marriage, siblings were unusually close, especially in the far-flung rural expanses of the region. But without question, the most crucial relationships a young girl maintained were with her mother and father.

While the planter's wife has been mythologized as a kind of do-gooding workaholic, there can be no doubt that it was indeed the mother on whose shoulders fell the burden of molding the moral fiber of a daughter. In her mother's eyes, a young girl could catch a glimpse of her own future, a projection of her life as a wife, and she was expected to learn from her not only the hard skills of household management, but also the softer skills of support, spirit, and seduction.

If, in fact, mothers shaped their daughters, then fathers shaped their

Left: Charles Jackson with his daughter Alice at her wedding in Linville, North Carolina. There is a particular tenderness between Southern fathers and daughters.

Below: At Dathel Coleman and John Georges's rehearsal dinner, the couple penned a special note of tribute to their fathers. GIBBONS

daughters' dreams. For a young woman marrying at such an early age, her father represented the absolute perimeters of the male universe; he was the only role model she had for her future lord and master.

Today, the passage from daughter to wife is not so monumental; with later marriages and established careers, Southern women rarely find that the so-called day of transfer takes them from the shelter of a father's wing to that of a husband's. The change of allegiance, from father first to husband first, now includes an intermediary step: self first.

But that still doesn't alter the emotional aspect of things. There is a particular tenderness between Southern fathers and daughters, a poignant echo of the Old South's brand of chivalry in which men protected their women and placed them on pedestals. Today's Southern father may have long since dealt with his daughter's independence, but nothing quite prepares him for the actuality of losing his little girl to another man, of watching the object of a lifetime of providing turn into a provider in her own right.

Fathers react to the business of weddings with all manner of attitudes. Some look on magnanimously, keeping mouths shut and pocketbooks open, while others seem to tackle the whole operation with the vigor of a tycoon masterminding a takeover. Traditionally, mothers have been the real powerhouses, corralling their daughters through an obstacle course of dos and don'ts with a steady hand. Nowadays, though, daughters stay single longer; their exposure to other looks and lifestyles gives them an edge their own mothers most likely never had as brides-to-be—a sharper image of what they want in a wedding and, more to the point, how to get it. Still, Southern mothers are another breed of cat, and I never underestimate them. There are plenty who do still

Above: Lee Rutherford and her mother, Laura. The whole wedding process—an odyssey of decisions, selections, and redefinitions—often becomes a reaffirmation of the bond between mother and daughter.

Below: On the day of the wedding, Dathel Coleman, the mother of the bride, pays close attention to the final details for Little Dathel. GIBBONS

orchestrate a wedding as might a field marshall, and very much with their daughters' blessings. I dare say that even daughters who know exactly what they want still hear their mothers' voices inside their heads with every decision they make—and with every tradition they break. For there is a kind of mystical communion between Southern mothers and their daughters, and whether relations are tight and easy or frankly ragged, it still seems important to both of them to have each other's sanction, to be reassured of that sense of continuity between them.

Spreading the News

There is perhaps nothing to compare with those first exhilarating moments of knowing you're going to be married; as if suspended in time, a couple is borne along on a current of happy excitement, conspirators sharing the wonderful secret of their commitment to tackle the rest of life as a team. But the secret is impossible to keep for long, and parents are usually the first to hear the good news, with close friends and the rest of the family following close behind. Often the unexpected presence of a ring does the talking, although engagement parties are still popular in the South. In the mid-nineteenth century, in Virginie Hermann's day, informing

every relative of the upcoming nuptials was de rigueur, and extended carriage trips to the many households that comprised a large Southern family meant the endless telling and retelling of the engagement and the wedding plans.

Etiquette has relaxed a good bit since Virginie Hermann made her engagement rounds, and spreading the news of a betrothal, not unlike the wedding itself, becomes a personal reflection of bride and groom. Some couples prefer to downplay the event, confiding the news in family and close friends, and letting word leak out to the rest of the world via the newspaper. Others, on the other hand, are delighted to be the guests of honor at a formal engagement party hosted by the bride's parents.

In the Old South, things were decidedly cozier; news of a proposal rarely surprised anyone, and meeting future in-laws was something of a non-issue since so often they were related.

Today, though, mobility is such that getting the two families together may present a challenge. Emily Post takes the position that the groom's mother should make the first move by calling the bride's mother to express her happiness over the news and to suggest a meeting of the two families. I'm not at all sure this is imperative; much depends on the ages and personalities of the bride and groom, after all, and today, it probably matters much less who makes a call to whom. What is important is the conveying of good feeling and the arrangement of some sort of meeting of the two families prior to the wedding day.

Getting Started: First the Dream

*I*f those first heady days of engagement find brides-to-be in a virtual dream state, it is not long before reality shakes them awake; now that they're getting married, after all, they have to actually get married, and pulling off this amorphous thing called a wedding often knocks the wind right out of them. Magazines bombard them with checklists: 101 things to do before you say "I do"; the complete countdown to wedding bliss; how to survive a wedding from tying the knot to toss-

Opposite: Some couples prefer to host a party for family and friends, saving the joyful announcement of the engagement until the end of the event. Use the great outdoors for your party. Greens and fresh flowers placed on a plaid cloth with matching napkins are a wonderful way to present a picnic spread. SKOTT

Right: Other couples are delighted to be the guests of honor at a formal engagement party at home. Greet guests with champagne and a colorful table at the front door.

ing the bouquet, and so on. Concerned friends and relatives don't hesitate to put in their two cents' worth. And the retail wedding industry—from bridal salons to the registry at local department stores—exerts its own subliminal pressures.

Best advice for dreamy brides-to-be? Don't wake up. At least not yet. Remember that, in the end, even small weddings are big productions, with scads of players all pushing their own agendas. To be sure, there are endless decisions to be made, people and services to hire. But don't fall into the trap of letting other people's panic coax you into leaping before you do plenty of looking—and thinking. The only sure-fire way to avoid being caught as a casualty in the fallout of wedding panic is to do some serious soul searching up front. Before you beat a path to the phone to book your church or country club, stop and think. Talk to yourself. And listen, carefully. Before you talk to anybody else, talk to your fiancé about who you both are, about how your wedding might best define you.

Left: What better way to get started on wedding decisions than a quiet breakfast with your mom at a possible reception site like the Antique Emporium in Texas?

Opposite: Patricia Egan and her daughter, Emily, plan Patricia's upcoming wedding to Vernon Brinson in New Orleans. Flipping through magazines and books is a good way to decide what kind of look you really want.

In this discovery phase of wedding planning, if you really give yourself a chance to articulate your dreams and expectations, personal preferences, as well as surprises, will surface. And finally, out of all the flotsam and jetsam, a distinctive style will emerge. Try it on and see if it fits you. And then, the tricky part . . . how to make it happen.

Developing the Blueprint: Organization and Action

*N*ow that you've got a handle on the dream, it's time to come down to earth. Budget is probably the most critical issue; it will shape many of the decisions to be made. (See "Who Pays for What" and "A Bride's Budget" on pages 233 and 234). But logistics are important, too. Bride's and groom's work schedules, out-of-town guests' travel, and availability of ceremony and reception facilities all bear on the selection of date and time. Most decisions interlock; a particular site, for example, may demand an afternoon or early evening ceremony, which then determines the degree of formality and, perhaps, tradition. The big picture is very much like a puzzle with a jillion little pieces to be juggled this way and that until they fit together. It's rarely completed in one sitting, and often the finished product metamor-

This is the time to dream, so make it a fun exercise. Forget about budget, forget about obligations. Just brainstorm. Think about weddings you've both been to, and what you liked and didn't like about them. Talk about the things that are most important to you: the ceremony, the food, the flowers, the people, the music. Talk about tradition—do you want it, do you need it, do your parents insist? Talk about place

and time and mood. Talk about numbers. Are you basically small and elegant at high noon in the apple orchard, while your fiancé is black-tie in a big hotel for eight hundred of your closest friends? Do strong attachments to different faiths pose some knotty problems? Well, now is the time to face the issues, not when it's all just a miserable memory. Consider, in the final analysis, what would make you both happy.

phoses a good deal from its original blueprint.

Some brides may consider hiring a professional wedding consultant from the outset. This is entirely a matter of personal taste. Many brides and their families bristle at the thought of a stranger's becoming intimately involved in their wedding, preferring instead to rely on the teamwork of mother and daughter, plus the help of a close family member to coordinate such activities as the processional, the cutting of the cake, and the tossing of

Right: Scott, a co-owner of Bud & Alley's Restaurant, picks herbs from the restaurant's own garden for Gail and Tom Hawkins's wedding feast in Seaside, Florida.

Below: At Jackson Square in New Orleans, florist Gordon Morey and his team, armed with buckets of lilacs, roses, delphinium, dogwood, and tulips, are ready to set up Cindy Brennan's reception. SCHERMAN

the bouquet. Others see a professional's role not as an uncomfortable intrusion but rather as a godsend. Here, after all, is a dependable expert who will shoulder the burden of organizing the infinite and the infinitesimal: taking measurements for the erection of a tent, coordinating the electrical needs of the band, booking courtesy vans in case of rain, lining up special rental of tables, chairs, and linens and making sure they are delivered, carting the wedding party's personal belongings from the church to the reception, seeing that the cake top is saved for the bride and groom, diplomatically sidestepping the snafus that arise when stepparents meet in the first pew . . . the list is endless.

Andre de La Barre, a special events coordinator and co-owner of Design Consultants, Inc., in New Orleans, comments: "A lot of brides—or their mothers—just realize the whole thing is too big for them to deal with. We do everything, if that's what they want; I may have a staff of thirty-two people with walkie-talkies for on-site coordination of a wedding ceremony and reception, and that staff will do whatever it takes to handle any problems without the bride's and groom's even knowing about it."

Without question, this is big business, and the highest level of professional quality is maintained from start to finish. Andre pinpoints where the real interests lie via exhaustive interviews with the bride; then, once budget is established, he is able to cut the corners he needs to, in order to give her what she wants at the price she can afford. Andre is like a time-management machine; for each bride, he maintains a file for every single detail of the wedding enterprise. He even calls the bride to remind her to get her blood test and get her change-of-address card to the post office. No item is left dangling, and no item is too insignificant to have a position of some prominence in one of those files. (See "Bride's Checklist" on pages 231–32). If you are inviting a thousand people to your wedding, this sort of staff-intensive, professional service may be your salvation. And salvation doesn't come cheap. For smaller appetites, on the other hand, this approach may seem overwhelming and a little too Madison Avenue. A different sort of wedding coordinator may better suit your sensibilities. Unlike de La Barre, whose firm may have a dozen clients a month, Brooke Lively, of Fort Worth, Texas, puts on only two to three big weddings a year and advertises exclusively by word of mouth. She offers a wedding package that includes consultation and on-site coordination for the rehearsal dinner, ceremony, and reception. She acts as general contrac-

tor, pricing all the subcontractors—caterers, bartenders, florists, rental companies—and offering a bride her choice.

Even if brides-to-be are entirely confident in that arena, more and more of them are finding that relying on a capable wedding consultant saves them money in the long run and spares them man-hours of hassling over the phone and in person with the

droves of service people who create the finished wedding product. All of which means they can relax and enjoy the event rather than becoming a slave to it.

One caveat: Word of mouth is probably the best voucher for a good wedding consultant, so don't hesitate to ask friends for their considered opinions. What counts is your ability to trust and work with a coordinator; if

The Coleman family's out-of-town wedding guests received fresh flowers and a detailed schedule of the weekend's events.

your personalities don't mesh, the relationship—and your wedding—will be a disaster. It's important to have no misunderstandings about areas of responsibility; you may be delighted and willing to pay someone to make sure buses can fit through the gates but may draw the line at having the coordinator open, catalog, and display your wedding presents. For many Southern brides today, career and civic commitments are not reason enough to consign wedding headaches to somebody else. Some brides thrive on the challenge of masterminding a wedding and prefer to get directly involved in every phase of the process, from decorating an unusual reception site to having a capable caterer prepare his or her own recipes to devising a whirlwind of activities for the out-of-town guests. The secret is facing up to—and relinquishing—the elements that aren't your forte. If food is your strength but flowers aren't, work out the recipes and presentation in intricate detail, but give your vision to a floral designer and let him have free rein.

Organization is a personal thing; for one bride it may mean a shoebox full of clippings and ideas, while for another it's a detailed planner with a rigid schedule to follow right up to the appointed wedding hour. There are magazines and books that outline the infinite steps to the altar, and it pays to check them out just to absorb the scale of what will be accomplished in the next several months to a year. Or you can rely on your mother's experience to pull you through.

When planning her Washington, D.C., wedding, Courtney Banks had specific ideas about how her wedding should look. She made a series of sketches of her ideas for the reception and worked with caterer, florist, and party planner to realize them.

the invitation. If you don't keep your perspective and your sense of humor, you may find yourself cratering under the demands and the cheap philosophies of everyone around you.

Forewarned is forearmed in this case. Simply know that pressure and stress are virtually inescapable twists and turns on this exciting, sensitive journey to the altar. Try not to lose your cool, and above all, don't fail to communicate and to compromise. Rely on your fiancé for strength, even when you disagree, and remember why you're getting married in the first place: to celebrate the joy of being with each other, not to stage a Cecil B. DeMille production.

Wedding Stress

At some point during wedding planning—and usually quite early in the game—most brides have a sinking spell that leaves them frazzled and fragile in the face of pressures that seem to emanate from just about every corner. Wedding stress is no joke, and should be neither overlooked nor underestimated. Remember, this is an emotional time for almost everybody close to the bride and groom. The bride and groom usually discover altogether new sides to each other, and sometimes the surprises are difficult to deal with. Settling major issues like the size of the guest list or questions of religion are often no worse in the headache department than the really niggly things like style and wording of

A Wedding of Earthly Delights at Evelynton Plantation, Virginia

*P*layer Butler and Mark Michelsen were engaged for fifteen months, so there was plenty of time for rational decisions and methodical planning. Player's mother, Noel Sengel, a criminal defense lawyer in northern Virginia, spearheaded the whole affair with cool persistence, meeting every deadline she set for herself with exacting precision and leaving no visible loose ends. No one was more surprised than she when she found herself an emotional shipwreck the week of the wedding. "Thank

goodness I was fine—shaky, but fine—on the day of the wedding," she recalls, "but all that week, I was just a mess. I could hardly speak. Every morning I would wake up and cry. You know, it's not like just having a big party; it's all that plus the unbelievable realization that your baby is getting married. It's a very emotional time. I would tell every mother to be prepared for the bride—and mine is a fairly organized, accomplished girl—to have an amazing attack of the nerves. Player got a fixation on a strand of her hair that wouldn't do right, and she was literally walking in circles.

Above: Evelynton Plantation, originally part of William Byrd's Westover Plantation, was named for his daughter Evelyn. Since 1847 it has been home to the Ruffin family, whose patriarch, Edmund Ruffin, fired the first shot of the Civil War. CROSS

Left: Upstairs in one of the manor-house bedrooms, Player's mother and bridesmaids toast the bride-to-be. CROSS

Normally I'm so organized, but there I was with my endless checklist, and I was so emotional I couldn't even read it. You need somebody to step in and take care of you both!"

Above: Noel Sengel and Player instantly saw Evelynton as a setting that had something for everybody; the adults would love the house and garden and the children could be turned loose to roll down the hills and play with the donkeys. CROSS

Right: The bridesmaids' floral chintz dresses were just the ticket for Player's hot July afternoon wedding. CROSS

The minute Player got engaged, she called her mother. She was in her first year of law school and had neither the time nor the inclination to handle wedding preparations. Player's parents are divorced and she grew up with her mother. Their closeness is marked by mutual respect and a lively sense of humor, as well as a shared vision of life and style; during the long planning process, they disagreed only once—when her mother tried to urge her not to give up her

maiden name. "I had no idea what I was doing," Player confides. "But thank goodness, my mother did. She kept a notebook, and it was great . . . she would call up with some choices, and tell me to pick A, B, or C. Then she'd call the next week with E, F, and G."

Although she'd never done it before, putting on a wedding was not the least bit daunting for Noel Sengel. She simply attacked the project as if she were preparing for a trial, keeping the myriad elements organized in a trial notebook from her office. In its various hole-punched sections, she listed the phone numbers of anyone and everyone she needed to contact, all the contracts and correspondence, deadlines, both immediate and further out, pictures of dresses and china and flowers. "Trying a case is a lot like putting

on a wedding," she notes with a laugh. "You subpoena witnesses, keep notes, set deadlines. . . . I even kept a tickler file just like at my office to remind me what I had to do and when."

The first order of the day was to sit Player down and put her through the paces of coming to grips with what sort of wedding she wanted: urban and sophisticated, simple and elegant, traditional or interpretive. They both decided they were after a kind of romance, decidedly Southern but not heavy-handed. The outdoors was important to Player and Mark, espe-cially as a setting for both ceremony and reception. "My religion is sort of nondenominational," Player says, likening it to a kind of pantheistic spiritualism that reveres the power and glory of nature as its own god.

They began looking at historic houses, and when they found Evelynton Plantation in Virginia's historic Charles City, they knew they'd come home. "I grew up in the country," says Noel, "in Buckingham County [Virginia] and I was used to a particular kind of entertaining. People got married at home and had parties. . . . There was this

Above: The flower girl leads off the procession-al. CASTON'S

Left: Player and Mark exchanged vows beneath Evelynton's rose pergola. CASTON'S

wonderful feeling of people flowing in and out of a big, old house with lots of lanterns in the yard and good food. Evelynton had that feeling for me, with its rolling hills and huge, old trees and the kind of hush of the boxwood garden and, of course, the beautiful open house with its wonderful flowers and antiques."

After a rained-out rehearsal the afternoon before, the wedding day was perfection. The formal boxwood gar-

Right: Annie Black, of Evelynton Plantation, designed these exquisite larkspur sheaf containers as a focal point for the table that was swagged and draped by Candlelight Linens. CROSS

Below: The happy couple is toasted by Player's father. CASTON'S

den, a traditional English quadrant design with fruit trees and a rose pergola, provided a lush summer palette for the crisp paper-white garden chairs. Guests sauntered in leisurely, stopping for minted ice tea before being seated in the garden.

After the ceremony, guests migrated back to the terrace, where two towering white tents kept the July sun off Catered Occasions' sumptuous country buffet supper of salads, fruits, and cheeses, plus cooked-to-order Chesapeake Bay crab cakes, grilled pesto chicken, and pasta tossed with a selection of sauces. The cake was

served with homemade peach ice cream on the side. As adults danced to the infectious rhythms of a swing band, children played with a gamboling herd of Nubian goats and a donkey tethered to a nearby tree.

"One of the reasons we loved Evelynton," says Noel Sengel, "was that we felt we were in such good hands there. There was such a distinctive style about everything, from the linens to the flowers to the whole attitude about putting a wedding together. We all seemed to be of one mind, and Player and I felt totally comfortable leaving the details of the reception to them. It was really like we were at home, only my house doesn't hold 280 people. This was the next best thing."

The Dress

Finery and Fantasy: The Stuff of Dreams

Of the myriad images that make up the collage of a woman's lifetime, there is perhaps none so telling as the picture of her as a bride. More than any of life's other milestones, it is a woman's wedding day that is most directly related to her own self-concept, to say nothing of the self she wants the rest of the world to know. The day is a symbolic threshold between the life she's known and the life she'll live; she has the rare opportunity to paint her own self-portrait, to indulge her dreams and fantasies in a

❧

Opposite: Lee Rutherford's vintage dress, worn by her great-grandmother, was the perfect gown for her country wedding. The children attendants carried small satin-, ivy-, and flower-covered hoops designed By Ron Barrett.

Right: Veils by Annie Heckler and Chris Endemetry of Atlanta.

kind of sacred iconography that paraphrases her own vision of herself to present company and preserves it for future generations. It's a weighty business, and she is determined to look the best she's ever looked.

There's something almost magical about a wedding dress. No other garment so completely transforms its wearer as does this simple envelope of pearly silk or satin. When a young woman first slips into heirloom lace or dupioni silk or sheer organdy, it all but takes her breath away. She becomes for a moment the Cinderella of her childhood memories, and an altogether new radiance emanates from her, as if she's jumped into a delicious new skin.

Amanda Adams of Birmingham, who was twenty-nine when she got engaged, had been vaguely lukewarm about the whole issue of her wedding until she spent a day at Anne Barge for Brides in Atlanta. "I had a ball," she says. "It was such a tangible thing, deciding on my wedding dress, that for

the first time since I'd gotten engaged, I actually felt like a bride. It was an important step, especially for my mother; she'd been dreaming about this day ever since she brought me home from the hospital."

There are many roads to the dream dresses of today's brides. Buying off the rack at a reputable hometown bridal boutique may be the most popular, but many brides treat themselves to shopping the signature

43

looking for; others haven't a clue. And the ones who think they know often change their minds quite radically before it's all over. Vera Wang, who founded the industry blue chip, Vera Wang Bridal House, Ltd., in New York, says: "A lot of girls now envision they'd look good in something that's very closely related to what they wear in their everyday lives. For example, a young professional who tends to wear Donna Karan or Michael Kors or Armani will walk in and say, 'Now, I don't want a big white dress. I want something sleek

Left: Wedding dresses by Jim Hjelm (left), Marissa (center), and Richard Glasgow (right).

Below: Something old, new, borrowed, blue. Mary Virginia Weinmann of New Orleans fufilled the age-old custom by borrowing her mother's veil, wearing a new Scassi dress, and adding violet-blue flowers to her bouquet.

collections of salons in bigger cities. If they have the pocketbook to match their fashion sense, they can go directly to the designer. Or they can have a local seamstress copy a favorite design from the latest couture collections, historical fashion books, or even an old movie. If they know their figures and have a sharp sense of style, that copy might just as well duplicate an original right out of their own imaginations. On the other hand, if tradition is everything, they may elect to wear their mother's dress, or remake their grandmother's or great-grandmother's. Or, if the family treasure trove turns up nothing that quite suits, they can hunt for a vintage wedding gown, if the reception is the right occasion for it.

Some brides have a precise notion of the type of wedding dress they're

Yves Saint Laurent designed this dress of white silk damask exclusively for Robin Robinson of Atlanta. For the headpiece he used a luscious silver and gold gazar in a leaf motif, echoing the embroidery of the dress. The veil of white silk tulle encrusted with stones was worn with the headpiece. SCHILLING

and modern.' They imagine their wedding day is going to be pretty much a romanticized extension of what they wear to work. But then they start trying on dresses and the next thing you know they startle themselves, as if they can't quite deal with the fact that they're wearing all this lace and tulle, and more important, that they actually like it. Suddenly, this isn't their everyday life; it's a once-in-a-lifetime fantasy. And I truly believe," she continues, "that everybody has two sides to their nature; everybody is both virgin queen and raging sex symbol, and a little bit of both comes out in a wedding dress."

Past Perfect, Future Perfect

*M*ost elements of today's bridal costume are direct descendants of nineteenth-century tradition. Although white dresses appeared sporadically on both the bride and her attendants throughout the centuries, the color was more likely a celebration

of peace and happiness than a symbol
of purity. White didn't become the
color of choice until about 1820 when
white satin and lace began to replace
the glittery brocades and silver
muslins of earlier days. By 1840, when
Queen Victoria married in white, it
was firmly established as the thing to
do, although brides continued to wear
a "best dress" that could be worn
again later, or even a two-piece outfit
that might make a nice transition as a
traveling suit for the steamer or train
they would board immediately following the ceremony. Marilyn Van
Eynde, associate director of the
Memphis, Tennessee, Woodruff-
Fontaine House, an 1870 historic
house operated by the Association for
the Preservation of Tennessee
Antiquities, says, "Often a bride had
to travel immediately after the service,
or perhaps the next day. She needed
something practical as well as fine."
One of her favorite items in a recent
Woodruff-Fontaine House wedding
costume exhibit is a wine-colored
dress worn by a woman who married
a minister. The bride was married in
the dress in 1882 in Charlottesville,

Virginia, and is said to have worn it
again at her fiftieth-anniversary party,
with very few alterations.

Veils, almost nonexistent in the
eighteenth century, came back into
vogue in the nineteenth century, too,
some say after a charming tradition
established by Nellie Custis, Martha
Washington's granddaughter, who
wore a lace veil at her 1799 wedding to
Lawrence Lewis—apparently in a
clever reminiscence of the day he first
glimpsed her behind lace curtains.

Wedding dress silhouettes have
more or less always followed the fashion of the day. In the colonial South,
as elsewhere, news traveled slowly,
and as a consequence fashion was
sluggish in effecting a change. Most
seventeenth-century women were
rabid for details of the latest mode in
fashion centers like London and Paris,
and in the days before fashion plates
they often relied on a quaint custom
known as "Coming Out Bride," in
which both bride and groom, with
self-conscious pride, modeled their
wedding finery and cutting-edge costumes every Sunday at church for a
month after their wedding.

Typically, of course, the life led by
colonials was not the life of the great
courts and capitals of Europe; the luxe
look of heavy brocade and handsome
silks was, for practical reasons, modified into homespun linen-wool blends
in the colonies. But the trapezoidal
shape of seventeenth-century
skirts still held sway.

The Right Shade of White

For brides who did select white,
an 1894 issue of *Ladies' Home
Journal* had this advice: "When
wearing a white gown thought
must be given to the becoming-
ness of the shade for after all,
there are as many tints in white
as in other colors; the one that
may suit the pale blond is
absolutely unbecoming to the
rosy brunette. Dead white,
which has the glint of blue
about it, is seldom becoming to
any one. It brings out the imper-
fections of the complexion,
tends to deaden the gloss of the
hair, and dulls the brightness of
the eyes. The white that touches
on the cream or coffee shade is
undoubtedly the most artistic
and best suited to the general
woman. However, in choosing it
one must be careful not to get
too deep a tone, which is apt to
look not quite dainty, and to
give an impression of a faded
yellow, rather than a cream
white."

The royal cachet had caught on with a vengeance by 1720, with the box-pleated Watteau back adding a royal sweep to favorite bridal colors of yellow and gold. By 1750 and through the end of the century, patterns joined colors as the popular picks of most brides. Figured damasks in pink, blue, and clear, undiluted yellow were very much the order of the day along with pronounced stripes and rich embroideries. Much as today, watershed events bent fashion one way or another, and certainly the fabled wedding of George Washington and Martha Dandridge Custis in Virginia's New Kent County generated plenty of mimicry. The widow bride wore a dress made in London, a heavy white silk shot through with silver, with a quilted satin petticoat underneath.

With the arrival of the nineteenth century, Americans began to exhibit their own fashion sense, although styles still hailed predominantly from London and Paris. Heavy weaves and embroideries gave way in this period to more diaphanous materials that celebrated the female form. Gone were the theatrical remnants of a century earlier, as French panniers and Elizabethan farthingales deflated into the classic Empire silhouette, with a high waist and a skirt as straight and fluted as a Greek column.

The landmark wedding of the century was the marriage of Queen Victoria, who by selecting a simple white satin dress accented with orange blossoms, permanently altered bridal garb. It has been said that in that age of submission and subjugation, the often restrictive attitudes of dress and behavior that women were saddled with led naturally to a wholesale penchant for dreaming and fantasizing about their weddings—the true beginning of the fairy princess bride.

By 1850, the silhouette was pushed to the outer limits of fullness with the popularity of the hoop skirt, generally attributed to Charles Frederick Worth, the founder of the notable Paris design house. This was an extravagant age, full of coquettishness and contradiction; the hoop skirt was, in a sense, fashion's chastity belt, isolating its wearer inside a force field of lace and petticoats, and yet women rather enjoyed tipping them up with feigned nonchalance to show off their lace-trimmed drawers.

The hoop skirt narrowed back to the bustle by the 1870s, and costumes grew elegant and stagy. But by 1900 the rebellious S-curve had again streamlined the silhouette in a look that gained immortality through the illustrations of Charles Dana Gibson. The 1920s blithely scrapped that look in exchange for a flattened chest and a dropped waist; while hem lengths rose to their highest heights—just below the knee—detachable trains and veils were endless. Although wedding dresses tended as always to remain exempt

Elaborate headpieces such as this one were introduced in the mid-nineteenth century.

from the radical trends of the day, a good number of preserved examples show the characteristic shaped hemlines and rhinestone, beaded, and metallic embellishments that enhanced cocktail dresses and ball gowns of the period.

With the Depression, a somber mood infected even bridal gowns, but with pleasingly elegant results. "The dresses of the thirties were really

Wedding Garb in 1855

I have a vision of the maiden in her white robe of heavy moiré and satin; the plain, pointed bodice laced up the back, the low-cut back and puffed "caps" forming the sleeves, the handsome moss trimming, the full gathered skirt, white kid gloves, dainty clocked stockings and white satin slippers guiltless of heels, while the tulle veil fastened by orange blossoms, enveloped the small graceful figure like an enshrouding mist.

It was my privilege, as first bridesmaid, to throw back the veil when the simple service was ended, and the young husband in black dress suit, immaculate gloves, with white waistcoat and tie of the heaviest brocade bent to bestow the first caress upon the trusting face uplifted to meet his own, in whose eyes shone the love of a life time.

There were but four attendants, two maids, a cousin and myself and two groomsmen. Our costumes were simple gowns of white English crepe over silk slips made after the fashion of the day with ample skirt and "baby waist"—a sash of moiré ribbon tied at the back, and gloves and slippers to correspond with those of the bride.

—from *An Account of an 1855 Wedding*, courtesy of Hermann-Grima Historic House

This wedding dress, which appeared in Godey's Lady's Book and Magazine, *was the latest fashion in April 1873.*

some of the most classic and sophisticated," says Caroline Rennolds Milbank, author of the definitive fashion history book *Couture.* "There was rarely any lace or beading, and the dresses tended to have high necks and long trains. This was the heyday of glamorous black and white movies, and things on the screen tended to look best when they were uncomplicated—all white satin, for example. It translated easily to real life. This was when the calla lily sheaf bouquet came into popularity."

The wedding dress generally thought to be the industry standard today—sheer yoke of tulle or organza, predominantly lace bodice, full convertible skirt with a train and a delicate sweetheart neckline—is a contribution of the 1940s, Ms. Milbank says. The 1950s, an epoch of unabashed prosperity, produced even fuller skirts. On the whole, wedding dresses during that decade tended to look more than ever like evening gowns, particularly those of Dior; hemlines for a brief period scooted up to the graceful ballerina or cocktail length, probably after the example set by Wallis Simpson, who married the Duke of Windsor.

Oddly, the turbulent 1960s delivered some of the most innocent wedding styles seen in over a century, with kerchiefs, Empire waists, pinafores, and other elements directly related to baby clothes. The 1970s, in contrast, felt the anti-establishment heat with a countercultural display of peasant and Mexican wedding dresses sporting big bishop sleeves and colored and batiked ruffles. Even so, the predominant styles of the day were princess lines and cream or white silk and satin.

Certainly the excessive 1980s took their cue as much from the royal wedding of Diana Spencer and Prince Charles as they did from the bullish stock market, and more stops were pulled out in the name of matrimonial bliss during this period than perhaps during any other. Although a relaxed, less ostentatious mode is predicted for the remainder of the 1990s, weddings in general, and wedding dresses in particular, seem reluctant to pull in the reins. As Caroline Milbank notes, "The dearth of pageantry in life today may be behind the fact that an elaborate wedding has become the only socially condoned form of excess. . . . The fantasy of being a beautiful bride and having the perfect wedding is particularly potent because it represents an attainable goal, far more likely, in fact, than the possibility of having a happy marriage."

On the other hand, most bridal salon specialists report a decided trend

Bustles are as popular today as they were in the 1880s.

toward marrying for the long haul, and hand in hand with it a sense of urgency about incorporating such traditions as heirloom garters and handkerchiefs and the various somethings old, new, borrowed, and blue.

The New Current

*J*im Hjelm, a thirty-year industry veteran known for his timeless designs, insists that tradition has never really been out, even though wedding dresses have followed a gentler version of fashion's curves. "Tradition never really left us, even when people were getting married in fields in the seventies. Tradition is tradition of the moment; you move with the silhouettes of the times, but you maintain a classic line. A bride doesn't want to look at her wedding portrait twenty years later and say, 'Oh my God, what was that?' She doesn't want it to be dated looking." Elegant designs and high-quality materials like silk shantung, silk taffeta, tulle, and imported lace lend further lasting charm to Hjelm's looks.

Vera Wang's bridal boutique, Bridal House Ltd., showcases her own collection of wedding dresses as well as those of major French, Italian, British, and American designers. Recently she's been designing wedding separates in two and three pieces, so a bride can have a full and dramatic silhouette but pare it down for the reception with a sexy slim sheath or a narrow, off-the-shoulder lace suit worn underneath. She's doing more gowns in ivory tones and even a few that have bands of color or pastel flowers. She sells plenty of tra-

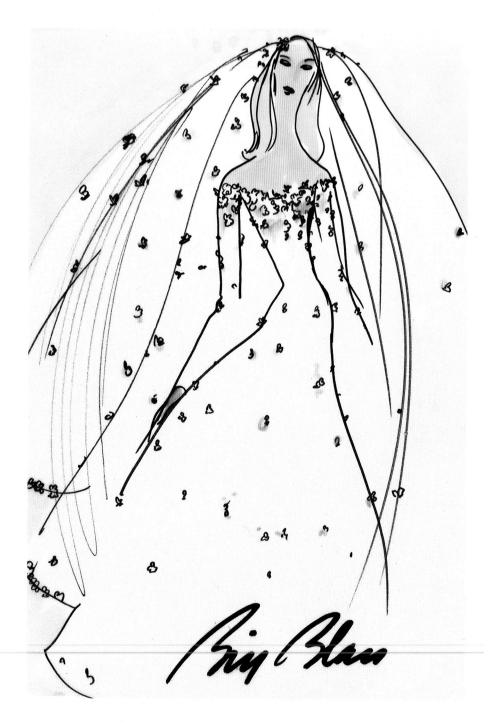

ditional Priscilla of Boston gowns with satin, lace appliqué, and beading, but she's also designing shirred body dresses of crepe or chiffon for the bride who refuses to leave her siren's song at the altar. "It's all about personal style in the nineties," she says. "I like to find interesting fashion and convert it into bridal wear. We've done dresses in damask, faille, brocade, short pouffy dresses, and even suits — a cardigan jacket with a skirt, for example. My clients, who have dresses custom-designed in my atelier, are really starting to take some steps, small steps though. I mean, I'm definitely not getting any bright red brides yet."

Of course, brides have craved old lace for eons, and the fine wedding outfits of any era were not complete without some generous incorporation of it, usually handed down from mother or grandmother to daughter with no little sentiment and ceremony. The renewed interest in handmade antique lace that sprang up in the 1980s continues unabated into the 1990s, and designers like Pat Kerr of Memphis, Tennessee, have capitalized on it with one-of-a-kind designs that are guaranteed to become the heirlooms of tomorrow. Kerr feels as if the recent tendency toward more serious, solid marriages is in some cerebral way tied up with the current fascination with old lace, a longtime collecting passion of hers. "A new, though classically shaped, wedding

Fantasy wedding dresses for the nineties designed by Bill Blass (opposite), Carolina Herrera (above), Jim Hjelm (top right), and Vera Wang (bottom right).

gown," she says, "combined with antique laces, luscious silks, and brocades, brings with it a real tradition of time."

Southerners in particular view their weddings, and their wedding dresses, with no small measure of pride and celebration. Says designer Bill Blass, "Southerners tend to take weddings more seriously than Northerners do.

They're serious, social occasions and their dresses tend to be serious costumes because of it. It wouldn't occur to me to actually design a dress as an heirloom, to be passed along to another generation. I definitely design for the particular bride and her tastes right now. They're older now, and they have a good idea of what they want."

Margaret Haughton, department manager and bridal buyer of the Dallas Neiman-Marcus stores, agrees. "Brides are more apt to try and make a personal statement these days. They're generally more knowledgeable about fabrics and lace and about designers." She finds more and more brides opting for all white or ivory weddings, from the bridesmaids to the mother of the bride to the flower girls—often with the intention of harking back to the historical precedent, but just as often for aesthetic reasons alone. She also sees a trend toward the whimsical, but achieved through silhouette and line rather than through excessive beading and sequins. And, she notes, most importantly there is a real movement toward dressing to be comfortable on your wedding day.

Pinning Down the Dream Dress

With such a rich history of wedding costume design and the endless opportunities of today's bridal marketplace, ferreting out that perfect wedding dress can be an overwhelming project. Fortunately, there are a

Helen Benton of Arkansas designed all the dresses for Laura Bowen and her bridesmaids.

number of influencing factors—size, season, time, site of the ceremony, desire for tradition, and degree of formality, for starters—that help weed out inappropriate choices from the outset. Then, of course, you need to do some looking. Perhaps the best place to start is the monthly fashion forum on wedding wear in the various bridal magazines. Comb their pages for the latest offerings, and check out the styles pictured in fashion history and couture books to begin shaping your dream dress.

Museums and galleries around the country periodically offer exhibits on historic wedding costumes that provide a wealth of information and inspiration. One of the premier permanent installations is the Woodruff-Fontaine House in Memphis; yearly exhibits draw from a repository of nineteenth-century clothing and accessories to present remarkably preserved wedding costumes from around the South.

It always pays to try on your mother's dress, if she still has it, even if it's not what you think you have in mind. The sentimental value is inestimable, and dressmakers can do marvelous things to tailor the design to suit your figure and sense of fashion. Aunts and grandmothers often have hidden treasures under their beds, and chances are they'd be honored to see you breathe new life into them on your wedding day. The most critical aspect is to try and force yourself to keep an open mind. Don't make the mistake of refusing to look past the dropped waist and sweetheart neckline you've always imagined yourself in; you may just cheat yourself out of a ravishing portrait collar that would have set off your neck and shoulders to perfection, or a soft satin sheath that would have been the ultimate for your garden ceremony, or a dramatic open back nipped in with flat satin bows from the waistline all the way to the hem of a three-foot cathedral train. And, for that matter, don't forget the back of the dress; it plays more than a cameo role in the ceremony, after all, and should be flattering and interesting as you stand at the altar. Trust your own instincts in the final analysis, but listen to other opinions along the way; you may be surprised.

Crystal Moffett and her mother, Louise, flew to Paris to have their dresses designed by French couturier Pierre Cardin. Crystal's dress is of white silk satin with a bustle on either side. MIKE POSEY PHOTOGRAPHY

Bridal Salons and Couture Collections

When a bride walks into the Saks Fifth Avenue bridal salon in New Orleans, says Christina Wysocki, "she'll start to design her wedding dress by the process of elimination. We'll talk about what she thinks she wants, some of the practical aspects of the wedding—time of day and year, etc.—and then we'll start looking at dresses. Maybe she'll like the sleeves in one, but not the neckline, the skirt in another, but not the fabric. We'll look at different shades of white. We try to encourage things one way or another, based on our own experience in fashion, but ultimately the dress has to feel great on her; it's very apparent when a girl finds her dress. She might try something that she's curious about, something I might not even have suggested for her. Then, once she puts it on, her whole face and body come to life, and she'll say, 'This is it!' She'll become absolutely radiant, and there's no question in anybody's mind that she's found the dress that will make her a gorgeous bride."

At Anne Barge for Brides in Atlanta, brides-to-be are offered expert advice. In these photographs sales consultant Matilda Dobbs helps Marie Berry choose dresses that flatter her tall and slender figure.

Above: Matilda Dobbs and Ruby Velasquez help Marie with the buttons of this Carolina Herrera dress of raw silk. Its wonderful details include a jeweled neckline and cuffs.

Below: A custom-designed veil by Crowning Touch beautifully complements this off-the-shoulder Glasgow dress.

Above: This Christian Dior dress features a low V back and a bustle.

Below: Ruby secures a wreath of fresh flowers to the veil. This dress of Italian silk is from the Marissa Collection.

Above: This Carolina Herrera dress features a white tulle skirt that is longer in the back. The handwork is of stones and pearls appliquéd on alencon lace.

Most bridal shops are able to coordinate veils and make recommendations on accessories and shoes after a firm decision is made on the dress. It's important to remember that the wedding costume, and in fact the array of the entire wedding retinue, must be considered as a whole. It's not unlike theater: while the bride is admittedly the dramatic lead, there remains a whole cast of characters—from groom to groomsmen to bridesmaids to children attendants—who must be outfitted in a manner that's cohesive and evocative when the curtain rises on the final act. Further, there are extra accessories like money purses, special garters, and luscious petticoats that a bride may want to spring for on this once-in-a-lifetime celebration.

Or keep an ear open for trunk shows in your local bridal boutiques. Player Butler and her mother made a ritual out of going to bridal shows. "It's kind of a throwback to the fifties," say her mother, Noel Sengel. "We had a wonderful time going to some of the shows around Washington. We found the dress at Woodward & Lothrop, but it was a real treat to take a few days here and there to watch a wonderful fashion show, essentially, and have champagne and croissants and strawberries. We found it gave us an idea of what was out there in various price ranges. It's fun, and a lot easier to visualize than just looking at magazine pages.

It's a little like being a fairy princess for a day."

Player settled on a portrait collar design by Richard Glasgow, who, being on hand at the show, also fitted her and made recommendations on her headpiece and accessories. The dress, dramatic in its simplicity, was elegant in a true white satin, luscious against Player's dark hair. "I wanted Player to look like Grace Kelly," Noel remembers. "She and I always loved the classic look of that time period; we didn't want a lot of lace, and I think we both wanted to see bare shoulders. Glasgow took a look at it on her, and said, 'Please, don't wear any jewelry at all around your neck. Keep the line really clean.' He designed the headpiece, which was essentially a flat bow in keeping with the back of the dress and a huge piece of tulle."

Brides-to-be from all over the South go to Yvonne LaFleur in New Orleans. Her dresses are customized, as are her dramatic one-of-a-kind headpieces. First- and many second-time brides may choose from a wide selection of antique lace that she has been collecting since 1971, antique wax orange blossoms from Germany, silk flowers from the Fromentine collection in Paris, sprays of pearls and rhinestones, and marquisette illusion. All of these beautiful trims are housed in antique armoires and cases from the Victoria and Albert Museum in London. Yvonne helps each bride-to-

be select a headpiece, taking into account such criteria as her hairstyle and the formality of the wedding.

Caroline Milbank, being well versed in couture, had a precise idea in her head of the just-so dress for her wedding day. She was vaguely disappointed by everything she saw on the retail market, and was particularly aghast at the prices. So, with a trusted local seamstress, she copied a longtime favorite evening gown from her own *New York Fashion* and landed her absolute dream dress for under $500.

Everything Old Is New Again

$\mathcal{I}$f good luck really does rub off, then there can be no more powerful talisman than wearing the wedding dress of a mother or grandmother. In the colonial South, when fashion was slow to change, the high cost of materials made virtually all apparel valuable; ladies' garments were routinely willed to daughters or nieces, along with favorite jewelry and undergarments. And although today's mores regrettably favor a disposable attitude toward clothes and other chattel, the South continues to set great store by hand-me-downs of all description; wedding dresses are no exception.

Bryce Reveley, a noted textiles conservator and owner of the New Orleans firm Gentle Arts, comments,

On her wedding day in June 1952 Betty Drennen showed off the exquisite detail of her dress.

"People are definitely more sentimental in the South. Heritage is very important to them. Land is in their blood, and they have a bred-in interest in their roots. It means something to them to wear their grandmother's lace or their great-grandfather's watch. I'm a little ashamed of it, but my family always used to say, 'Well, she's awfully nice, but you know she had to buy her silver,' as if the thought of not having generations behind her to inherit it from was the most pitiable thing on earth. That sort of thing still actually matters in the South, and weddings are the most obvious display of that kind of sentiment." An authority on preserving and caring for antique textiles, Reveley also reconstructs and redesigns old gowns and wedding accessories. "There's a tremendous sense of love and continuity that comes with being able to say, 'I'm the seventh person in my family who's worn this dress,'" she notes.

When Jennie Hart Forbes was married in April 1990 in Chattanooga, she was the eleventh family member and fifth generation to wear an heirloom dress made in New York in 1873. Jennie's aunt, Betty Drennen of Birmingham, is the primary caretaker of the dress, a heavy silk and satin design accented by rose point lace; after each wearing she stores it in an acid-free box—ordered specially from the New Orleans Museum—at the family homestead, Hawthorne Heights, in Union Point, Georgia. The dress made its debut on Betty's paternal great-grandmother, Addie Collier, and since has been altered slightly by each bride to suit her own tastes and times: Betty's grandmother Katherine Sibley Bryan added leg-o'-mutton sleeves and illusion at the neckline, aunt Virginia Bryan McCulloch fashioned the rose point lace into a V-neck, while Betty, who wore the dress in 1952, changed the lace into a lightly ruffled bertha. The full ruffled skirt has not been changed, although each bride has brought her own headpiece to the ensemble. (For advice on saving and preserving your dress, see page 242.)

In most cases, heirlooming and refitting a vintage dress still falls well short of the cost of buying a new dress. For brides with a special eye to history, Bryce Reveley suggests looking under the antiques category in the newspaper classified section, checking out church rummage sales and estate sales, or buying a dress from a reputable vintage garment dealer. Her own wedding dress was literally found in the trash by a friend living in Dallas.

But, she warns, there are pitfalls to antique dresses. You have considerably less control over the outcome of a shored-up vintage dress than you do over the known quantity you select off the rack, and you may as well accept the fact that you're probably not going to be as comfortable as you might in a new dress. Textiles are perishable, and even a reinforced dress is guaranteed to be fragile. Learn how to wear it, she cautions, and spring for the undergarments that will best protect and set it off. Be mindful of dancing with too much abandon, and try to keep your father from stepping on your hem when he kisses you. And above all, check with whomever is responsible for keeping the dress for the proper permissions before doing any alterations. (For Bryce Reveley's advice on preserving wedding veils, see page 241.)

Heirloom Records

Chronicle your family's wedding heritage by starting an album or wedding portfolio. As Bryce Reveley suggests, be sure to include names and dates as well as photographs and newspaper clippings. Jot down comments or remembrances, and contact living relatives for their own souvenirs of the day. Take particular note of a dress that's handed down from generation to generation, citing the particular embellishments and changes made by each bride; other memorabilia such as watches, necklaces, lace, tussie-mussies, or any other sentimental items that make it from one wedding to the next also bear a mention. Remember that wedding petticoats can be made into beautiful christening gowns; include notations and photographs of the recycled gown in its new incarnations.

These flower girls wore handmade dresses of cream batiste and white lace at their aunt's wedding in Birmingham. CHIESA

in helping you create a flattering look that will stand the test of time and in accommodating the most becoming type of headpiece to your face and hairline.

Shoes should, above all, be comfortable, for the bride must meet and greet, dance and dip in her wedding slippers. Try them out, walk around in them for a day or two before they carry you down the aisle. Wonderful accents of beading and bows, sequins and even rhinestones create a sense of finery in wedding footwear for the

Left: Antique lace and wedding accessories from the collection of Bryce Reveley, New Orleans.

Below: For Amanda Adams's at-home wedding in Birmingham, Duff was suitably attired in a lace garter. GIBBONS

Luscious Odds and Ends

*A*ccessories to the wedding gown often bring tradition into the picture for a bride. Perhaps the most important accessories are her headpiece and veil. Old family lace may be used, or pearl- or satin-edged tulle in various lengths depending on the for-mality of the occasion. Styles vary; for some brides, a gorgeous point lace mantilla may create the right mood, while for others a crown or wreath makes the point. For still others, a simple bow or bandeau or spray of fresh flowers offers an elegant but minimal look. It pays to play around with the options before committing; your hairdresser should be invaluable

Trousseaus

The word *trousseau* originates from the French term *trousse*, or bundle, referring to the fact that a woman "bundled" together with her dowry created the de facto marriage package for a suitor. Formerly, Southern brides assembled first- and second-day outfits—and sometimes as many as a week's worth—to be worn after the wedding, the postnuptial wardrobe falling only slightly behind the wedding dress in importance. Nowadays, however, with the median age for brides being older than ever before, chances are a girl has both career and casual wardrobes well in hand by the time she marries, pushing the lovely concept of a trousseau into obsolescence. Today, the custom generally translates into a nice new set of going-away clothes, usually a smart suit and hat or a chic traveling dress. But it seems a shame to let a charming custom wither on the vine; at the least, treat yourself to some new lingerie or a few new accessories to mark the beginning of your new life.

bride who wants her costume to be complete. On the other hand, wedding shoes hardly make the splash a dress and veil do, and for economy-minded brides, they can be a real savings area; an inexpensive peau de soie with a comfortable heel does the trick nicely, or even ballet slippers, leaving you some residual funds to apply toward other elements of the wedding garb. Grass stains are one of the big enemies of elegant wedding shoes, so beware; but don't let finickiness put a damper on your fun, either—you can always dye them later.

Often handed down, handkerchiefs can be essential when emotions are running high; it is said that a bride who cries on her wedding day never sheds another tear about her marriage. One charming custom invites each bride to monogram the handkerchief before passing it along to a sister or daughter.

The garter represents one of the oldest wedding traditions still practiced today. It may be old, new, borrowed, and/or blue, and is often removed by the groom at the close of the reception and tossed to a lucky bachelor, then destined to be the next to marry. Vera Wang and Pat Kerr offer special designs in old lace and nice satins. Pale blues, creams, and whites are the most requested, but Vera has made up sexy black garters for brides who like to spice up tradition with a little shock effect.

Money purses are an integral part

Beading added a sense of finery to Robin Robinson's wedding shoes. SCHILLING

of the bride's raiment in some cultures and faiths. Often made of exquisite old lace, they represent another opportunity for establishing ritual within a family, by being passed along from generation to generation. The bride carries a money purse during the reception so that guests may offer monetary wedding presents at any time. Brides may also consider a wedding purse in beautiful old lace or seed pearls and sequins so that they can have handkerchief, lipstick, or compact handy during the reception.

Depending on her dress, the season, and the time of day, a bride might wish to incorporate a nice pair of kid gloves into her ensemble, but as Bryce Reveley, always to the point, says, "Very few wedding costumes need gloves, and they just add problems, in my view. If you insist, well then go on, but you'd better practice ahead of time, especially the exchange-of-rings portion of the ceremony."

Dressing the Wedding Party

The wedding tableau should be considered as a whole, and that whole should be more than the sum of its parts. Certainly, the bride and her wedding array command center stage, but the groom and his groomsmen and ushers, the bridesmaids, flower girls, and ring and train bearers all figure into the composite; with a little planning the big picture should have all the resonance of an Impressionist painting.

The degree of formality is set by the type of wedding and reception, the time of day, and the setting, all of which generally influence the size of the wedding party as well. Those decisions firmly made, a bride can proceed

For a Nashville wedding, the bridesmaids' dresses of pale pink taffeta took a simple, pared-down cue from the bride's more elaborate wedding gown.

to narrowing the field of color and mood as she moves closer to dressing the wedding party.

Historically, brides have seemed just about incapable of choosing bridesmaids' dresses that didn't irk the girls who wore them in one way or another. Over the last few centuries, bridesmaids' dresses have essentially mimicked the bride's wedding gown in

color and style, although in the 1930s and 1940s, the custom shifted to pastels in organdy and tulle, with the maid of honor in a different color or a slightly fancier version of same to spotlight her for the crowd. Currently, there are few limitations on the available choices, other than those of etiquette. In the last few years, considerable effort has been made by many brides to select

it's a matter of courtesy to include a maid of honor in the decision making, don't try to cater to the whims of everyone from your individual bridesmaids to your mother-in-law-to-be.

Grooms' and groomsmen's apparel has always presented less of a snafu,

Left: Dathel Coleman chose two-piece dresses designed by Angelle Parlange of New Orleans for her bridesmaids. The off-the-shoulder portrait collars echoed the neckline of Dathel's Glasgow gown.

Below: For the evening ceremony, John Georges of New Orleans and his groomsmen opted for black tuxedos with bow ties and cummerbunds.

that elusive dress "that can be worn again."

Suiting up a bevy of bridesmaids with no particular average height, weight, or coloring is no mean feat, especially when price is indeed an object. The best bets are to look for hues that create a nice backdrop, styles that avoid the trendy or overwhelming. Think of silhouettes that flatter a variety of figure types and colors or prints that don't garishly assume control of the scene. Try, too, to be mindful of budget, remembering that the dress is only one of many expenses your bridesmaids will incur just to be in your wedding. Probably the most crucial point to master is the fact that the choice is ultimately the bride's; while

Children are always a treat to outfit for the wedding; although special thought should be given to including them in the ceremony, they do make adorable additions to the whole. Eton collars for boys and beautiful eyelet or organdy for girls are just a few of the myriad options.

with styles ranging widely from the ultraformal black full dress or tails with white shirt, piqué vest, and tie for an evening wedding to a blue blazer, gray trousers, and loafers combination for casual daytime affairs. Etiquette dictates that weddings with ceremonies beginning before 6:00 P.M. are daytime events. The morning suit—a cutaway coat with gray striped trousers, gray vest, ascot or tie—is a favorite formal ensemble before sunset. Add a top hat, spats, or gloves if you feel daring. For a less formal look, a groom might consider a gray stroller and striped trousers with a dapper homburg. For the semiformal evening ceremony, the attire has traditionally included a black tuxedo with bow tie and vest or cummerbund. And for the hotter climate, a white dinner jacket with formal trousers might be a fun alternative.

A Marriage Made Near Mobile

When Lee Rutherford's great-grandmother died in 1988 at age 99, she left behind, among other things, two exquisite vintage dresses. Lee's grandmother had the dresses cleaned and repaired, and when Lee saw them, she knew instantly that one of them would be her wedding dress. "I had always had in the back of mind," she remembers, "the idea that I wanted a country wedding that was both elegant and simple, where people could take off their shoes if they wanted, but still enjoy a feeling of beautiful flowers and wonderful food and a special country setting. Elegant, but not stuffy in any way. And for that kind of wedding, it just seemed that an heirloom lace dress was the perfect thing. I knew from the start that I didn't want a new dress, and something with a long train just seemed out of place. Neither of these

dresses had actually been wedding dresses, but they seemed just right for what I wanted; I tried on both of them, and chose the one that looked the most flattering."

The dress, an ankle-length design of remarkable old rolled lace, had a fitted waist and short sleeves. A minimal change made to the original choker neckline—one panel of lace was removed—left a more flattering square neck that suited Lee. Further, the orig-

Above: The entrance gates at Chasley were decorated with pineapple-shaped topiaries. These pineapples, symbols of hospitality, are made up of seed pods, strawflowers, chrysanthemums, pecans, moss, and fresh green boxwood, and topped with two dozen aspidistra leaves.

Left: The reception was held at Lee's family seat, Chasley, situated near the tiny village of Franklin, Alabama. The plantation, built in 1827, is used for holidays and special family occasions.

inal eighteen-inch waist was brought into more reasonable 1990s proportions, and elegant covered buttons were added to the back to replace hook-and-eye closures. Her veil was designed by Yvonne LaFleur of New Orleans.

All the events surrounding the early October wedding weekend had about them a quality very like that of this hand-me-down dress: an unforgettable sense of place, of time, of family, and of ritual—all the things that make the South the South. Throughout—from the country bridesmaids' luncheon held at the 1824 Masonic Hall, to the groomsmen's pontoon-boat fishing party, to the rehearsal dinner held at Sumner's family's lovely Mount Pleasant home, amid tables draped effectively in burlap and antique quilts to the wedding-day hunt breakfast to the ceremony and reception themselves—there reigned the unaffected

air of gracious hospitality, of Southern plenty, of old family homesteads and relatives reminiscing.

The wedding was held at 4:30 P.M. at the River Ridge Methodist Church, a charming 1890s structure erected on land generously deeded by a Rutherford family ancestor. Because there was no air-conditioning, all windows were left open, allowing the sweet scent of locally gathered wildflowers planted in window boxes to drift inside.

In keeping with the relatively tiny size of the church and the casual outdoor reception at the Rutherford family seat, Chasley, Lee went about grooming her wedding party with a clear, logical approach. "I certainly had fall in mind when I was thinking about the colors and the feel, although things are always pretty green around here at the beginning of October. It's more like late summer, just turning."

Above: Lee and Sumner share a dance.

Left: Instead of dropping petals or carrying bouquets, the children carried small satin-covered hoops decorated with ivy and flowers.

Right: During the reception the children all took rides in the Rutherfords' hay wagon.

Opposite: The River Ridge Methodist Church, built by the Rutherford family over a hundred years ago, was decorated simply and elegantly with arrangements of ivy, ginger, Casablanca lilies, daisies, larkspur, tallaberry, floribunda roses, and pittosporum. The pews were adorned with daisies, fern, and pittosporum.

Luckily we had a cold snap, though, so leaves were starting to change." Lee and Sumner agreed on a simple costume for the groomsmen: blue blazers, white shirts, creamy trousers, and brown loafers. The tie, a rust-colored foulard, nicely echoed the bridesmaids' dresses—a coppery silk taffeta copied by a local seamstress from a favorite dress out of Lee's own wardrobe. "It's really hard to work out a dress that looks flattering on lots of different peo-

Right: The rehearsal dinner was held at the country home of the groom's parents, Ann and Marion Adams. Decorations included a wagon filled with baskets of goldenrod, and tables decorated with Ann's antique quilts and bouquets of wildflowers and gourds.

Below: The bridesmaids' luncheon was held at a Masonic lodge built in 1824 in Perdue Hill. Pumpkins, wildflowers, antique plows, and cotton baskets filled with corn husks, flowers, and gingham-wrapped champagne bottles created a rustic atmosphere.

ple," she notes. "I knew I wanted something clean and straight, and I'd always liked this dress of mine. I thought it might actually be wearable again." With its graceful square neck and back, cap sleeve, straight silhouette, and layered hem, the dress complemented the lines of Lee's wedding dress nicely and indeed proved wearable after the wedding.

For the country setting, Lee had envisioned the bridesmaids in straw hats from the very start. "I didn't want anything sweet or frou-frou," she says, "but something very like the country. It was fun. We went down to the wholesale market and picked out dried flowers and woven ribbon to go on them." Instead of letting bridesmaids' bouquets take a reserved back seat to the potent hue of the dress, she opted for a burst of unabashed color; the bridesmaids carried loose French-braided sheaves of mixed cut flowers in fuchsia, pink, orange, purple, and yellow, all the colors of a late summer garden against the autumnal canvas of their dresses.

Lee and Sumner had eight children serve as flower girls and boys, all of whom are young cousins, nieces, and nephews on both sides. A picture of

*Top: The groomsmen awaiting their instruc-
tions.*

*Bottom: For her bridesmaids, Lee chose cop-
per-colored dresses and straw hats decorated with
dried flowers and raffia.*

children attendants in a French brides
magazine gave Lee the seed of an idea
for her young attendants' attire and
flowers. Instead of dropping petals or
holding bouquets, both the boys and
the girls carried small satin-covered
hoops. (For instructions for making a
wedding hoop, see pages 219–20.) To
communicate to a seamstress the specific idea she had in mind for their outfits, Lee combed through dozens of
pattern books and magazines. She
wound up with white socks, midshin
cuffed trousers and cummerbunds,
white shirts, and big lace collars for
the boys; for the girls, the same lace
collars capped off straight creamy
white dresses.

The overall wedding canvas—from
the blue blazers to the straw hats to
the dreamy children's ensembles to
Lee's own heavenly lace heirloom—
created a perfect picture of fall; it was
exactly what the church, with its
breezy open windows, and gracious,
white-columned Chasley called for.

The Invitations and Parties

Presentations and Parties: Harbingers of Happiness

*T*here was a time when news of an upcoming wedding was spread by the posting of banns or public notices, and with about as much enthusiasm as roll call. The curious practice, said to have originated with Charlemagne, was an attempt to avoid intermarriage at a time when, among other reasons, random indiscretions frequently blurred lines of ancestry. Public notices, too, were the most efficient method of disseminating information in a day when

❦

Opposite: At Leslie Daubenberger and Bobby Lorton's rehearsal dinner, clear tents trimmed with tiny lights created a romantic atmosphere.

Right: Ann Penn of Fort Worth used a magnolia blossom motif on the invitations to her son's rehearsal dinner in Nashville.

personal invitations were a rarely indulged luxury. The custom carried over to Colonial America and is still practiced today in some churches, predominantly Catholic, but with a happily modified raison d'être: nowadays, the congregation is made aware of a couple's marriage intentions not so they might comb the family trees for undisclosed lines of kinship but because it is considered their duty to foster the healthy marital relations of one of their flock, much as might conscientious godparents.

Today, spreading the joyous news of a wedding is a multilayered affair, and in passing along the word certain forms of communication are better suited to certain groups than others. There are people in both the bride's and groom's lives, for example, whom they'll want to inform immediately, in person or by telephone if distances don't permit a face-to-face encounter; parents, grandparents, siblings, and particularly close friends usually fall into this category. This is also just the

time and place for a handwritten note to godparents or cherished aunts or uncles—the time investment is frequently less damaging than that of a phone call, and the distinctive pleasure of receiving anything handwritten these days should in no way be underestimated.

For that broader circle of social and business acquaintances, an engagement announcement in the newspaper will suffice. Local newspapers have individual sets of guidelines for what is

Wedding invitations in the South are usually traditional, though some brides opt for the unusual. A trip to Jamaica for Karen Sherman's wedding was one of a kind, so she had invitations hand painted (top center). Larry Morse of Little Rock created a formal invitation with a white moiré bow and gold trim (right).

customarily printed, and you'll save yourself an inordinate amount of time by asking the society editor for specifications—have a form sent to you if one is available—before spending man-hours on an epic account with a lot of extraneous material. Ordinarily, a black-and-white photo of the bride-to-be is required along with information concerning her parentage and schooling, her fiancé's parentage and schooling, and the proposed wedding date and location, if known. Some newspapers, especially in smaller towns, permit more luxurious detail.

Then, of course, there is that select body of friends, family, and acquaintances the bride and groom will wish to invite to the wedding and/or reception—thus arises the practical need for a wedding invitation. Since the invitation is a lasting memento of the occasion, to say nothing of the important first impression made on guests, it pays to give more than a fleeting thought to selection of paper, typeface, and style. If your wedding is formal and your aim is tradition, there are two correct choices: white cotton rag engraved with black ink or ecru cotton rag

engraved with black ink. Wording is third person with the bride's parents listed, at least figuratively, as hosts, requesting the honour of your presence at the marriage ceremony of their daughter, whose first and middle names only are given, along with the full name of the groom, preceded by the title Mr. or Dr. For invitations to the reception, the pleasure of one's company is requested. Also requested

today is the favour of a reply—conspicuously absent from earlier invitations, to which a prompt, gracious reply was the natural conclusion drawn by all recipients—and without the advance reminder.

Regrettably, however, ours is not a perfect world: parents are divorced, deceased, or remarried and often don't give their children away at all, so these days chances of textbook wording on a wedding invitation are slim. Naturally, there are plenty of commonsense solutions to these matters of etiquette and extended families, and a proper invitation is attainable for virtually anyone, no matter how convoluted her family history.

Having said this, more than a passing mention should be made of the fact that the wedding invitation as we now know it is really a product of the twentieth century, which makes quibbling over what's correct and what isn't something of a moot point—assuming correctness has something to do with outlasting trends. While there are certainly recorded instances of engraved, third-person invitations in the historic South, most wedding invitations took the sensible form of notes or letters, handwritten by the mother of the bride. For weddings of a manageable size today, this is still a perfectly proper and quite lovely option. If the bride has lived under her own roof sufficiently long and is uncomfortable with the idea of being given away by her parents, she may find it silly for anyone other than herself to pen the notes. Jackie Slutzky, graphic artist and owner of Pace's Papers, a fine stationer in Atlanta, frequently revives the gracious old tradition by making a plate of the mother-of-the-bride's handwritten invitation and engraving it on fine paper stock to send out for small weddings.

In the nineteenth century, invitation cards not much larger than today's business card became increasingly popular. These engraved invitations simply stated the names of the bride's parents, who inevitably did the hosting, along with the date, time, and place and the names of the young intendeds in the lower right-hand corner. Simple, but unflaggingly elegant.

After World War I, the double-fold invitation that is today's standard-bearer became firmly entrenched, although commonly it was the formal oversized (or embassy) version requiring an extra fold before being slipped into the envelope. It also tended to be personalized, with a blank line left for writing the invitee's name by hand. (Nowadays, the all-purpose variety capitalizing on the convenient word

Preserving Invitations

For decades, brides have held on to their wedding invitations as permanent keepsakes. A thin gold frame is probably the most formal format, but more whimsical versions include laminating invitations on trash baskets or large pillar candles and lacquering them on the tops of wedding boxes or hope chests for storing other wedding memorabilia—the garter and sixpence, other party invitations, copies of favorite rehearsal dinner toasts, dried flowers from the bouquet. My mother-in-law decoupaged all my debutante party and wedding party invitations along with lace and bits of fabric on a hope chest; years later, it's a heartwarming souvenir of a very happy time. Mary Virginia Weinmann of New Orleans was given a gorgeous camellia bowl with her wedding invitation etched on it as a thoughtful present from friends.

Now Rhonda Aguillard of Legacy in Fort Worth, Texas, preserves wedding invitations for brides via the time-honored art of quilling. The invitation is delicately bordered with tiny bits of rolled paper and seed pearls, placed in a shadow box, and then mounted on burgundy or teal velvet before being framed in a gesso-look frame. Another of her coterie of dedicated Texas craftsmen affixes dried flowers to the invitation, either in a small swag or bouquet; then she watercolors the foliage and ribbons or bows and coats the finished product in protective plastic. The bride has only to slip it into the frame of her choice.

"your" is used almost exclusively.) Tissue paper, originally used to blot drying ink, is obsolete from a practical point of view, but is used occasionally for the fun of it.

Of course, wedding invitations have long since broken out of their traditional confines, as older and second-time engaged couples with definitive ideas about marriage and the occasion of it have attempted to put their personal stamp on the celebration—and often without sacrificing good taste. The most successful of these, I find, are the ones that announce themselves for what they are: sometimes just a refreshing new look at the marriage ceremony, such as an invitation to a warm social, and sometimes spiritual, gathering at which a marriage ceremony will be taking place. Handled with a light, sensitive touch, nontraditional wedding invitations do indeed communicate much to the recipient about the bride, the groom, and the event, and are often just what's wanted for an individual occasion.

I must confess that, for me, the classic, understated elegance of the genuine article—complete with its fine papers, dark inks, and proper wording—has no legitimate equal. But then times do change, even in the South.

❧

Since the wedding invitation is a lasting memento of the occasion, it pays to give more than a fleeting thought to selection of paper, typeface, and style. SCHILLING

Christina Wysocki of Saks Fifth Avenue in New Orleans laughingly confided that she reluctantly accepted the appearance of stamps on wedding invitations. In her day they were strictly hand delivered on a silver tray by the bride's mother's domestic servants. Jackie Slutzky settled the distinction in her mind this way: "If the wedding is in a house of worship," she says, "then the invitation should be traditional, but if it's in any other place—a country club, a botanical garden, at home, etc.—you can do something different." Even for the something different, though, Jackie uses the finest paper (much of it imported from France) inks, and interesting old plates; she globetrots on a regular basis, scouring fine shops in the world's cultural centers for a peek at the best offerings to take back to her shop. In the final analysis, then, the debate over what's proper in wedding invitations is far from over, and is probably a matter best left to etiquette experts (see "Formal Invitation Etiquette," pages 235–36).

If you do decide on a formal invitation, your first steps should lead to a good local stationer; there, after poring over the sample books, you'll finally settle on a style of paper and a typeface that suits you. Wording may leave you scratching your head, however, even if yours is a straightforward family situation. Martha Woodham, the society editor of the *Atlanta Constitution* and author of the monthly column "Modern Manners" in *Elegant Bride* magazine, says that although the queens of etiquette frown on it, she is not bothered by seeing divorced parents on the same invitation, if they get along. As to whether stepparents should join the real parents in doing the inviting, she insists an absolute ruling cannot be made; if you've been all but raised by your mother and stepfather, for example, and have had virtually no relationship with your real father, it makes sense to include the stepfather on the invitation. A commonsense/good manners approach should prevail, frankly, over anything etched in etiquette books. The real pitfall in today's extended families, she says, is the pressure, or perhaps genuine desire, to include four sets of parents on an invitation, especially when the bill is being shared by the bride's and groom's real parents and their new spouses, as well, perhaps, as by the couple. "Remember," she cautions, "a wedding invitation is not a Broadway show. The invitation is not a list of credits and, perhaps unfairly, is not meant to be a reflection of who's picking up the tab for the event. And if there's friction between divorced parents," she adds, "you might consider having the mother do the inviting to the church and the father do the inviting to the reception. Or have both the bride's real parents issue the invitation but put their names on separate lines."

Managing your Guest List: Best Bets for Organized Invitations

The task of assembling a master guest list from the support lists provided by your parents, your groom's parents, possibly grandparents on both sides, to say nothing of your groom's and your own lists, can be exasperating at times. No one ever sticks to the requested number limits, and you can count on everyone's being less than efficient at providing the proper names, spellings, and addresses. Often there are confusing overlaps, especially when bride and groom are from the same town, opening up additional spaces, but to which side's credit? And then, of course, there's the inevitable paring down of the list, the often endless thinking and rethinking of whom to invite and whom you must regrettably eliminate. Many brides find the guest list the most onerous item in the enormous organization chart of wedding planning.

Following are a few tips for controlling the list before it controls you.

• Numbers are driven by several factors: budget, personal preferences, selection of site for ceremony and reception, and so on. Consider all these influencing factors and come to a firm decision with your fiancé's and your parents' input about the size of your guest list. Then the hard part: stick to it.

• Customarily the guest list is chopped into thirds, one each for bride and groom, bride's parents, and groom's parents. This is not etched in stone, however; if the groom's family is from out of town, they might take a quarter, while your parents take half and you and your fiancé take the other quarter. Be mindful of all the players here, and use both common sense and sensitivity in coming up with a workable formula.

• Ask your groom, your parents, and his parents for a maximum list. Be specific about how you'd like the information provided: full name with appropriate titles and correct addresses with zip codes, for example, if it's to be a traditional, formal invitation. You might even run off copies of a basic format leaving blanks for information requested; this will make it easier for them to compile, infinitely easier for you to read, and subtly remind them that you do indeed need every bit of the requested information. Then come up with your own list (you and your groom may compose your list together). Insist on a reasonable deadline and, again, stick to it. Then see where you are. If there are overlaps, note them, and inform parents they may add more names. If you find major number overruns, don't be ashamed to ask parents to trim the list, no matter how difficult. As for your own list, sit down with your groom and discuss each uncertain invitee; think long and hard about why you want to invite them, and remember: this is your wedding ceremony, not a party to pay back social debts or to curry business favors.

• Once you've got a handle on the list, establish a card file—for both ceremony and reception, if necessary—with a section for backup invitations. Transfer each name and address to an individual card. This makes the frequent shuffling and changes of mind easier to deal with. BUT: It's also important to create a flat file, either typed or computer-generated, and alphabetized for quick and easy counting. For the calligrapher or whoever is doing the addressing working from a flat list is far simpler than rifling through cards.

• Be certain to allot plenty of time for proofreading invitations for spelling and other errors.

Then there is the matter of the actual printing and the current battle royale over engraving and thermography, a printing process that inexpensively duplicates for all but the most discerning fingertip the look and feel of engraving. Some argue that economy-minded brides should stand firm on good-quality paper with 100-percent-cotton fiber content over less desirable wood pulp and opt for thermography, letting etiquette mongers run their idle fingers over invitation backs until the cows come home.

Most wedding invitations are apt to require enclosure cards of one type or another. Reception cards or ceremony cards may take several forms. And you may wish to include pew cards or "Within the Ribbons" cards for close family. "At Home" cards furnish the new address of the bride and groom, as well as the names they'll be using. Though an abomination to Miss Manners, the reply card is more and more in evidence as an integral part of the wedding invitation since, alarmingly, it seems the formal reply—or often any reply at all—is considered optional behavior these days.

Carter Bowden, of PS The Letter,

one of Fort Worth's premier stationers, has finally caved in to the reply-card union, however, and while he sees a trend toward the proper, traditional, and formal—99 percent of his clients opt for engraved Crane ecru paper with black ink—he advises considering reply cards. "The easier you make it for guests to reply, the higher the response rate. You must add a stamped, pre-addressed envelope, too,

or few will respond properly." He adds that better than 60 percent of his customers do order reply cards now.

You may also wish to send out wedding announcements to out-of-town friends and acquaintances. These should be engraved or printed following the format of your invitation, and sent the day after the ceremony.

Mary Rose and Martha Wailes of The Stationer in New Orleans suggest

A collage of bachelor and bachelorette party invitations. For the guys, a trip to Las Vegas and a fishing expedition on the Alabama River. For the girls, a weekend in Aspen and a tubing adventure in Virginia.

that invitations should be ordered about three months before the wedding date. Plan on a good week for hand-addressing, more if a calligrapher is used. Most stationers will arrange to give you outer and inner envelopes before the actual invitations and enclosures are finished, so addressing may begin in earnest. Consider sending out the invitations at least four weeks in advance of the wedding date; when regrets come in, it's considered proper to ask others from a second, backup list up to two weeks before the wedding.

Many fine stationery shops have computerized calligraphy capabilities for addressing inner and outer envelopes with a flourish at a fraction of the cost of the actual handwork.

Parties, Parties, Parties

In the South's infancy and adolescence, when the region was predominantly rural and big-city diversions just something to dream about, Southerners developed—perhaps in self-defense—a kind of hospitality that frankly doesn't exist anywhere else in the country. On isolated plantations and farms, opening heart and hearth to family and good friends was the only legitimate entertainment around, and just about anything constituted an occasion for celebration. Even funerals became institutions of great merry-making; weddings tipped the scales. Innumerable parties, dinners, dances, and showers could be squeezed out of one such happy affair, blessedly breaking the monotony of daily routine in the broad country expanses. The excitement of buying new materials and sewing frocks, of planning a special menu and activities for house guests, and of making the endless preparations all combined to create an occasion of almost unbelievable festivity.

Historically, little has tarnished Southerners' love of going to parties—and little has changed in the way they give them. True enough, entertaining has gotten more complicated, and tea and crumpets in a maiden aunt's parlor is probably more exception than rule nowadays. And yet, whether they're entertaining at home or at a favorite commercial establishment, Southerners still have a distinctly languid, comfortable way of making their guests feel at home. Perhaps in a throwback to their own frontier days, they're instinctively creative hosts, always looking for inventive ways to spur passionate and amused conversation. Food, flowers, a little faded glory, and sometimes even a touch of farce combine in a perfect balance that gives their parties a palpable difference. Weddings provide the ideal canvas for creating individual, unusually special parties, and, as harbingers of the fun to come, the accompanying invitations are wonderful opportunities for artistry.

There are a number of parties traditionally associated with weddings, and with the exception of an engagement party, most tend to take place during the wedding weekend. Some are designed merely to honor the bride and groom, others as thank-yous to the wedding party, and still others as entertainment for out-of-town guests who've made a special and appreciated effort to travel to the wedding. Renay Levenson, whose daughter Kathy was married in January 1992 in Atlanta, notes, "Southern weddings usually span an entire weekend of festivities—luncheons, brunches, rehearsal dinners, parties for out-of-town guests after the wedding—and include close relatives, bridal party, and out-of-town guests. Friends host many of the events and sometimes festivities start several months in advance."

Much as invitations, the parties that go hand in hand with a particular wedding speak volumes about the bride and groom. Some couples prefer to downplay the preamble of festivities, concentrating on an elegant, special ceremony, while others positively revel in the excitement of being center stage at rounds of celebrations that begin a full year before the wedding. No strangers to parties of all description, Cindy Brennan's legendary restaurant family virtually raised entertaining to another plane. And yet as a working bride she felt it made sense to restrict the parties that friends and relatives graciously offered to the four-day peri-

Drayton Hall Plantation in Charleston, S.C., is a favorite site for parties of all kinds.

od surrounding the wedding; that way, out-of-towners could make the most of the weekend, and local friends wouldn't overdose on the event before it happened. Though Leslie Dauben-berger and Bobby Lorton were both living in Tulsa, they had met in Dallas, where she was in school. They decided to hold engagement parties, a host of showers, cocktail parties, bachelor and bachelorette dinners in various locales where they'd lived and developed last-ing friendships, as well as luncheons and brunches, plus a full plate of activ-ities for guests and attendants during the wedding weekend.

The Engagement Party

*T*raditionally, the engagement party was given by the parents of the bride anytime after the joyful announcement was made to immediate family. Nowadays, it is also considered entirely proper for the parents of the groom, both sets of parents, or even the bride and groom to host this party, if they wish. Often, however, a bride and groom urge parents to skip the event altogether in favor of marshalling funds for the wedding to come.

The format of an engagement party may be formal or entirely casual, rang-ing from a seated dinner to a cocktail buffet to an outdoor barbecue. It can be held at home or in a restaurant or private club. Often the occasion is a surprise announced by the father of the bride or by the bridal couple, fol-lowed by a touching round of toasts.

Often, when a couple lives away from home, friends elect to host an engagement party for them. Janet Mosely and Tom McMahan, for exam-ple, were living in Fort Myers, Florida, when they decided to get married. Janet's boss and her husband gave them a wonderful country supper in honor of their engagement. Their farm-house was the perfect setting for grilled oysters and a groaning board of tooth-some country food, and they gave Janet and Tom an unforgettable corsage out of the rare orchids they grow. Charlotte and Shy Anderson of Little Rock, Arkansas, had conducted the lion's share of their courtship between flights—she is public relations director for the Dallas Cowboys, and both of them travel extensively for business—so the appropriate spot for their engage-ment party was an airport hangar full of parked planes; the site was decorated festively with oversized model airplanes suspended from the ceiling.

Dinners and Cocktail Parties

During the months preceding the wedding, friends and family often give parties of all description to honor the engaged couple. You may find yourself overwhelmed by all the generous offers. It's important to be gracious in accepting them of course, but also to adopt a pragmatic approach to planning. Trying to coordinate and successfully merge guest lists—your colleagues at work and his, your college friends and his, your childhood friends and family, his—can be a dizzying prospect. Extra organization and reflection will help you sort through the list so as not to overlook anyone, while at the same time avoiding duplication of the same combination of guests at every party.

For hosts and hostesses, there's a whole universe of particulars to be addressed. Often, they are mixing two disparate groups of people with no established common interests, and just as often they're faced with entertaining a group of people who've seen each other at half a dozen parties already

✿

David LaVoy of Atlanta created this tabletop of flowers for Jill Shoffner's engagement dinner at her parents' house. He incorporated the family's antique candlesticks and Canton porcelain, giving the table an elegant touch.

given in honor of the bride and groom. Luckily, there are innumerable angles for successful parties—themes and otherwise—and inspiration is everywhere.

Never overlook the changing seasons as an anchor for your parties; food and flowers coordinate perfectly to create the right mood. And it's always fun to instigate an instant conversation starter by asking guests to come in costume. Sometimes the guests of honor are the only theme necessary, at other times it may be in everyone's best interest to offer diversion in a different form: a hayride after a country supper, a relaxed pool party, or a wine tasting with interesting wine and food pairings, for example.

Kathy Levenson and David Rubenstein of Atlanta were given a surprise bowling party by some friends. Invitations and silk-screened T-shirts were hand delivered to forty guests who were taken to a local bowling alley by way of a mystery bus. Twenty lanes had been reserved and decorated with congratulatory banners, and drinks, dinner, and casual dancing followed in an evening of great merriment.

Seven couples hosted a Famous Lovers party for Dathel Coleman and John Georges at the Napoleon House in New Orleans. Guests were invited to come dressed as famous lovers and eat, drink, and dance the night away. Betty Hunley, who has her own sta-

tionery and graphic arts firm and designed the invitation—a shiny lipstick red card with a kiss on it—says, "Our project was to come up with something that gave the message that you were supposed to dress up like a couple, but we didn't want to give out any ideas."

The Wedding Weekend Events

More and more frequently, couples are opting for a healthy dose of parties surrounding the wedding. Out-of-town guests have made the special trek, after all, and even a frazzled bride wants them to feel that their presence has not gone unnoticed. The various parties that flank the wedding are the social platforms for reunions of all sorts: family, old friends, college friends, business acquaintances. But particularly, they offer a bride and groom the chance to spend time with the very people they have chosen to be in the wedding with them. These parties become poignant occasions for reminiscing about old times and looking ahead to the future. Most wedding weekends include a bachelor party of some description (and often a bachelorette or spinster dinner), a bridesmaids' luncheon or tea, a rehearsal dinner the night before the wedding, and a luncheon or brunch for friends and out-of-town guests the day of the wedding—or an open house or after party if the wedding is early. Additionally, there might be a luncheon or brunch the day after the wedding.

Martha Woodham also notes a tendency on the bride's and groom's part to put together a four-day festivity package for their guests, often with the couple staying on to the end. She recalls one couple who married in Texas but were to live in Atlanta. Interested in putting two as yet unintroduced groups of family and friends

Right: For a less formal tea, invite your guests to play volleyball, horseshoes, and croquet. You could serve Long Island iced tea and mint juleps with assorted finger foods. ECKERLE

Below: You might consider a formal tea at a historic plantation such as Drayton Hall on the banks of the Ashley River, Charleston, S.C. Have tables set up with crisp white linens, elegant china and silver and decorate with freshly cut peonies.

at ease, they dubbed their Thursday soiree an Opening Ceremonies party and asked everyone to wear something that suggested their home state. This, of course, precipitated a lot of animated conversation as guests tried to guess whence everyone else hailed. The next day, there were golf and tennis tournaments for the wedding party—and anyone else with an interest—followed by a tour of Coors Brewery. The formal church ceremony on Saturday was followed by a kick-up-your-heels reception at a local cowboy bar; the groom was actually kidnapped from his bus en route by well-wishers in a pickup truck and later deposited at the reception, where two-stepping and fireworks proceeded apace.

• Bridesmaids' Luncheons and Bachelor Parties

Traditionally, the bride honors and thanks her bridesmaids via a tea or luncheon before the wedding, while the groom is given a bachelor party as a final farewell to whatever joys being single may have held for him. Bridesmaids and friends may also treat the bride to an unruly night on the town as a symbolic final hurrah. These parties now assume all shapes and forms, however, and brides and grooms show their individuality by choosing between innumerable types of entertainment.

In a very casual prelude to their white-tie evening ceremony and reception at Anderson House—

Washington, D.C.'s exclusive home of the Society of the Cincinnati—Meg Garretson spent her wedding day sailing with her bridesmaids on the Chesapeake Bay, while her fiancé, Ned Carter, held a golf tournament for his groomsmen. A Fort Worth groom painted Atlanta red with his buddies, while his Nashville fiancée chose to cart her bridesmaids off to New Orleans for a weekend of jazz and Sazerac well in advance of the wedding. Player Butler's bridesmaids surprised her with a limousine and champagne for a night of barhopping, while Kelly Howell of San Antonio and her bridesmaids were given a relaxing (and rejuvenating) poolside primping party by her mother-in-law the day before the wedding—but more importantly, the day after Kelly's bachelorette party. "The Polishing," as Frances Strange referred to it, was the perfect chance for the girls to unwind and catch up with each other; they sunbathed and swam, had manicures and pedicures, and feasted on cold tenderloin with hot/sweet mustard sauce, red pepper pasta salad, and an assortment of pickup sweets.

• Rehearsal Dinners

Historically, a tea or luncheon was given on the day of the wedding rehearsal by the bride's parents, although it is far more common today for the parents of the groom to host a dinner following the rehearsal. It is both permissible and increasingly common for other hosts to enter the picture here, and etiquette books favor whatever is comfortable financially for everyone involved. The dinner is as often casual and relaxed as it is formal, and may as easily take place outdoors under the stars as in a private club's banquet rooms.

Player Butler and Mark Michelsen's very traditional rehearsal dinner was held at the Bull and Bear Club in Richmond, Virginia, with a commanding skyscraper view of downtown, dinner of beef tenderloin, and especially witty toasts from the overwhelming number of lawyers in attendance, Player and Mark among them.

For Matt Strange and his fiancée, Kelly Howell, father Don Strange, of legendary Texas catering fame, hosted a no-holds-barred evening at the vintage Waring Store, a nineteenth-century general store in Waring, Texas. Mexican chefs cooked specialties on site; antique Coca-Cola machines and rustic carts and wagons

Table Toppers decorated this "bachelor-night-out" table with a white satin underlay and a black scalloped overlay gathered in folds and topped with red satin flowers. Vintage bow ties double as napkin rings; the mint julep cups are the groom's presents to his groomsmen.

At Kelly Howell and Matthew Strange's rehearsal dinner in the Texas Hill Country, drinks were served at the long bar, which was simply decorated with fruit and a few greens. An old doctor's buggy at the end of the bar was used to hold champagne and flowers.

were filled to brimming with vegetables and fruits; old-fashioned counters were stacked high with mouthwatering homemade fruit pies and tarts alongside oversized coffee urns, and picnic tables were covered with red-and-white checkered tablecloths in an informal decorative touch.

For their unusual rehearsal dinner, Libby and Jim Landis of Slidell, Louisiana, took family and friends out for a ride on an antique fire engine; dinner was an old-fashioned barbecue, and toasts were made with great fanfare against the clanging of the fire-engine bell.

• Luncheons, Brunches, and After Parties for Out-of-Town Guests

For the many guests who make a point of coming to your wedding, a nice breakfast, brunch, or luncheon the day of the wedding offers a gathering point for old friends to catch up with one another, and for new ones to become acquainted. When family and friends suggest giving a party in your honor, this is one important slot they might think about filling, especially if the wedding falls later in the day or in the evening.

Some of Lee Rutherford's aunts and friends held a special day-of-the-wedding hunt breakfast at Perdue Hill Plantation, complete with enormous cauldrons of turkey hash, an array of home-baked breads, spoils-of-the-hunt sausage, grits, and a whole galaxy of pies and tarts. In the spring and summer, Maline McCalla, a dear friend of Lady Bird Johnson and a comrade in the cause of wildflower dissemination and preservation, frequently gives a bride's good friends and out-of-town guests a wildflower box-lunch party on the day of the wedding. For this relaxing, low-key event, the setting is central. Maline spreads antique quilts randomly about, reserving draped round tables or decorated picnic tables for older attendees; lunch—a delectable south-of-France medley of *pissaladière* and miniature chevre-and-onion confit tartlets, fresh fruits, and good cheeses—comes in white cake boxes or rustic baskets tied with tiny ribbons and a bouquet of wildflowers.

Equally important, if your wedding is held at midday or in the afternoon, an open house or casual after party offers guests evening entertainment. Members of the wedding party might consider inviting any interested guests to join them at a local bar or nightclub, or failing any organized activity, the bride might provide out-of-towners with a welcome basket containing a good list of evening entertainment about town.

Some couples host the wedding weekend themselves, offering not only a wedding ceremony but an unforgettable trip for family and friends. On the Friday before their wedding, Gail Satterwhite and Thomas Hawkins, who married in Seaside, Florida, organized a sail on the *Flying Eagle*. That evening, guests were invited to a

Lee Rutherford and Sumner Adams were given an "After the Hunt" breakfast at Perdue Hill Plantation, a hunting lodge built in 1848. Hostesses served grits, wild turkey hash, hot fruit, and homemade pies. The table's centerpiece depicted a woodland scene fashioned out of wildflowers, mushrooms, bark moss, a bird's nest, and a wild turkey.

rehearsal dinner with beach music and tiki torches, plus a tropical buffet of crawfish, shrimp, teriyaki chicken, catfish, andouille sausage, and margaritas. The party continued later that night when Gail and Thomas got together with the wedding party and close friends for dancing at a local beach club. On Saturday morning, Gail's mother hosted all the girls at a champagne brunch. The gazebo wedding

and reception were held that afternoon, and on Sunday guests were treated to a farewell brunch at the honeymoon cottage.

Kelly Miller and Richard Sanders of Nashville decided to treat their guests to a Caribbean cruise instead of just another wedding, so off went ninety of their friends and close family for an extended weekend on the *Nordic Princess*. The Nashville contin-

gent hosted a party Thursday night, and Kelly's parents, from Atlanta, hosted a bon voyage party Friday night in their stateroom. A rehearsal luncheon was held Saturday in one of the ship's lounges, and on Sunday the entire party took private boats to an island for snorkeling and swimming. The forty-five-minute ceremony was held aboard ship at sunset on their return, with enraptured passengers looking on from the upper deck.

All in the Family: Entertaining the Children

*C*hildren are a welcome addition to some weddings, downright crucial to others; particularly in the event of second marriages, it's important to make children feel included and very much desired as participants. But keeping them occupied during the often lengthy parties and proceedings takes a little forethought. Instead of relegating them to rounds of insufferable grown-up conversations, consider children's tables with special menus, party favors, and tabletop games. Older children might serve as baby-sitters or party coordinators. Or consider a specially organized evening for children that runs parallel to the adults' party: Bingo, Casino Night, special drawings for prizes, circus clowns, and fortune-tellers all promise to keep younger guests properly amused.

Gail Satterwhite had babysitters entertain the children at her wedding with coloring books and bicycle rides. Lee Rutherford offered young guests ice cream cones and carriage rides. Courtney Cowart of Atlanta wanted children to come to her ceremony and reception in Atlanta, and sent out a

❧

Left: The Bunting children are making bouquets and potpourri in their own playhouse for a Birmingham bride's wedding brunch. GIBBONS

Below: Ann Penn worked out a special children's table and menu for her son's rehearsal dinner at the Belle Meade Country Club in Nashville. The menu included shrimp cocktail, curly fries, filet, and ice cream balls for dessert.

Favors and Welcome Baskets

Whether it's altogether necessary or not, Southern hostesses have an almost instinctive need to mother their guests. For wedding party members and out-of-town guests in particular, a thoughtful bride can make all the difference between an expensive weekend hassle and a convivial get-together with old friends. Here are a few ideas that will make your guests feel more than welcome.

• Pull together history and sightseeing information on the city or area where your wedding is to be held. Include informative maps, walking tours, points of interest, and other attractions that might entice them when they have free time between organized activities. Send this information with a warm note once you receive an acceptance, so guests can plan for the weekend in advance.

• Reserve blocks of rooms at discounted rates at a choice of local hotels in different price ranges. Send telephone numbers, rates, and identifying characteristics ahead of time. (If it's financially feasible, pick up the tab for members of the wedding party, or invite them to stay at your house or your parents' house.)

• Send a welcome basket to hotel rooms. Include a favorite bottle of wine with a corkscrew, confetti, old photos, fruit and cheese, or items pertinent to the locale. Include a printed, typed, or handwritten schedule for the weekend, with all the whos, whys, whats, whens, and wheres, not to mention the hows— special transportation available, suggested dress, and so on. This lets everyone know what's in store, and will help keep you and your various hostesses on schedule throughout the weekend.

• Arrange a welcoming reception for out-of-town guests in a designated room in the hotel. Have the announcement of the event beautifully penned on scrolls that are then sealed with gold wax and tied with gold and silver ribbons. The scrolls can either be placed in guests' rooms or hand delivered. When the guests arrive at the reception, they are greeted by the best man and maid of honor, who offer refreshments and show a videotape of you and your fiancé welcoming everyone and detailing the weekend's events.

Courtney Cowart McHale of Atlanta planned numerous activities for the children at her wedding, including a picnic in the park.

personal note to her guests explaining that there would be lots of activities for their children all weekend long, including trips to the zoo and ice cream parlors, with baby sitters available throughout.

Tying the Knot in Tulsa

Leslie Daubenberger and Bobby Lorton met in high school in Tulsa, but didn't start seeing each other seriously until her freshman year in college at Southern Methodist University in Dallas. Five years later, he proposed, and over the next nine months they toasted and were toasted by friends and family in a veritable round robin of creative parties. Although Leslie's family had lived in California for some twenty years, Bobby's family is fourth-generation Tulsa and, as owners and publishers of the morning daily *The Tulsa World*, they are inextricably tied to the city. This wedding and all its attendant parties brought together everything that is irreducibly Southern with a fresh injection of fun and glamour from the West Coast.

With strong family ties in both California and Oklahoma, Leslie and Bobby had two engagement parties. First on the docket was a champagne brunch hosted by her parents, Sharon and Charles Daubenberger, at the Bel Air Bay Club in Pacific Palisades, California. The brunch was a reunion for all the friends Leslie had grown

Above: Linen court-jester napkins were painted with gold trim and gathered with napkin rings featuring framed pictures of Bobby and Leslie as children. The favor boxes, engraved with the name of the bride and groom and the date, held chocolates.

Left: Chrissy and Suzanne Collins help their mother decorate the tables for the prewedding watermelon party. They even add plastic ants for a real "picnic" effect.

Opposite: The Lortons' backyard and garden provided a spectacular setting for the rehearsal dinner. Bobby and Leslie's table was draped with a special cloth designed and painted by artist Tim Trapolin. Personalized with their names and the date, it can be laundered and used again on their first or fiftieth anniversary.

up with, as well as the friends of her parents who had been like second parents to her throughout her childhood. Back home in Tulsa, the Daubenbergers and the Lortons co-hosted a large cocktail party for some two hundred friends to announce the engagement locally.

Winding into the home stretch for the June 1 wedding, the May calendar was full of dinners and cocktail parties all given by friends of Leslie and Bobby. A Mexican fiesta with mariachis and margaritas at the Southern Hills Country Club started the ball rolling. The next weekend, best man Doug Pielsticker and his father, Jim, took Bobby, his groomsmen, and assorted fraternity brothers and pals— about thirty of them—to Las Vegas for a weekend of gambling, shows, and general carousing, including the "Bye Bob" invitational golf tournament, complete with "Bye Bob" T-shirt favors. Not to be outdone, Leslie and company took off for Aspen, where Bobby's sis-

ter lives, for a weekend of shopping and barhopping.

Home again, they were swept into a magical at-home Hawaiian luau that transformed friends' indoor tennis courts into a tropical paradise, followed by the "The Guys and the Gal" theme of a Christmas-in-May dinner party and a "La Dolce Vita" party thrown by aunts and uncles, with plenty of wine, pasta, and romance.

Leslie and her mother, Sharon Daubenberger, attacked the wedding with systematic organization, equipping guests with all the pertinent information on party times and places and making everyone feel utterly welcome. A golf tournament was sponsored on

Above: For the rehearsal dinner chef Philippe Garmay prepared a mixed seafood grill painted with avocado crème frâiche.

Left: The wedding party arrived by trolley from the church. The bridesmaids were splendid in midnight blue full-length suits, accented by portrait collars and plunging necklines.

Friday by Bobby and his father for all the groomsmen and out-of-town guests, while sisters and sisters-in-law hosted a very formal bridesmaids' luncheon. Bobby's sister, Tracie, owns T. A. Lorton, the sophisticated local gift and bridal registry shop, so the luncheon, held at her house, bore many of her signature decorating touches on the tabletop and throughout with a refreshing garden theme. Leslie took the occasion to give her bridesmaids engraved silver bottles as a thank-you for being part of the festivities.

The rehearsal dinner was hosted by

Bobby's parents and held in their terraced backyard, a cascading panorama of decks, pools, fountains, and yawning expanses of manicured lawn canopied by gracious old trees. Roxana Lorton, with the help of her talented daughter, Tracie, designed the tables, each set with special napkin rings holding assorted baby pictures of Leslie and Bobby—instant conversation pieces.

Bobby's aunt and uncle Susie and Fulton Collins offered a haven for recuperation the following noon at a casual poolside lunch. The watermelon motif took its cue from an invitation asking guests to "take a slice out of Bobby and Leslie's wedding day."

Following a traditional ceremony at Trinity Episcopal Church, an extraordinary reception was held at the Philbrook Museum of Art, formerly a private estate (and available to corporate and individual patrons for private use). Guests flowed out into the mag-

nificent sculpture and formal gardens for drinks and hors d'oeuvres, before being treated to a lavish seated buffet dinner. After the cake cutting, dancing, and tossing of bouquets and garters, Leslie and Bobby dashed away by limo to their private plane, bound for a first night at the elegant Mansion on Turtle Creek in Dallas, and then on to a wedding trip in Hawaii.

Above: At the Philbrook Museum in Tulsa, Louisette Brown, Pam Hayne, and Tim Trapolin of New Orleans's Anything Grows created a showstopping pedestal arrangement of just-picked feverfew, trumpet vine, and wild maple at the base of the rotunda's fifteen-foot-tall sculpture.

Left: In her Christos dress of ivory silk satin, Leslie helps Bobby with his slice of wedding cake.

The Presents

The Tradition of Giving

*T*he tradition of giving wedding presents to a bride and groom is as old and venerable a part of the celebration as the marriage ceremony itself, although the concept has changed shape considerably along the way. Nowadays, the presentation of an engagement ring is an accepted harbinger of the merriment that lies ahead, and the convention of offering a young engaged couple the fundaments of a new menage has become second nature to most wedding guests, going hand in hand naturally with

❧

Opposite: Gifts brought to Player Butler and her groom on the day of the wedding were placed on an antique four-poster bed in the front bedroom at Evelynton.

Right: Mary Virginia Weinmann received a bottle of champagne decorated with flowers and an antique silver chalice. Bouquet by Rohm's in New Orleans.

wishing them the best for a happy life together.

Well-wishing had no particular place in the original picture, however, when women were kidnapped rather than courted; the "engagement" ring of the day, given by a woman's captor, was a symbol of bondage and ownership rather than of everlasting love, and the honeymoon referred not to a glamorous vacation but to a period of time after which the captor could stop looking over his shoulder for signs of a rescue by the stricken girl's family.

Impersonal as it may seem today, marriage as a cold-blooded contractual arrangement benefitting father and husband was certainly an improvement over the abduction scenario. Until the eighteenth century, dowry and bride price were openly discussed, and depending on the time or place, women were routinely bought and sold, bartered and virtually horse-traded just as any other commodity. Money and personal property were used in these transactions, and every-

thing from pigs and cows to land, slaves, and family silver entered the bargaining arena.

While in the 1700s there was at least an imagined freedom of selection practiced among courting couples in the colonies, the pressure on families to marry off their daughters accelerated plenty of nuptials; making a nice match between estates was at least as important as looking for a good relationship. Betty Washington, George

Washington's younger sister, was married to widower Fielding Lewis in May 1750; not quite seventeen years old, she brought to the marriage a handsome dowry of 400 pounds sterling and two female slaves.

Setting Up Housekeeping

*I*n the predominantly rural South, from the first quarter of the eighteenth century right through the nineteenth, isolation was still very much a way of life, and family, rather than the marketplace, provided the emotional and physical safe harbor for children undergoing rites of passage. When belles became brides, often as little more than children, they relied heavily on their mothers to assist them in making the transition from mere maidens to household managers. As more experienced housekeepers, mothers and aunts paid regular visits to help them settle into their new domiciles and domestic roles, and were often the sole sources for building up

Opposite: Tracie Lorton of Tulsa says, "Wedding presents don't have to be silver anymore. You might focus on the bedroom rather than the dining room." Consider a bed tray with accompanying tea service or a pair of needlepoint pillows.

Right: In the nineteenth-century South, wedding presents tended to be small and personal.

the requisite inventory of soap, candles, bedding, and other household needs. It was generally the mothers and aunts who came forward with the necessary trousseau items for young brides: gloves and handkerchiefs, bed jackets, garters with sterling silver clips, and complete first-, second-, and third-day outfits, from the petticoats and camisoles all the way to the dress gloves and hats, that were part of a young woman's everyday toilette—and all in a highly charged secret ceremony that was the very hallmark of feminine tradition.

As for furniture and other major household appointments, it was common practice for both sets of parents to supply their newlywed children with an ample store. Presents of any significant value were either part of a specified dowry or given by close family members. Noland Fontaine of Memphis, for example, built a smaller version of his mansion across the street for his daughter and her groom as a wedding present. According to Marilyn Van Eynde, associate director at the Woodruff-Fontaine House, some typical wedding presents recorded for 1898 included an oriental rug, a barley twist table for a plant stand, a nice pair of hurricane lamps, pictures painted by amateurs, cups and saucers, lace tablecloths, vases, compotes, and personal bureau items such as hair-

Quite the reverse, in fact, during some epochs when, royalty aside, it was considered in lamentable taste to give a wedding present at all unless your relationship with the bride or groom was well established.

Bridal Registry

*I*n earlier days, great rosters of wedding presents, particularly when received by royalty and landed gentry, were published in the newspaper—often with donors' names—in part to satisfy the curiosity of local layfolk, but principally to help steer other well-wishers away from duplicating items that had already been received. Less than delicate to be sure, but a basically sound formula, and one that has evolved into what is now known as the bridal registry, a fairly efficient commercial enterprise that makes a bride's tastes and preferences known ahead of time to guests shopping for her wedding present.

The turn of the twentieth century marked the first forays into commercial bridal registries, when shops began keeping lists of wedding pre-

brushes, powder boxes, and hair receivers (a storage box for combed-out tresses).

In the South, then, those crucial items a young girl needed to run her new house in the prescribed manner—silver, china, crystal, linens—were inherited rather than received as formal wedding presents from guests; apart from what was offered by par-

ents, wedding presents tended to be small and personal and given only by family and close friends—a glass place card holder, for example, or a lace handkerchief or doily or perhaps a special book of poems. Invitations to guests who were not intimates of the family did not bring with them an obligation to spring for a wedding present, as is so often the case today.

sents that had been purchased and sent to brides; in that more subtle manner, they could counsel would-be guests in making an appropriate selection, gently guiding them away from pieces that had already been sent. Stores soon began urging brides to preregister their tastes in china, crystal, silver, and linens to eliminate some of the guesswork for guests.

Frank Bromberg III of Bromberg's, a 155-year-old exclusive jewelry and gift shop with eleven stores throughout the South (including Underwood's), notes, "There are many more choices to make now than ever before. In our store alone, girls have 45 china companies and over 500 patterns to choose from. Very often," he says of the more than 1,000 brides registered each year at Bromberg's, "they have inherited china, and are interested in something special to mix it with, or perhaps just a special set of occasional china."

Rhonda Aguillard of Legacy in Fort Worth agrees that brides "want to be more wardrobed, and have things that will mix and match and be used together for a lot of different occasions. Service plates are coming back," she notes. "People my age don't have servants, but with a well-trained husband you can wait a table with service plates and still have a beautiful formal meal and use all those little goodies and accessories and not kill yourself. We try to [help a bride] look ten years down the road, where you're going to be able to do it all so you have some-

A Few Pointers for a Successful Bridal Registry

• It pays to make several visits to the marketplace when you're choosing china, silver, and crystal. Don't make snap decisions in a day, and don't forget to consult your fiancé. Remember: These patterns will have a prominent place in your house and your life for a long time; allow yourself the luxury of letting first impressions sink in.

• Think realistically about your current life-style and how you want it to develop after you're married. If lead crystal seems to collide with your rapid-fire pace or casual entertaining format, forget it and move on to less formal alternatives. If you already have your grandmother's gorgeous Flora Danica china, register for camera equipment instead. The point is to be both practical and creative; there's no reason to stand on a tradition that no longer has a place in your life, and there's every reason to paint a descriptive picture of that life-style for guests on the hunt for the perfect addition to it.

Don't overlook bookstores, antiques shops, hardware and gardening stores, gourmet shops, and any specialty stores pertinent to your interests.

• For first looks, remember to shop during off-peak hours, when you're likely to get a salesperson's undivided attention. When you're ready to register, schedule an appointment with a registry consultant; you'll minimize interruptions and make the most of your time.

• Remember to cover the waterfront pricewise. Don't be afraid to register for a few high-end objects, even if it's hard to imagine you'll really receive them; friends and relatives may prefer to pool their resources in order to buy you something special and substantial. On the other hand, don't forget to include a good variety of inexpensive items for those whose budgets may lean that way, as well as for appropriate shower presents.

• Keep in regular contact with the stores at which you've registered. Let them know what you're receiving, and make certain your own register agrees with theirs. Be clear from the start about their policies for exchanges, time limits, and so on.

thing to grow into and use along the way."

Now, particularly with later and second-time marriages, it is entirely customary for brides, along with their fiancés, to register not only for such standard articles as china, silver, and linens, but for more contemporary goods as well—audio and video equipment; sporting goods; gourmet cookware and kitchenware; tickets to theater, ballet, and opera or to sports events; artwork; travel-related articles; and any items that fall into particular collecting genres. Guests may respond by selecting specific items the bride has registered for, or they may simply be enlightened by those preferences as

When you get back from your wedding trip, take some time, at your breakfast table, to enjoy some of the gifts you've received. It might be the right moment to start on those thank-you notes, too!

🌿

Inventive Wedding Presents

Sometimes a little ingenuity and imagination make up for wherewithal in coming up with one-of-a-kind wedding presents. Some off-beat ideas for creative guests:

• Put together a book of certificates for special-occasion dinners to be home-cooked by you for the bride and groom.

• Take photographs of the whole wedding procedure, from the engagement party to the bridal showers to the rehearsal dinner and reception. Make an artistic collage with initials and wedding date in rich calligraphy and select an interesting frame.

• Send a special flower arrangement the first of every month until their first anniversary. Take advantage of what can be gathered locally: spare berried branches in January, for example, forced narcissus bulbs in February, lush sprays of forsythia and quince in March, and so on.

• Create a luxurious old-world tablecloth by hand painting plain linen with a brocade-look fruit-and-flowers border and lush center medallion. Hand paint napkins to go with it.

• Put together a fabulous collection of cassette tapes with a romantic theme.

• An invaluable source for wedding gifts of all kinds is *The Wedding Fantastic,* a catalog put together by Kathleen Mahoney of San Francisco.

to her general level of taste, opting to choose something suitable as a surprise.

Brides disseminate their bridal registry information by word of mouth only, and often they do their guests a service by registering in more than one city if, for example, they live and work away from the hometown in which they're to be married. Many bridal registry shops have computerized systems that facilitate purchases and selections in stores in several different cities. Rich's in Atlanta, for example, has twenty-two stores throughout the South (it's known as Goldsmith's in Memphis). Says Pam Parker, "We have a very user-friendly system at Rich's. It can be overwhelming making selections. Our consultants walk around the store with a bride and get a good idea of what she's after. We have a worksheet with categories and we just begin filling in. The consultants are really pros; they advise here and there. Then every bride comes up on a computer printout that tells a shopper everything she needs. All the stores are compatible."

Andrew Morton, a fine gift and bridal registry shop in Knoxville, Tennessee, even has a chauffeur who

task of completing them, while formerly the exclusive burden of the bride, may now be shared by bride and groom. Since there is a grace period for sending wedding presents, there is a corresponding grace period for acknowledging them; few brides conquer the full stack of acknowledgments within six weeks of the wedding, but it is unacceptable to let them lag longer than six months. The best way to tackle the job is not to let yourself get too far behind. While the prospect of writing hundreds is almost paralyzing, it only takes a moment to pen five notes.

Displaying the Presents

Inviting people over for a cup of tea or a glass of sherry and a glimpse of the wedding presents was a time-honored tradition in the South. While schedules for most women have long since made an anachronism out of the old practice of paying calls, it is still

delivers all the wedding presents to the bride's house.

Some brides and grooms opt for donations to a favorite charity in lieu of wedding presents. This is a matter for word of mouth only, but most organizations will send the bride an acknowledgment of such a gift, so she can make a note of it and respond.

Since it is mandatory to acknowledge every wedding present with a handwritten thank-you note, it is also critical for brides to keep a fairly meticulous record of the presents they receive. Collecting the proper information at the time a present is unwrapped will keep later mix-ups to a minimum. Most department stores and gift shops sell wedding present registers with neat ledgers for noting the description of the item, the name of the donor, the store it came from, and the date it was received; most also come with corresponding stickers in a fairly foolproof backup system. Martha Wailes and Mary Rose of The Stationer in New Orleans created their own wedding present registry book, with enough room for recording five hundred presents.

Thank-you notes should be written on plain or engraved notepaper. The

customary in the South to showcase wedding presents for friends and family as a measure of gratitude and pride on the part of the bride and groom. Ordinarily this is accomplished in the mother's or the bride's dining room, or perhaps in a less used room by way of rented tables and risers. An artistic eye for display often combines place settings and gift items interestingly, although some brides prefer to place like items together. Normally, only one of a particular item is shown. Fresh flowers are always a nice addition.

For brides who have neither the time nor the inclination to come up with a decorative scheme, there's always the possibility of relying on a mother, aunt, or artistic friend for creative aid. Presentations, a small com-

Gilding the Lily: Variations on Gift Wrap

The best presents come in packages that are presents in themselves; consider making your wrapping paper a keepsake instead of a throwaway. Think about incorporating some of the following "containers" when packaging your special wedding presents:

• Fabric-covered or hand-painted hatboxes
• Exquisite imported sheets or pillowcases tied with wired French ribbon
• Hand-painted bakery boxes
• Unusual baskets decorated with fresh herbs, flowers, and ribbons
• Monogrammed cotton handkerchiefs
• Oxidized copper or verdigris watering cans
• Glass fishbowls or bubble bowls for a see-through wrapper

(For instructions on how to wrap a hatbox with fabric, see pages 218–19.)

This bride opted for a more formal display of gifts. The candles, flowers, and mirrors add a dramatic touch.

pany in Atlanta, is in the business of making an attractive splash of wedding presents. The owners, Lou Winship and Katie Jackson, make a preliminary visit to the house and survey both the space and the expected number of presents. They landscape the space using attractive damask-covered risers or, in the case of rented tables, white damask cloths accented with silk braid and handsome Chippendale risers and plate stands. They encourage brides to group elegant presents on one table, casual ones in another area, and shower items in yet another spot. They spruce up the resultant tableau with cut flowers, which they refresh on their weekly visits to incorporate new presents into the design.

The custom may rub you the wrong way, but don't be too quick to dismiss it as old-fashioned nonsense. Your mother's and grandmother's friends will enjoy it, and it makes for a relaxing occasion to get together informally for tea or drinks with old friends.

Wedding Showers

Although filling out china and silver patterns may have been beyond their ken, colonial and antebellum friends and neighbors were quick to lend a domestic helping hand to newly married couples by way of old-fashioned poundings and infaires at which they lavished them with kitchen and pantry staples, tools, thread—all the domestic stuffs now considered standard fare for wedding showers. Always popular in the South, the bridal shower is thought to have had its origins in Holland, where a disapproving father forbade his daughter's marriage to a penniless miller by refusing her a dowry. Sympathetic village folk, always a soft touch for a love story, sprang to the couple's aid, showering the bride with all the necessities. The father, it is said, also softened, permitting the marriage and throwing in a generous dowry for good measure.

An interesting variation on the bridal shower appeared in mid-nineteenth-century Memphis. The so-called Lavender Bridge was a ladies' get-together, either for tea or for lunch and cards. All the participants wore lavender in some form or fashion, and tea and bridge tables were draped with special lavender cloths and accented by lavender sachets; personal presents were offered as the women chatted and lent a helping hand to the bride-to-be on her quilting or sewing.

Although wedding showers waned in popularity after the 1950s in the rest of the country, they have seen little abatement in the South, perhaps because its frontier and plantation roots run deeper than might be expected. Even today, there is a sense of community response to a wedding engagement in the South, and family and friends are quick to spread their best wishes and hospitality to the bride and groom.

Bridal showers used to be exclusively that: all-female gatherings for tea or luncheon in which the bride's attendants and family and friends bombarded her with all the things she would need to organize her kitchen and boudoir, including free advice. Now, of course, the concept of the happy homemaker is relatively obsolete, and showers frequently honor both the bride and the groom.

Showers are not usually the domain of family members; they're given by close friends or bridesmaids, and the informal gatherings that surround them may take innumerable forms. Whether for cocktails, luncheon, or supper, a warm camaraderie reigns as friends of bride and groom come together to offer their support of the new couple's stab at setting up house. One caveat: If you're the recipient of more than one shower, try to organize your guest list so as not to invite the

Wedding Present Co-op

There's strength in numbers, so get together with friends and marshall your resources to create a smashing wedding present that's personal and useful. Consider these ideas:

• Make a VCR all the more special by starting a great film library of romantic or comedic old classics to go with it.

• Create the ultimate honeymoon bed with a luxurious set of Egyptian cotton sheets, pillowcases and shams, plus nice wool blankets with monogrammed blanket covers.

• Stock a great honeycomb terra-cotta wine rack with interesting vintages in red, white, and blush. Add twelve nice large tasting glasses, plus a sturdy corkscrew. You might consider a special bottle to be saved until the first anniversary.

• Consider season tickets to the symphony, ballet, opera, or to sporting events, and add the appropriate afterthought: a monogrammed pewter flask for football games or opera glasses for the theater.

• If the wedding is timely, get together with friends and decorate the newlyweds' house for their first Christmas together; the gift certificate might be a special-edition ornament.

• Make up a certificate book for a series of romantic dinners out on the town at favorite elegant restaurants and local hot spots.

• Put together some honeymoon necessaries: a great underwater camera or a camcorder, foreign language translation and phrase book calculators, versatile lightweight luggage, or even monetary contributions arranged through the couple's travel agent.

• Create an instant garden for do-it-yourself landscapers. Do a rough landscaping sketch of the space, roll it and tie it with an ivy ribbon; nestle the plan among a variety of perennial shrubs, assorted seed packets, his and hers gardening gloves, trowels, and shovels.

Right: For a pottery and ceramics shower, ask guests to bring pieces from the bride's everyday pattern. All pieces are from Les Rubans.

Below: For a garden shower, give gardening-related gifts. The topiary heart, whimsically shaped ivy plants, and cherub are from Petit Jardin.

🦅

same groups to more than one. But if you want to include them a second time, be sure to make a personal call telling them not to feel obligated to bring you another shower present.

Although showers may be of a general nature, themes bring the boundaries of gift-giving into a sharper focus for couples who have particular needs. Kitchen showers, boudoir showers, collecting showers, round-the-clock, and alphabet showers are but a few of the possibilities. Leslie Daubenberger was given a special-occasions shower

by college friends in Dallas, and each invitee was charged with finding a suitable present for a particular landmark occasion in a newlywed's entertaining schedule. Appropriately, from her sister-in-law Tracie Lorton she received a silver pillbox filled with aspirin for a first dinner for the in-laws. Her sister, Robin, gave her an iron rabbit rose holder for a first Easter lunch.

A Nashville bride was given an alphabet shower. Invitations instructed each guest to bring a present beginning with a certain letter, and the net

result was a collection of usable, creative kitchen and bathware: a good steel colander for C, a great enamel omelette pan for O, an extra large bottle of Vita Bath for V, among others.

Charlotte Anderson of Little Rock, Arkansas, had an "Around the World in One Romantic Evening" shower in which friends brought her baubles and trinkets particular to different ports of call: from Ireland, a beautiful set of linen placemats and napkins; from Portugal, a collection of colorful ceramic ware; from London, a stylish umbrella; from Russia, hand-painted eggs. Kelly Howell of Dripping Springs, Texas, was given a wonderful basket shower at which the hostesses provided six unusual baskets, one for each major area of her house: kitchen, bath, linen closet, dining room, bedroom, and library. Friends were invited to bring a special present for a particular basket, each color-coordinated with Kelly's new house plans.

And note that grooms are more than bit players in the wedding, and more and more often are honorees at wedding showers. Use the wedding shower as a good excuse to throw a party for the bride and groom, with more emphasis on party and less on presents.

Presents from the Bride and Groom

While the bride and groom are on the receiving end of most of the presents associated with weddings, it is their singular joy to return the favor at certain points during the prewedding festivities. Ordinarily, a bride will select special thank-you presents for her bridesmaids and the groom for his groomsmen as a tangible acknowledgment of their appreciation for support and participation in the wedding ceremony. Additionally, the bride and groom will present a special token of their appreciation to hosts and hostesses of showers and parties given in their honor. The bride and groom may elect to celebrate the occasion by giving a wonderful present to each other, as well as by thanking their parents (or other sponsors of the wedding) with a one-of-a-kind acknowledgment of their time, efforts, and love. And although the reception is considered a present of sorts for the guests, brides may wish to give them a special favor as a keepsake of the occasion.

For a Christmas-ornament shower in Atlanta, Jan Shoffner created a small topiary Christmas tree decorated with papier-mâché angels and nosegays of freesia, paper-whites, and plumosa tied with white and gold satin ribbon. The topiary was given to the bride as a memento of the occasion.

Consider giving your bridesmaids a gift that might some day become an heirloom — a silver picture frame, a lace pillow, a cameo pin, or a silver jewelry box.

• For the Attendants

Presents for members of the wedding party are traditionally given at the rehearsal dinner or on the separate occasions of a bridesmaids' luncheon and a bachelor dinner. The mementos given to bridesmaids and groomsmen by the bride and groom are part gratitude, part affirmation of friendship, and part souvenir of the occasion. Ordinarily they're personal articles meant to be longlasting reminders of the bride and groom and of their festive wedding ceremony. Mrs. Beau Clinton of Fifth Seasons, a gift shop in Little Rock, Arkansas, notes that because of their personal nature, engravable items are singularly more popular than any others for wedding party presents. "Silver letter openers, wine stoppers, money clips, Jefferson or julep cups are good choices for groomsmen," she says, while, "silver frames, dressing-table accessories such as makeup brushes, powder boxes, and compacts, bud vases and pewter or silver containers make nice selections for bridesmaids."

At Cindy Lee and Thomas Coke Bates's rehearsal dinner, groomsmen were surprised by waiters bearing mint juleps for them to sip in a special toast; the engraved silver cups were theirs to keep. Jean-Baptiste Ducruet, an architect in Connecticut, and his bride, Linda, gave the entire wedding party miniature watercolors executed by him. Mark Michelsen gave his groomsmen monogrammed silver money clips with built-in Swiss army knife accoutrements; Tim Draper provided disc cameras ensuring plenty of merriment and no lack of photo coverage of the rehearsal dinner; and Ned Carter gave each of his groomsmen a dramatic nocturnal photograph he'd taken of the White House and framed as a memento of his Washington, D.C., wedding.

Susan Williams gave her bridesmaids beautiful monogrammed boudoir pillowcases, while Player

Butler gave her attendants crystal makeup brushes. With only three attendants, Nancy Broadbent was able to give wonderful silver serving pieces she'd recently picked up in the London silver vaults. Meg Garretson needle-pointed round boudoir pillows with her bridesmaids' initials, each in colors specially chosen to accent their particular decors. Marcie Hughes picked up the tab for her bridesmaids' wedding shoes and gave them each an engraved silver shoe horn to go with them. Lisa Harrison gave each of her bridesmaids an Evelynton Plantation Battersea box filled with homemade potpourri as a special memento of the wedding site.

• For Hosts and Hostesses

An immediate expression of gratitude is called for after a party or wedding shower given in the bride and groom's honor. Prior to the event, verbal thanks are all that is needed, along with strictest cooperation in submitting guest lists and addresses. After the event, a small thank-you present— which needn't be expensive—along with a prompt thank-you note underscores the honorees' sincere appreciation of the effort and expense that went into a lovely party. Brides may consider wonderfully packed gift baskets full of gourmet edibles or assorted teas and coffees or perhaps soaps and potpourris.

Potted plants or orchids dressed up in surprising wooden or tole containers, a special basket arrangement, a rich Rothschild garden of various planted blooms, or a moss window box with fresh flowers all make for nice keepsakes. Brides may also wish to send a dramatic floral centerpiece to their hostesses on the day of the party. Don't overlook your father, the most important host; consider taking a six-pack of his favorite beer, emptying the contents of one bottle, filling it with a loose bunch of wildflowers in a natural bouquet, and attaching a special note.

• For the Guests

Wedding favors are a special gesture from bride and groom to all their wedding guests to thank them for being a part of the occasion. In the best European tradition, dragées, or coated almonds—often in beautifully packaged boxes—were given to wedding guests to spread the good will and good luck of the bride and the groom. The custom has long been practiced in the South as well. Brides often bundle them in tulle tied with tiny satin ribbons.

Cake boxes monogrammed with the names or initials of the bride and groom and the wedding date were a common historic wedding favor in the South; the convention, still practiced today, makes for a lovely take-home favor.

Wedding favors may come in all shapes and forms, as long as they take a strong directive from the style of the reception and the personalities of the bride and groom. For ecology-minded, nature-loving couples, monogrammed wildflower seed packets to take home and plant might be the perfect finale to a grand occasion. Polaroid photographs of guests make an inexpensive, fun reminder of the event. Edible offerings—tiny monogrammed boxes of chocolates, cookies, or mints in heart shapes, for example—are always appropriate. Or, if the floral design of a reception follows a particular theme, reduce it to a miniature keepsake for guests—tiny terra-cotta pots of violets or Johnny-jump-ups or diminutive rose topiaries, for instance.

Dathel Coleman gave her bridesmaids a canvas pillow that was designed and hand-painted by her mother. Each pillow was personalized with the bridesmaid's name and the initials of the bride and groom.

Capitol Contributions: A Sophisticated Soiree in Washington, D.C.

*M*ost weddings are occasions of overwhelming joy. But some seem to elevate joy to a new plane altogether, redefining the term at every level and for everybody involved—from the bride and groom whose vision it is, to their newly linked families, to the professionals whose expertise make the final product unforgettable, to the guests whose hearts virtually swell at such an obvious outpouring of love and caring. Courtney Banks and George Pappas's wedding in Washington, D.C., was the absolute

paradigm—an event so beautifully personal, so charged by the spirit of giving, that it practically oozed happiness from every pore. Said Washington party planner Marylin Bradley, who coordinated key aspects of the reception, "I've covered many weddings in my life, but never have I seen so many people smiling."

Nancy Kingsley, the mother of the bride, had a more delayed but equally

Above: Marilyn Mueller, of Criollo Chocolates, created Courtney's dramatic five-tier cake, which was filled with delicious combinations of chocolate, topped with French meringue buttercream icing, and decorated with pastillage flowers.

Opposite: The National Museum of Women in the Arts provided a warm and enchanting ambience for the wedding reception.

Left: George enjoys a cigar with his brother and best man, Niko. FLANDERS

❧

positive reaction to the proceedings. "It's funny," she comments, still recovering from all the excitement a week after the wedding, "but once you're in the throes of the night, you become sort of a zombie. It's not until afterwards that all these fragments of memories come back and you begin to see how special it really was. The phone calls and letters [from friends and family] have just been overwhelming. From start to finish, it's been an unbelievable joy; the whole process was like a wonderful new bond between Courtney and me. I'd have to say that the wedding really was a tribute to

her, because she has been such a gift to me."

In fact, the wedding itself was a treasure, and to everybody associated with it—a finely tuned collaboration of amateurs and experts, in which many creative heads came together and, playing off one another's enthusiasm and innate style, turned out a thing of perfectly remarkable beauty and relevance.

Courtney, a graduate of the Maryland College Institute of Art, is accomplished in a variety of media and now certified to teach art. She had very specific ideas about how her wed-

ding should look, having amassed reams of clippings from magazines and books to give focus to her own vision. And she had distinct ideas about where the reception should be.

Courtney had fallen in love with the National Museum of Women in the Arts, a luscious space in its own right and one of her pet projects to support and foster; the museum opened in 1982 and features the work of women artists from the 1600s to the present. Holding

her reception there not only signaled her patronage of a relatively new institution but also afforded her 240 guests a special private showing of its beautiful galleries. It was a wonderful chance to share this new treasure with friends and family who most likely hadn't seen the space.

Working with caterer Susan Gage, floral designer Barbara Rudolph, and Marylin Bradley, of Creative Parties, Courtney realized her dream installation—a high-style, ultraromantic elegance, sweetened with nostalgic Victoriana and yet tailored with all the crispness of a Viennese confection. Courtney sketched renderings of the spaces, the tables, even the cake to create a starting point, and then freely brainstormed with all the professionals until they'd honed the look to a turn. Fabrics carefully and deliberately cho-

sen to enhance the delicate veining of the galleries' extensive marble created a veil of rosy pinks and peaches in moiré, taffeta, and tapestry with the whitecap of antique lace overlays; centerpieces were intentionally uncommercial—loose cascades of open garden roses tangled appealingly amid cherubs of varying heights and formal branch candlesticks; food and bar service—upscale regional butlered hors d'oeuvres and an elegant French-service seated dinner—were as if from another more gracious epoch; heart shapes were everywhere—in special ceramic serving pieces, on the dessert

Above: The youngest members of the wedding party take a break. FLANDERS

Left: Invitations to the engagement dinner, the rehearsal dinner, and the wedding, place cards, and table cards with gold-leafed borders. Letters to family and friends were printed on notecards depicting holdings in the museum's collection.

table, on the hors d'oeuvres trays, and even as favors for all the ladies. Helen Pappas, the mother of the groom, covered satin heart boxes with delicate laces and trims and filled them with an odd number of sugared almonds, a Greek tradition symbolizing for bride, groom, and guests the bittersweetness of life; the odd numbers—three, five, or seven—are indivisible, representing eternal love and the ongoing strength of the new marriage. Having seen her mother-in-law's keepsake heart-shaped box from her own wedding, Courtney was enchanted with the custom; Helen found the boxes and contributed the heartwarming homemade favors as her present to wedding guests in honor of her new daughter-in-law.

As befits the best of Southern families, both sides of this wedding are rooted in absolute bedrock. Having tragically lost her father at an early age, Courtney felt she had a lock on extended American family dynamics, since her widowed mother remarried twelve years ago, adding six stepbrothers and stepsisters to her own family of five children. Nancy Kingsley actually met her husband through her children. Their own wedding found nine of the combined eleven offspring at the Episcopal altar with them, after which they all headed home to a reception (and coincidentally post-football-game) dinner Nancy had cooked herself.

"What's so fantastic," Nancy Kingsley remembers, "is that Courtney, who comes from the most unique, comfortable stepfamily situation, suddenly found herself in the midst of a Greek family, where the whole Greek community is like an extended family. When you already have a family that means everything to you, and then you find yourself so warmly accepted and loved by a new family, it's really something extraordinary."

As if to set a tangible example of their community of love and support, five couples, longtime friends of the grooms' parents, gave a special prewedding brunch in honor of Courtney and George. Most of the hosts are second-generation Greeks who have known each other since living in Washington and even back in Greece. In a moving toast, one hostess explained why there were five of them giving the party by saying, "We have a long history of loving and caring for each other and supporting each other through thick and thin. It means everything to all of us. And now, what we want to give you, George and Courtney, is the continuity of that support; we're behind you and we're here for you, whenever you need anything."

The ceremony, held in the Bethesda Presbyterian Church, was a brilliant and moving amalgamation of two ser-vices, drawing heavily on Greek ritual and symbol. Courtney's brother Michael escorted her down the aisle but he did not give her away alone; instead, both families rose in response to the question, in essence giving their children to each other. In a touching mini-ceremony, George's best man, his brother Niko, presented the Greek Orthodox priest with a pair of floral crowns tied together with satin ribbons; the silver tray used to carry them was later presented to the groom as a wedding present from his groomsmen. The priest then crowned Courtney and George, symbolically naming them king and queen of their new household and pronouncing that, thus blessed, their house would flourish, opening its doors with warmth

Above: The bride and groom take a spin on the dance floor. FLANDERS

Left: Courtney's bridesmaids' deep burgundy velvet dresses with portrait collars beautifully complemented her own gown. FLANDERS

and generosity, never knowing a stranger. Later, at the reception, Dan Kingsley introduced the priest and bid him say a special grace before dinner, as if to mark the beginning of Courtney and George's new life together.

Note: We are grateful to the National Museum of Women in the Arts for granting us permission to photograph this wedding on its premises.

The Flowers

Flowers to Have and to Hold

Wedding flowers have been through no fewer gyrations over the years than have wedding costumes. In this century alone, the bridal bouquet has come full circle not once but twice. Nothing is more fascinating than flipping through vivid old newspaper accounts that document the dramatic yet quite natural evolution from controlled nosegays to loose, lush sheaves and back again. It is in those yellowed clippings that you find the lovely wax orange blossoms of the 1890s and the sweet shower

Opposite: For Leslie Daubenberger's bridesmaids, Mary Murray designed bouquets of tulips, freesia, nerine lilies, astilbe, and campanula, loosely tied with a braided French ribbon.

Right: Animal topiaries, dressed up for the occasion, greeted guests at Lynne White's party in New Orleans.

bouquets—very often lily of the valley—so typical of the turn of the century; it is there that you notice the delicate 1910 cascade bouquet ballooning by the 1920s into a kind of hand-held perennial bed, usually upstaging the short flapper dresses of the day and the brides right along with them; it is also there that the Deco-inspired 1930s reaction makes an appearance, with ultrachic sprays of callas as a floral mirror of the times—slender, cylindrical, streamlined. The 1940s bouquet grew full again, but rounder this time and entirely lacking the waterfall proportions of the 1920s; favored posies were garden roses, stephanotis, gardenias, and tuberoses. Wedding write-ups from the 1950s show a melange of bouquets, generally rounded and full, some of the tight nosegay variety, others of short, manageable cascades. Often, in a nostalgic throwback to earlier days, prayer books were carried in lieu of a bouquet and decorated minimally with tiny satin ribbons and

orange blossoms, wild clematis, or lily of the valley.

The 1960s and 1970s saw brides scooping up wildflowers and wrapping the stems in a grandmother's lace handkerchief. More color crept into the picture, although lighter shades of pale were still what it was very much about. Mrs. John Page Williams of Charlottesville, Virginia, remembers the lengths her daughter Betsy Poist went to just to be able to carry lilies of the valley, as she herself had thirty

Elaborate wedding bouquets were typical at the turn of the century.

🌿

years earlier. "By 1970," she recalls, "you couldn't seem to find lilies of the valley for love or money. Finally we just gave up and raised them ourselves. We planted the pips in little pots about six weeks before the wedding, and wound up with buckets full of them to take to the florist—who, of course, was overcome. And Betsy nearly drove him crazy by insisting on having single white roses in the middle of the bouquet with the lilies of the valley around them. The night before the wedding," she continues, "she came rushing in, saying, 'I've found the roses!' which she had, growing on the roof of my mother's garage. We went over at 6:00 the next morning, snipped them and ran them over to the florist, and somehow he did something to them so they didn't drop petals."

Somewhat prescient in horticultural matters anyway, Betsy's choice of bouquet for her bridesmaids was not surprising either. She had gathered armloads of Queen Anne's lace from the rolling hills of Goochland County, west of Richmond. To these she added blue cornflowers, marguerite daisies, and delphinium bought at a flower stall in downtown Richmond. She wanted the stems left loosely tied, but completely unwrapped. "I want it to look like they just stopped by the side of the road and gathered them right up out of the fields," her mother remembers her saying emphatically, and well before the pendulum had swung away from the discipline of tight bouquets. Her own bridesmaids in 1940 had carried just that, circular nosegays packed tightly with peach geraniums; they had also worn straw hats brimmed in the same way to go along with dresses of pale gray starched organdy over peach taffeta.

The 1990s have answered the unhinged extravagance of the 1980s by developing a fascination with the compactness of French bouquets; with the preciseness of a beautiful paperweight, scads of different blooms—freesia, roses, orchids, stephanotis, tuberoses, white violets, sweet peas, lisianthus, even big blossoms like peonies—are bunched tightly together in a small, perfectly round nosegay, and then wrapped in satin and cinched up at the bottom with a spectacular fat French ribbon, shirred and wired to achieve a baroque effect. But it must be said, too, that apart from the current interest in tight bouquets, the 1990s have also brought a catholic appreciation of all styles of bouquets. Brides and their floral designers take all the elements into consideration now; the dress, the bride's figure, the veil, and the general mood of the wedding all have a direct impact on bouquet choices.

Wedding flowers may have changed silhouette and substance time and time again, but they've always been there. Since the moment men and women felt compelled to sanctify marriage with a ceremony—and probably well before—flowers have been an integral part of the proceedings. Orange blossoms, symbolically appealing because they both bloom and bear fruit, are reputed to date back to a twelfth-century Spanish legend. Made standard fare by Queen Victoria, who wore a diadem of fresh orange blossoms, they were used almost exclusively in connection with weddings for years—Cornelia Vanderbilt had them shipped fresh from Florida to cap off the lace veil and satin slippers she wore at her legendary 1924 wedding at Biltmore House in Ashville, North Carolina. From about the 1830s on, when means were more limited, wax orange blossoms were worn, according to textiles expert Bryce Reveley. Wax flowers, she notes, were treasured and handed down from mother to daughter for generations. In the course of resurrecting vintage lace veils, she has

David LaVoy's circular "petit" bouquet of princess spray roses, freesia, and stephanotis, dressed with ivory and white wired French silk ribbons. David tied single stephanotis blossoms to the hanging satin dress ribbons.

restored wax orange blossoms she considered to be 120–40 years old.

If orange blossoms have had the most distinctively matrimonial identity over the years, they were significantly predated by fresh herbs—by tens of centuries. Very much a part of early Greek and Roman weddings, herbs were thought to ward off evil spirits and to shower the bride and groom with untold good fortune. Today's

brides may consider using herbs in wedding bouquets or in tabletop arrangements; rosemary for remembrance and lavender for devotion are frequent choices. Coles Jackson, for example, used fresh lavender for a fragrant aisle runner at the wedding of one of her daughters in North Carolina. Petals/Colonial Herbs in Columbus, Georgia, among other distinctive wholesalers, packages rose-

mary and lavender for strewing on a departing bride and groom.

According to Marilyn Van Eynde of the Woodruff-Fontaine House in Memphis, during the eighteenth century and well into the nineteenth, the formula bouquet had yet to appear. Wedding flowers tended to be garden flowers or whatever was blooming at the time. "They were gathered loosely and attached to a fan or a bible, or just carried as a simple bouquet. Elaborate wired bouquets didn't really come in until the 1920s."

"Fans," Bryce Reveley concurs, "were frequently used, particularly special wedding fans made of mother-of-pearl and lace. They were gorgeous and functional, too, and they were carried open with a bouquet or held closed with streamers coming down." Cinched up with a light cascade of lily of the valley or a clutch of orange blossoms, the wedding fan might make a wonderful reappearance today.

The language of the fan was only slightly less complicated than the language of flowers, which Victorian-era lovers also had a passion for. Young ladies believed flowers to be a great source of communication with the opposite sex. A column entitled "Language and Sentiment of Flowers," published in a popular magazine from the period, reads: "an extended and sometimes important correspondence may be carried on by the presentation of bouquets, single flowers and even leaves; the charm of

this interchange of thought largely consisting in the romance attendant upon an expression of sentiment in a partially disguised and hidden language." The writer then encourages the reader to learn the list of over 250 flowers and their sentiments, since any ensuing conversation "will depend upon intimate knowledge possessed of the language of flowers and the variety from which to select." The writer goes on to describe a typical scene of a courting couple: "The gentleman presents a Red Rose — 'I love you.' The lady admits a partial reciprocation of the sentiment by returning a Purple Pansy — 'You occupy my thoughts.' The gentleman presses his suit still further by an Everlasting Pea — 'Wilt thou go with me?' The lady replies by a Daisy, in which she says — 'I will think of it.'"

In our greatly expanded world market, we often take for granted the marvelous availability of cut hothouse flowers, but in the eighteenth and nineteenth centuries, wedding flowers were greatly restricted, and war,

among other hardships, left an imprint on many a marriage. Mrs. John L. Williams, for example, married in Richmond, Virginia, in 1864 toward the end of the Civil War. Not a flower was to be had anywhere, but enterprising family members managed to fashion a novel headpiece for her nevertheless. Looking to the barnyard for inspiration, they created a smashing circlet of white duck feathers that was worn for the occasion, and preserved. Still extant well over a century later, it has been treasured and worn by family members over the generations.

Floral Designs: Getting Started

The floral scheme for a wedding is a composite made up of three interlocking components: personal flowers, ceremony flowers, and reception flowers. Personal flowers refer to those flowers that are worn or carried by the wedding party and close family members — the bridal bouquet and headpiece, bridesmaids' bouquets and possible headpieces or loose flowers for the hair, boutonnieres, corsages for mothers and sometimes grandmothers, strewing flowers, basket flowers and/or hair flowers for younger attendants. The ceremony flowers are the arrangements, garlands, topiaries, swags, badges, chuppah decoration or pew markers that a bride might select to adorn the church, synagogue, or secular ceremony site. The reception flowers, often the priciest part of the total design, decorate the reception area; if the reception is at a private club, restaurant, or hotel, or if it is at the parish house of the church, the scheme may boil down to a few simple buffet-table arrangements; if, on the other hand, it is held outdoors under a tent or at any of a number of wonderful alternative spaces that benefit from an injection of fantasy, brides may be in the market for a major installation of fresh flowers, fabric, and other special effects for buffet tables, entrances, stairways, and dining tables.

Without discouraging prudent planning, it's best not to jump the gun where wedding flowers are concerned. Like all the other elements of a wedding, the flowers don't exist in a vacuum; to a large extent, they are dictated by the many other selections a bride makes in defining her wedding—the season, the time of day, and the dress, for starters. As Bobb Wirfel, a partner in Houston's In Bloom, Inc., who at one time worked with the late Houston floral designer Leonard Tharp, notes with caution, "You really need to have a wedding plan first, before you attack the flowers.

Weddings are much more personalized than they ever used to be, and all the things that fall into a wedding plan have a tremendous impact on the flower treatment: the church, the reception site, the dress, the brides-

For Robin Robinson's reception at the Piedmont Driving Club in Atlanta, lush bouquets were displayed in large cast-iron urns that were specially painted for the event by florist Ryan Gainey. SCHILLING

Casablanca lilies, Queen Anne's lace, viburnum, eleagnus, delphinium, larkspur, and roses are just a few of the flowers used for the arrangements at Robin Robinson's reception. SCHILLING

maids' dresses, the mood . . . to say nothing of the particular likes and wants of the bride."

Wirfel and his partner, Scott McCool, generally schedule a lengthy first meeting with the bride and her mother to get a sense of the basics. They look at the various restrictions at the church and what the reception site entails, and they get a good feel for the dress and the wedding-party clothes. "What strikes me most," Wirfel notes, "is that brides these days know a lot more about flowers than they ever used to . . . and I've been making up bouquets for a long time. There are very few who don't have definite ideas; they may not be horticulturally informed, but they've seen pictures in books and magazines—they're more sophisticated and exposed than ever."

Personal Flowers

• The Bridal Bouquet

Traditionally, the bride's bouquet has been white with the refreshing interspersement of ivy for fidelity, but the choices for today's bouquets are essentially limitless. Apart from consideration of the site, season, and formality of the occasion, a good bit of thought should be given to the dress and the physical character of the bride. There are three basic types of bouquets: a circular nosegay, a hand-tied arm bouquet, and a loose cascade. Some suit styles of dresses and figure types better than others. A tall, slender bride in a satin tulip skirt, for example, might benefit enormously from a sheaf of graceful callas that would be overpowering on a more petite bride. A full skirt with a dropped waist, especially when there's special decoration at the hip—panniers, for example, or a cluster of fabric roses—seems to demand a tight nosegay that doesn't fight with the dress. The creamy tones of a vintage gown do well with a mixed palette of pale-colored blooms such as champagne roses, viburnum, orchids, stephanotis, even pale peach parrot

Checklist for Your Wedding Florist

• Do plenty of looking first—at friends' weddings; at wedding, flower, and entertaining books; at old photographs—and think about how flowers fit into the dream-stage concept of your own wedding. If you're getting married at a small country church with a garden reception following, think about English garden flowers like snapdragons, foxglove, and open roses for a natural, unstructured feeling, or maybe knotty baskets of lilac, peony tulips, and variegated ivy; if you're trying to transform the country club where every one of your friends has already gotten married into an all-new environment, think about chair-back decorations with beautiful but manageable nosegays of pansies or sweet peas all caught with silk braids. Decide whether you're after casual country or elegant urban, whether you want a dewy, just-picked look or unapologetic chic.

• Paint as clear a picture as you can for your florist. Bring your dress and one of your bridesmaid's dresses if possible. Pictures or swatches will do, but nothing beats the genuine article. Know what groomsmen are wearing, and discuss setting, season, time of day, and formality. Have a firm count

of the number of bouquets, boutonnieres, corsages, and so on that you'll need.

• Wedding flower budgets can be as little as $500 or as much as $500,000. Have a clear idea of what your budget is, but don't be inflexible. Often, your florist can translate your costly dream into reality by suggesting appropriate shortcuts. And sometimes relaxing the purse strings just a little makes that critical difference between the make-do and the truly memorable.

• Discuss all aspects of the job with the florist: personal flowers, ceremony and reception flowers, cake decoration, and so on. Ask to see pictures of his or her work.

• Ask questions and listen. Don't feel pressured if you're not knowledgeable about flowers. Remember, that's why you've hired a professional in the first place. If you are a little more savvy horticulturally, it may be even more important to keep an open mind. Two heads are usually better than one, and you may find your good ideas will become great ones with the input of your florist; he or she may suggest flowers you never thought of or alternative arrangements guaranteed to dazzle you and your guests. Don't forget florists have a lot of experience; it's their job to interpret the spirit you want to convey and at the best price.

• Be prepared for weather not to cooperate. You can't control it, so there is little point in getting yourself into a swivet if it's a cold spring and the dogwood you counted on doesn't bloom in time. Keep an open mind and establish workable alternatives up front; if the dogwood refuses to cooperate, you might discover that weeping cherry, delicate pear blossoms, and quince—all in bloom a bit earlier—make an even more luscious show. Above all, leave the last-minute scrambling for substitutions to the professionals.

Dathel Coleman used white silk cording as a unifying decorative motif for her daughter's ceremony and at-home garden reception. Here the cord is tied around a table centerpiece.

The choices for today's bouquets are essentially limitless. Jill Shoffner's bridal bouquet consisted of spray roses, pale peach and white full-blown roses, and lily of the valley. SCHILLING/VERANDA

tulips. An oyster satin A-line gown is luscious with an arm bouquet of white delphinium, lavender, white Dutch iris, and tiny sprigs of bouvardia.

Shirley Heumann of Rohm's in New Orleans offers several pointers on the bridal bouquet. "Most of all," she cautions, "don't make it too big or too loud. You don't want the bride to be overwhelmed by the bouquet, after all. For a pure white dress, you can think of white roses, phaleonopsis orchids, stephanotis, lily of the valley, and gardenias."

Ultimately, then, the bride's bouquet should suit her. I can't think of a more appropriate match for the dress of dark-haired Leslie Daubenberger than her lavish bouquet of alba lilies,

pink peonies, white Canterbury bells, double tulips, bouvardia, campanula, lisianthus, pink and white astilbe, Ariana and Lady Di roses, and clusters of lavender and white freesia. Cindy Brennan had to have her favorites, peonies and dogwood, while Kathy Levenson carried a classic design of white spray roses, Osiana roses, a touch of stephanotis, and lilies of the valley in a contemporary English nosegay with narrow satin ribbons and hot-glued tea roses cascading from it.

• Flowers for the Bridesmaids

The bridesmaids' bouquets generally play off of the bridal bouquet to create a cohesive whole that takes into account the mood and palette of all the dresses. Old rules of thumb dictated that many of the same flowers were to be used in both, but that the silhouettes should differ—a graceful cascade for the bride, tighter nosegays for the bridesmaids, for example. Additionally, color was allowed to creep into the bridesmaids' bouquets. Now, of course, there are no rules beyond what looks and feels right to the bride.

Most florists discourage settling on a color scheme per se. It's too limiting and too pat. Instead, they say, decide on a palette—a range of hues—and deal with what the season has to offer. You'll save money and wind up with much fresher bouquets if you work

with, rather than against, nature. And yet, that doesn't mean the strains of a theme can't inch into your floral design. What could be more appropriate for a September country wedding than bouquets of wheat and lavender girdling tightly packed curly lettuce or kale and parsley? Or even a heavenly bouquet of late-season hydrangeas, faded on the bush to soft pastels? And for a steamy July wedding, why not a nosegay of zinnias or a full bouquet of fresh basil, Dusty Miller, sage, and lavender for a true kitchen-garden appeal? For spring, could anything be more appealing than bright nerines with droopy wisteria and a few dendrobium orchids or blue hyacinths and pink tulips with loose spires of fuchsia Japanese magnolia? And at Christmas? Traditional English boxwood with a profusion of gloriosa lilies. Or even purple kale, red peppers, and paper-whites.

Long admired for his wedding work, the late Leonard Tharp operated a celebrated flower boutique in Houston before founding the Conservatory of Floral Art in Alexandria, Virginia. Says longtime partner Tom Stovall, "Leonard always did all the personal flowers for a wedding the day before, which seemed to astound people. But for a big wedding, that freed up so much more time the next day for whatever flowers needed doing at the church and reception. Actually, we found the bouquets really came out much lovelier after a day of crisping in the cooler;

Leonard used to call it 'hardening up.'" Tharp kept them in plastic bags and added ribbons and final fragile touches just before the event.

Sue Paciocco of Alamo Plants and Petals in San Antonio remembers a favorite wedding for which she created a different bouquet for each bridesmaid—yellow tulips, pale pink bouvardia, hot pink nerine lilies, pale peach blush lilies, peachy pink sonia gerberas, pale blue delphinium, dark blue iris, lavender Dutch daisy poms, and a clutch of purple violets for the flower girl. Tabletop flowers might coordinate in this manner, with seating assignments at the iris table, for example, or the pink tulip table.

New York floral designer Ronaldo

Maia's favorite bouquet for a bride or bridesmaid is an old-fashioned nosegay of parsley and paper-whites with galax leaves, violets, and grape leaves. One of the more delicate combinations, he feels, is lily of the valley with freesia, baby roses, nerines, pear

Above: Lee Rutherford's bridesmaids' bouquets were placed on a dining table during the reception, creating a lovely spontaneous arrangement of variegated weeping fig, Woburn Abbey and sonia roses, and gerbera daisies trimmed with peach wired French ribbon.

Right: Jan Shoffner's bridesmaids carried Christmas wreaths of pink roses, peach tulips, white freesia, fern, and peach satin ribbons for her "at home" Atlanta wedding. Wreath by David LaVoy.

blossoms, and tiny orchids. Above all, he cautions, don't try to put everything in one bouquet. Bouquets that masquerade as window boxes do anything but flatter a bride or bridesmaid. Don't consider anything larger than 10–12 inches in diameter.

Some brides may consider using old-fashioned silver tussy-mussies as part of the wedding-party scheme. These charming Victorian-era posyholders with attached ring chains for easy carrying make wonderful presents for bridesmaids, in addition to lending an heirloom aura to the wedding party. They also offer a nice opportunity for embellishment; old lace or tulle and even wired French ribbon are a beautiful accent to a cache of blooms.

Flower girls and young attendants may carry diminutive bouquets similar to the bridesmaids', or small baskets of fresh flower petals for strewing down the aisle to make way for the bride.

David LaVoy's richly colored bridesmaid's bou-
quet of fuchsia and purple freesia, and Lady Ioca
roses, tied with peach wired French ribbon.

Amanda Adams thought a smilax garland might serve as a kind of floral
nursemaid for the children in her wedding, keeping them together and giving
them something to do with their hands;
her friend Betty Drennen designed the
garland with three detachable bouquets, so that each child would have an
individual nosegay after the ceremony.
Lee Rutherford revived the old English
tradition of festooning hoops with
flowers for children to carry, while
Courtney Cowart of Atlanta had her
child attendants carry evergreen hoops
at her Christmas wedding. (For
instructions for making flower hoops,
see pages 219–20.)

Brides of earlier eras placed their
wedding bouquets at gravesites in the
cemetery. Today, bouquets may be
dried and retained as keepsakes or
given to hospitals or nursing homes.

- **Headpieces and Flowers**
for the Hair

Wax orange blossoms were once the
wearable flower of choice for most
weddings. Now all manner of blooms
are worth consideration. Bandeaux,
crowns and circlets, and Juliet caps
with attached veils are all suitable for
the crowning glory of fresh flowers.

Bob Derr of Occasions, Flowers by
Bob in Hampton, Virginia, loves to
weave delicate orchids into French-
braided hair. On the other hand, nothing is lovelier than a chignon style for a
bride; Dallasite Stephanie Logan kept
her long hair through the wedding just
so she could wear it up, French-twist-
ed and secured by a fat barrette covered elegantly with a magnolia blossom
and attached to a short tulle veil.

Flower girls may wear something as
simple as a gardenia tucked behind an
ear or elaborate braids of tulips, stars-
of-Bethlehem, camellias, tiny roses, or
even less formal flowers like renuncu-
lus or anemones.

There are a number of other elements of the bridal attire that benefit
from fresh flowers. In the earlier part of
the century, brides often bordered their
trains or the hems of their dresses or

veils with fresh flowers. Even wedding slippers were an appropriate spot for fresh blooms, making the bride feel bedecked from head to toe. You might consider having your dressmaker sew stem pockets around the hem of your dress; you could insert into them gorgeous orchids or lily of the valley or orange blossoms, kept fresh with small single-flower water vials available at floral supply stores.

• Sons and Lovers, Mothers and Others

Groomsmen wear a boutonniere that complies roughly with that of the groom. Leonard Tharp was adamant about the proper form of boutonnieres and would implore his students to use a single flower only when making them. Let corsages be corsages, after all, he would say, and leave the lavishness where it belongs—on the ladies. A small white or champagne rose, a sprig of stephanotis or freesia, or a tiny orchid all carry an appropriate, understated message as boutonnieres. Ringbearers wear a similar boutonniere.

Mothers of the bride and groom, grandmothers, and other special family members the bride may wish to single out often wear a corsage pinned to the dress or on the wrist. Just as frequently, today's brides may choose to have a small nosegay made up for the mothers, or offer a single stem plucked out of their bridal bouquets.

Ceremony Flowers

*S*heila McQueen, protégé of Constance Spry and head of the legendary Constance Spry design school in England, considers weddings inseparable from flowers, and the church the principal showcase for them. "Sometimes," she notes with some dismay, "I see more money and effort being spent on the flowers for the reception, on the principle that the guests will be in the church for only about three-quarters of an hour, whereas the reception may go on for several hours. Well, I feel that the church quite definitely has priority. In the church, while waiting for the service to start, everyone can enjoy look-

Above: At Lee Rutherford's wedding, the flower girls wore wreaths of satin ribbons, roses, and stephanotis in their hair.

Opposite: At a recent Nashville wedding ceremony, topiaries of pink and white open roses and hydrangea adorned every fourth pew. The bases were camouflaged with moss, variegated ivy, and curly willow.

ing at the flowers and all the trouble you have taken will be appreciated."

Before devising a master plan, investigate the restrictions on floral decoration at your church, synagogue, or other ceremony site. Some churches are quite strict about what can be installed and by whom, often preferring the ladies of their own altar guild to make necessary floral decisions and complete the handiwork. Candles are often a problem as well, so check on the limitations you'll be working within before being disappointed when your grand scheme falls outside of the vestry guidelines. Time considerations are critical, too. Bobb Wirfel installed one of his biggest church decorations in even less than the menacing forty-five-minute window allotted by the cathedral. "We had seventeen people at work," he remembers, "and we put up thirty-eight pew markers [lengthy cascades of roses, orchids, and gardenias that were as impressive as the bridesmaids' bouquets], a floral arch, garlands on the choir pews, and a wonderful white and foliage treatment on the altar. We finished in thirty-seven minutes."

Church decoration runs the gamut from hanging pots of geraniums in tiny sunlit chapel windows to stately pew ends topped with massive candelabra erupting in a lava flow of hothouse hybrids. But informal or formal, small and warm or large and majestic, most churches require some decoration—at the altar, in the windows, at the door, or on the altar steps. General church-decorating caveats: Don't forget that the congregation may stand for the better part of the ceremony; keep arrangements high and boldly visible so they'll make a dramatic impression even on guests seated in the last rows. Subtle compositions will be wasted on

Flowers to Throw at the Bride and Groom's Departure

• Potpourri, either loose in great silver bowls or in interesting baskets, or wrapped in tulle bundles tied with tiny satin ribbons. Try wrapping potpourri in hand-painted or silvered doily cones. Or consider using only one type of dried blossom—rose petals for example, or white dogwood—loose in a gorgeous container.

• Fresh flower petals—roses, camellias—whatever's in season. Pass them around in pretty china or silver bowls.

• Birdseed, either bundled in tulle or tiny fabric packages or disguised in satin or brocade roses.

• Wheat grains, in a wheat sheaf container—the perfect environmentally correct rice substitute for fertility and good fortune.

the altar and should be reserved for windows where they can be examined at closer range. For the altar, bouquets of brilliant reds, oranges, and pinks have become as popular as whites once were, but don't despair if your church allows only greens—mixed foliage such as croton, eleagnus (with its heavenly fragrance), kale, and any of the variegated varieties can be as interesting as colorful blooms.

Altar arrangements need not take their cue from bridesmaids' bouquets, if that seems too contrived, but the wedding tableau should be considered as just that: a conglomerate of soft, cohesive hues and textures. Pew markers are a lovely addition, although for the budget-conscious they may be as simple as nice bows or ribbons. Don't forget windows and even the font, a magnificent spot for a loose shower of foliage and blooms. Chuppahs offer an opportunity for spectacular floral decoration in fat, lush garlands of evergreens or solid blooms—hydrangeas, roses, peonies, or a lavish mixture. They may even be made entirely of natural materials like curly willow, and then festooned with clutch bouquets, swags, and garlands.

For Janet Mosely's wedding in Highlands, North Carolina, the tiny 1895 chapel, with its stained-glass windows depicting bucolic local mountain scenes and the rich patina of its dark, carved-walnut walls, needed very little decoration. Outside the church, foxglove bloomed in luxurious fullness.

Flowers inside the church were the strict domain of the altar guild, which, spearheaded by Janet's grandmother, added full, appropriately uncomplicated arrangements of roses, wild hydrangeas, spider chrysanthemums, and Queen Anne's lace, all in beautiful old silver tureens.

The man-made restrictions of an organized house of worship can seem insignificant compared to the challenge of playing alongside nature itself. Within the natural theater of a breathtaking outdoor setting, a florist's arrangements may be relegated to bit parts. Generally, it is a bad idea all around to compete with nature by trying to fill up the panorama with a lot of big arrangements; the problem is, they'll never be big enough, and if they are, then you have to question the choice of site in the first place. Let the garden introduce its delicate palette little by little. As the guests wait for the ceremony to begin, they'll absorb everything they should, and in garden rather than Hollywood time—a tangled skein of glorious fragrances from earthy mulch to the heady scent of a medley of blooms; the soft graduation of shades from pale to deep; birds talking to each other overhead; lighting

❧

Sweet Pea, the Bunting family cat, enjoys the fragrance of freshly cut flowers from the family's garden. Pansies, snapdragons, roses, and Mexican sage are to be used for a bridal bouquet. GIBBONS

here and there. Likewise, leave the ocean backdrop of a beach wedding well enough alone; give the historic house with its warm antiques and soft oriental rugs plenty of room to breath; let the at-home wedding site show off its personal treasures without being overwhelmed by floral artifice. These types of secular wedding sites are usually chosen for very special reasons; it's best to let them carry the melody and have flowers provide the grace notes, rather than introducing a whole new song in a different key.

In the Texas Hill Country, where Matt and Kelly Strange were married, yawning stretches of rolling hills,

pierced intermittently by live oaks, a meandering brook, and wandering livestock, provided more grandeur than a medieval cathedral might have; even four hundred seats seemed fittingly insignificant in this open-air temple, leaving guests with an unmistakable, and quite moving, message about creation and continuity. Here it would have been almost preposterous to do more than lay a floral claim on the lovely corner of nature that Matt and Kelly had chosen for the recital of their vows; pew markers and a great pair of green and white bouquets, designed by Sue Paciocco, were full and lovely yet appropriately humble in the presence of the awe-inspiring natural setting.

Gail and Thomas Hawkins chose the oceanfront of Seaside, Florida, as their altar. With a cerulean sky and crashing waves for a backdrop, their gazebo wedding *en plein air* needed little more than mandevilla vines to complete the picture; bright, trumpet flowers all but disappeared into the natural setting, while still adding that imperceptible but just-right touch of tropical color.

Amanda Adams wanted to let the dramatic architecture of her parents' conservatory—a circular, sun-drenched garden room whose expan-

For Gail and Thomas Hawkins's reception at Bud and Alley's Restaurant, Michael Redman created three-tiered arrangements of wildflowers, rubrum lilies, miniature sweetheart roses, delphinium, gardenias, and roses.

sive Palladian windows give onto the pool—stand on its own as an at-home altar of choice. "The last thing I wanted to do," she says, "was to overdo things with flowers. It wouldn't have made sense for the space. I was after subtlety—in color and feeling. We just used pale roses in big bouquets, and tied the sconces with French ribbon."

Save the grand gestures for hotel ballrooms and rented halls; they agree

with each other. The appealing emptiness that makes commercial spaces so versatile and convertible also thrives on frequent makeovers from lush interior landscaping. This is the moment for instant floral architecture—the kind that creates pews by placing blossom-studded topiaries at the end of each row of rented ballroom chairs; apses from virtual walls of bamboo spewing cymbidium orchids from every opening; altars out of "trees" of freshly cut redbud and yards of antique brocade. This is not the time for restraint, but rather for the big, the bold, and the unabashedly beautiful.

Reception Flowers

*T*he sheer breadth of floral decoration available today for wedding receptions is mind-bending. No less a personal statement than the ceremony, the reception and its accompanying flowers paraphrase the bride's personality with eye-catching beauty and fragrance. The options are as unlimited as the number of sites, spanning the spectrum from cut garden flowers in the parish house to dazzling installations in

For a Nashville reception, Mark O'Bryan entwines ivy around a large trellis that will be covered with garden roses and potted hydrangeas.

venerable old country clubs to brilliantly orchestrated themes suited to myriad outdoor environments. The bride's vision and the site provide the keystone of the design, although simple settings don't always beget simple flowers, any more than fancy settings necessarily equal fancy installations. Sometimes the location stands on its own, be it simple and pared down or ultra-elegant and high style; on the other hand, standard sites sometimes demand a floral facelift, while the most blue-chip backdrops, outside and in, often crave the complement of a clean line rather than cranked-up virtuosity.

Themes can work if they're handled with aplomb. For the Thanksgiving wedding of Sally and Lawrence Smith's son, Michelene Gary filled the lovely but otherwise bare ballroom of the 1927 Virginia Beach hotel Cavalier-on-the-Hill with a virtual forest of cut pine trees—140 of them—each strewn with tiny white lights, a mound of shiny red apples at its base. Tabletop arrangements were of Holland flowers, red apples, and starched paper-whites. "Even more than the visual impact," Michelene remembers, "was the incredible fragrance that arrested you the minute you walked in."

For another Thanksgiving-season reception, Jane Carter of Atlanta and London hired the renowned London-based floral designer Kenneth Turner and Atlantan David LaVoy to decorate the elegant Piedmont Driving Club. Twenty-foot oak trees were cut and

greenhoused to preserve leaves; the reception decor was based on a virtual forest of oaks, each with a custom-built table surrounding it and a mass of fresh vegetables and flowers at its base.

Often a site obstacle becomes the mother of a grand invention. Janet Mosely's reception at the charming Highlands Inn, thankfully rescued from certain demise by owners Pat and Rip Benton, is a brilliant example. Molly Craven took a lengthy stage, a permanent fixture of the facility threatening any design element introduced, and unflinchingly packaged it as if it were the very cornerstone of her scheme. By sheathing it in lattice trailing with smilax and shored up by ficus trees and potted plants, she had the beginnings of what would become a forty-foot-square, twelve-foot-high mountain garden, replete with fountains and figurines, walkways, garden banquettes, and fantasy tree arrangements—four-foot, six-foot, and eight-foot trunks crowned by enormous bouquets of rhododendron, roses, and wild galax.

And what about transforming the venerable old country club into something guests haven't been treated to a few hundred times before? Rusty Glenn of Dallas doesn't hesitate to create a structurally all-new environment. One of his signature devices is an iron armature, custom designed to surround a doorway or a mantel, to form a screen behind the cake table, or to create a smashing tablescape or even individual centerpieces. "I've got a great welder,"

For a Houston wedding, Bobb Wirfel created tall table centerpieces of roses, blue hydrangeas, gloriosa lilies, French tulips, and euphorbia. A small nosegay of greenery and green and champagne grapes rested at the base.

he confides. "I'll look at a space and these images come to me in the middle of the night practically about how to treat them. Of course my welder thinks I'm bonkers, but I'll have him create an iron frame with rods coming off it at different heights to hold potted plants, candles, and an assortment of floral cages with oases for cut flowers. Then the client has a one-of-a-kind installation with tremendous movement and interest.

"I like to use natural materials like grapevine, wild grasses, birch branches, that sort of thing. But particularly," he continues, "these armatures give me a frame to incorporate blooming plants with fresh cut flowers. You get so much punch from that look, especially when azaleas are in bloom or caladiums or hydrangea or even things like kalanchoe and geranium, nothing necessarily fancy. You get so much look from them, and then, of course, the client can take most of it home and plant it for the summer."

A Presidential Wedding Reception

The state rooms were profusely decked with flowers, palms and tropical grasses. The large windows at the South side of the oval Blue Room were hidden behind a foliage that touched the ceiling. Tiered below were various shaded plants accented by red geraniums and white lilies. The fireplace was filled with celias and small pink flowers and on the mantel was a bed of red roses with the monogram "C-F" in white. On the opposite wall was a bank of red roses and purple pansies with the date formed by yellow pansies. Above the door from the main corridor were the words "E Pluribus Unum" worked in blue immortelles on a deep red background.
—Account of the wedding reception of President Grover Cleveland and Miss Frances Folsom

Nuptials in Nashville: A Touch of England in Tennessee

*E*nglish roots run deep throughout the South, and in one prominent Nashville family, the British heritage that shaped the genealogical tree has also influenced a lifetime of collecting, entertaining, and outdoor pursuits. It also gave daughter Robin's wedding its very distinctive colors. Of course, English tradition can hardly be discussed without mention of the U.K.'s virtual obsession with flowers and gardens, a fascination that has not been lost on this family. The bride's particular passion for roses, for example, provided the cornerstone of a floral scheme that made the whole wedding

unforgettable. Throughout the reception a lovely feeling of al fresco lushness—accomplished by a brilliant symphony of floral chintzes, trailing ivy, and Chippendale planter box topiaries, lattice trellises, and lofty interlocking tents all spectacularly lit—could not help but call to mind the breathtaking lay of the English countryside and the lavish ease of English country entertaining.

Above: Throughout the reception, a lovely feeling of lush openness—achieved through a combination of floral chintzes, trailing ivy, and Chippendale planter box topiaries—evoked the verdant charm of the English countryside.

Left: Robin's bridesmaids prepare for the big event.

Above: Even the graceful bell-shaped wedding cake, designed by Evelyn Blair, was decorated with pastillage bouquets of pink and white roses.

Right: A happy Robin and Richard make their exit. CHIESA

The rose theme began early in the planning stages—with the dress. Favorite designer Arnold Scaasi came up with a mesmerizing and appropriate design in white satin—a fullish skirt with a bodice that might have been a rose garden in bloom, encrusted as it was with appliquéd organdy blossoms. The bridesmaids' dresses, full-length off-the-shoulder taffeta in pale but intense pink took a simple, pared-down cue from the wedding gown—a single rose at the center of a dramatic portrait collar.

Robin and her mother worked closely with Mark O'Bryan of the Tulip Tree in Nashville to develop a master floral plan for the church and reception. Roses figured prominently throughout, from the front doors of St. George's Episcopal Church to the wedding party flowers—Robin with a bouquet of all-white sweetheart roses and her bridesmaids with pink and white roses, as well as a single pink sweetheart at the base of their French-braided hair. It was a picture-perfect composite, with the heady essence of the lush blooms perfuming the air.

The bride and her mother had never imagined the reception as being anywhere but at home. Their graceful Greek Revival house, with its elegant proportions and captivating collection of English antiques, provided a genteel

Right: In the pool, Mark O'Bryan added a floating cherub decorated with roses, caladiums, ivy, and maidenhair ferns.

Below: Two massive bouquets of roses adorn the doors of St. George's Episcopal Church.

entree to an open-air evening of feasting, toasting, dancing, and celebration; most of the festivities took place under the canopy of a series of tents masterfully insinuated into a richly landscaped backyard.

The touchstone was a luscious chintz Robin and her mother found for the tablecloths, its creamy ground splashed with the pinks and greens of cabbage roses. As a complement to the cloths, a dance floor was designed and

fabricated in a varnished creamy background with a floral border and dazzling floral medallion; the four corners of the dance floor were marked by fifteen-foot lattice pyramids interlaced with pots of blooming hydrangea, ivy, and, again, virtual hedges of open garden roses. Tent poles were softly embellished with thick English boxwood garlands studded with roses, and occasional and dining tables all bore a series of rose topiaries in miniature Chippendale planter boxes, a one-time side business of Robin's mother. The combination of diminutive tabletop versions of the dance-floor pyramids with double- and single-ball rose topiaries created a floral feast for the eye.

Along the perimeter of the tents, oversized Versailles tubs were planted with calladiums, ferns, and hydrangeas in bloom, visually beckoning guests to the landscape beyond: to the pool—set off by a floating fountain with lovely garden statuary—and the pool house, where the children enjoyed their wedding feast.

Waiters offered hors d'oeuvres to guests before a seated dinner at Robin and Richard's reception, in an elegant departure from the traditional Southern cocktail buffet; a simple first course of artichokes vinaigrette was followed by rare tenderloin with bearnaise sauce, fresh squash, and tiny haricots verts. The dessert—a light, bittersweet chocolate mousse—was the perfect comple-

ment to the wedding cake.

Dancing to Peter Duchin's legendary orchestra insured a festive evening for wedding party and guests, many of whom were meeting for the first time, having traveled some distance to be there. The lovely evening was a tribute to Robin and Richard, not only reflecting their distinctive taste and lifestyles but also mirroring the warmth and devotion of their families and friends, and, in return, it was an unforgettable thank-you present to their guests.

Above: Richard poses with some family and friends.

Left: For her son's rehearsal dinner, Ann Penn worked with Brice Evans to create these lush centerpieces of green grapes, pears, and caladiums in glass urns.

The Ceremony

Observance of an Ideal: Selecting the Sanctum, Styling the Vows

*M*ethods of courtship and proposal have come a long way since the Sunday in 1047 when a frustrated duke (later to be known as William the Conqueror), unsuccessful after seven years of pursuing Matilda, daughter of the Earl of Flanders, ambushed his elusive paramour on her way home from church, rolling her in the dirt despite her formidable garb and striking her repeatedly to be sure the point was well driven home. Oddly enough, she was impressed, and consented to

Opposite: For Lee Rutherford's wedding, all the arched windows of the church were opened wide. Florist Tom Bailey filled the window boxes with asparagus fern, pittesporum, and daisies.

Right: St. Louis Cathedral in Jackson Square, New Orleans, site of Virginie Hermann and Joseph Landreaux's nuptial mass in 1835.

the marriage, which went ahead without incident some five years later at his Normandy castle. Less violent courses of courtship thankfully won the day, paving a more traditional and acceptable road to the altar. And while engagement has spanned the spectrum, from the touchingly understated—a young Breton had only to carry a young lady's umbrella in public to announce their upcoming nuptials—to the extreme, the actual marriage ceremony itself has changed very little over the centuries, and remarkable strains of sameness link even the most disparate religions and cultures.

Throughout the ages and across the globe, marriage has been, at its essence, a covenant between a husband and wife and their god, and often, as a consequence, between their families. The so-called contract has been backed by a dowry made up of assorted assets, cemented by the symbol of a ring, and solemnized in various forms and fashions by a figure of religious or civil authority. True, in

some earlier periods marriage was "not so much a union of hearts and souls as the joining of a strawberry patch and two fields of wheat," as Ethel Urlin aptly notes in *A Short History of Marriage.* The attendant ritual of marriage, however, has clung to its fundamental language quite remarkably throughout the ebb and flow of social etiquette and folkways.

In the early Christian church, for example, during the first centuries A.D., marital couples were already known to

137

join their right hands at the altar and to exchange rings; they also sanctified the event with a sacerdotal veil—which covered both bride and groom, much in the tradition of the Jewish chuppah—and allowed themselves to be crowned with myrtle after the pronouncement as a sign of victory and innocence.

In the colonial South, with its overwhelmingly rural character, most wedding ceremonies were performed by a minister at the bride's house. The trend continued to dominate through the antebellum period and straight up to the turn of the century, although the earlier establishment of urban centers like Charleston, Richmond, and Atlanta had spurred church weddings for city dwellers. In predominantly Catholic Louisiana, on the other hand,

cathedral weddings had long been the norm, as spiritual beliefs governed the notion that God lived in the church, and religious functions by rights were expected to take place there, shielding worshipers from the pedestrian distractions of the unconsecrated homefront.

Marriage ceremonies tended to be short, especially non-Catholic ones, and most were held during the week, contrary to the current tradition. The event itself was rife with superstition in its

Above: The bell tower of the Church of the Good Shepherd in Cashiers, North Carolina. Church bells have summoned guests to weddings for centuries.

Left: At the turn of the century in the South, most wedding ceremonies continued to be performed by a minister in the bride's house.

Opposite: The Church of the Good Shepherd. Throughout the South, the character of wedding ceremonies tended naturally toward the Anglican because of the predominance of English settlers.

Weddings for All Seasons

Although local weather patterns and personal schedules overwhelmingly determine the timing of today's nuptials, earlier wedding days were often set by superstitions. Lent was out for good reason, and May had long since carried a pall of bad luck. For the ancient Romans, May was the month of festivals for the dead, whose anguished souls, it was thought, haunted the living at this time; centuries later, it was still thought that a marriage in May would portend death or disaster. June, long the optimum marriage month, is but one choice nowadays, for weddings regularly dot all twelve months of the year. From a floral point of view, April wins hands down despite dicey weather, and with the widespread use of air-conditioning, the stifling months of July and August are no longer ignored. Holiday weddings are increasingly popular for the vacation days they guarantee, and for the special spirit that attends them.

every aspect, from the chosen day and hour of the service to the wedding supper or breakfast that followed it, to the trousseau, to the crossing of the threshold of the new abode. One after another, ancient ditties, old saws, and rhymes, charmingly naive to today's reader, attest to the heartfelt belief that happiness and prosperity depended heavily on choosing not only the proper mate but the proper time to marry him.

It was thought, for example, that the luckiest day for a man to marry was the day of the week on which he was born. For the bride, however, this didn't hold; her best bet was to be married on her groom's birthday. A common verse reserved for marrying couples went like this: "Monday for wealth, Tuesday for health, Wednesday the best day of all; Thursday for crosses, Friday for losses, Saturday, no luck at all."

Throughout much of the South, the character of wedding ceremonies tended naturally toward the Anglican because of the predominance of English settlers. But on the frontier, where other extractions played a more significant role, and in Florida and Louisiana, where Spanish and French influences colored the culture, traditions of the mother country were guarded and preserved. Prior to European settlement, Indian traditions varied from tribe to tribe, although the involvement of a contractual merger symbolized by an exchange of spoils of the hunt and the ceremony of dance were common themes to most. A notable exception was the Florida Seminole tribe, whose marriage ceremony involved virtually no fanfare. On a day selected by the consenting parents of the bride and groom, the groom arrived at the bride's house at sunset. This seemingly insignificant act fulfilled the marriage contract; it pronounced them husband and wife and allowed the two to set up a new menage in the camp of the wife's family, as was also the custom of the tribe.

Today, wedding ceremonies are more personal than ever before; as one of the most pivotal rites of passage, the content and location of the ceremony stand as a meaningful metaphor for the bride and groom themselves. Practices that were unheard of a century ago—writing your own vows and reading them, incorporating elements

of two different faiths into one unified ceremony, getting married outside the church or home—have become accepted today and, by their prevalence, almost orthodox. Although most couples still marry in a family church, many chapels and churches no longer expect or require couples to be part of their congregations. Often the type of ceremony a bride and groom are after will suggest a church—an expansive cathedral for a large, formal wedding at night, for example, or the charming honesty of a plain country chapel for a small noon wedding.

Cindy Brennan and Eddie Davis were married in the majestic Holy Name Catholic Church in New Orleans. GREVY

Secular Sites

Brides and grooms may decide on virtually any secular site for a wedding ceremony—from historic houses to hot-air balloons, from botanical gardens to romantic riverboats, from the seashore to the ski slopes. The Cherry

International Wedding Traditions

By and large, the marriage ceremony that developed in the Southern colonies came from England, although immigrants from Scotland, Germany, Ireland, Spain, and France, as well as African slaves, held fast to their native culture's wedding traditions. You might consider incorporating and updating some international matrimonial traditions into your own ceremony. A few suggestions:

• **Africa** Tribal chiefs traditionally bound the bride's and groom's wrists with plaited grasses as a symbol of moving forward through life as one. Ask the minister to tie your wrists with local wild grasses, wheat for fertility, or with a garland of red columbine (anxious and trembling) or honeysuckle (devoted love, fidelity) or phlox (our hearts are united) or Canterbury bells (constancy). Have him read a special prayer for this distinctive portion of the ceremony.

• **Turkey, Morocco, India** The bride spends five days prior to the wedding preparing for the altar by taking a series of ceremonial baths for purification. She then anoints the body with special oils, and sisters and friends paint her hands in intricate designs with a henna dye. Consider first-class pampering to get relaxed for the big day. Get plenty of sleep that week, and treat yourself to a massage, facial, manicure, and pedicure. On the wedding morning, have a makeup artist and hair stylist put on the finishing touches for a gorgeous bridal look.

• **England** The bride traditionally walked to church with her attendants, preceded by a young maiden strewing flowers all along the way. Try walking with the congregation from the church to the reception site if it's a feasible distance. If not, have a flower girl strew petals all the way down the aisle to make the path of your married life a bed of roses.

• **Germany** The bride and groom consecrate the marriage by holding candles festooned with flowers and ribbons. You might consider lighting a unity candle or having a trio of candles—one for your family, one for his, and one for the new family your marriage will create. Have your mother light one, his mother another, and the two of you the third, from the joined flame of the first two.

• **Bermuda** The wedding cake is topped with a young sapling to symbolize the growth and fruition of a new life. For a garden or outdoor wedding, think about incorporating a tree planting into the ceremony. Have the sapling already in the ground; then have the minister bless the tree with a special prayer or homily on the nurturing of your love and life together. You and the groom might shovel a bit of soil over the tree with a beribboned spade and sprinkle it with holy water.

• **Japan** The bride and groom become husband and wife when they sip from a single cup of sake. Present the wedding couple with a *coupe de mariage* (an engraved, double-handled silver goblet). During the ceremony the officiant may ask the bride and groom as well as both sets of parents to sip from this goblet, symbolizing the union of the two families.

Blossom, a stately riverboat that plies the Potomac, has the singular distinction of offering captains who do double duty as ordained ministers.

When the ceremony site offers neither a classic aisle nor a traditional altar, the bride and groom often create new parameters for a personal sacred space. It may be an aisle of fountainside steps leading the bride to an altar of green grass underneath a cluster of towering walnut trees; it may be the familiar fireplace in her parents' living room, topped by a family portrait and framed by the instant architecture of rented gold bamboo chairs; it may be a cavernous ballroom "landscaped" with folding-chair pews and a flower-bedecked chuppah. Whatever the setting, these alternative ceremony sites, by virtue of an enormous infusion of personal spirit and soul, become their own sort of hallowed hall and sacred ground.

Finding your dream wedding site takes a little sleuthing, but there are lots of places to start. As always, the recommendations of friends and family are priceless, but don't forget to poll all the professionals who have an opportunity to view alternative sites for a living. Having worked at these facilities, their input is critical; they will have a solid feel for how flexible the site is, what sort of restrictions come into play, what time of day is best, and so on. Local chambers of commerce are a wealth of information as a rule, providing listings of unusual banquet facili-

Account of a Florida Indian Wedding

A description of the marriage ceremony of an unnamed Indian chief and his bride from the notes of a French expedition to Florida in 1564:

. . . the king, ready to find a wife, ordered the tallest and most beautiful daughter of his followers to be chosen. This young woman was brought to him on an animal skin litter, fitted with a canopy of leafy boughs to shade her. Carrying the matrimonial litter were four strong men. Two more men walked alongside the litter holding fans up to shade her. Trumpeters blowing horns made of bark and hung with small oval balls of gold, silver and brass walked in front of the litter while beautiful girls walked behind it carrying baskets of fruit. Their costumes were skirts of Spanish moss and decorations of pearl necklaces and bracelets. Bodyguards brought up the rear of the procession.

The king waited for the queen on a special log platform built for the occasion with his most important followers sitting on benches below him. When the newly selected queen arrived, she was seated on the king's left as he congratulated her and told her why she was chosen. A dance by ceremonially dressed young girls followed. All the men and women had pierced ears in which hung small oblong fish bladders which, when dyed red, looked like "light-colored rubies."

—from *The Southern Bride's Notebook* (Maison Blanche Publications, 1983)

ties and wedding sites; and usually a call to the local art museum will also turn up other good leads, if the museum itself does not permit private affairs. The yellow pages are also an obvious but often overlooked source; try listings under wedding facilities, banquet facilities, or rental spaces. Remember county parks and local universities, which often have quite elabo-

Opposite: This altar, overlooking the pastures of Dr. and Mrs. Benjamin Caldwell's Inglehaum Plantation in Franklin, Tennessee, offered the perfect setting for their daughter Trudy's marriage to William Henry Byrd, Jr. SCHILLING

# A 1937 Wedding Ceremony in Historic Westover Church

In 1937 Kirkland Ruffin Saunders wrote a history of Westover Church in Virginia's history-rich Charles City County, as a kind of two-hundredth anniversary present to the parish. Actually, the church had been established much earlier, around 1637, making it one of the earliest Episcopalian churches, but it was moved in 1737 from its original site on Westover Plantation by owner William Byrd's wife to its present site on Evelynton Plantation. Mrs. Saunders gives a personal and, as she puts it, "non-historian's history" of the church and its parish, detailing, among other interesting items, the wedding ceremony of Ellen Douglas Bruce Crane, whose family had rescued Westover Plantation after the ravages of the Civil War:

What would I give for an account of all the weddings in Westover Church or even for a list of the married couples. . . . It is altogether fitting that the most recent ceremony at Westover Church should have taken place April twenty-fourth in this year of celebration [1937] and the bride have been a daughter of Westover! Each time there is a wedding, some one is certain to say, "The church has never before looked so lovely"; but this time it is true. There were only two decorations, dogwood and ivy, and yet the effect was magical. . . .

To soft strains of music the vested choir boys of All Saints Church, Richmond, standing in a group near the organ, sang "The King of Love My Shepherd Is." There were other appropriate hymns and anthems in their boyish soprano voices and then the sound of humming as though angels in the distance had taken up the glad refrain. The boys' organist sounded the wedding march and, following the groomsmen, three fairy-like little girls in small editions of the bridesmaids' dresses came up the aisle. . . . The bridesmaids, fresh, young and lovely, were like flowers growing in a garden.

Then came the bride, Ellen Douglas Bruce Crane, handsome and stately, a vision in ivory satin and bride's veiling. She came on the arm of her father who was to give her in marriage. . . .

Again the thrill of marching music and the long line of lovely ladies and handsome men, slowly filed down the aisle. Joy there was but the restrained joy of gentility, an atmosphere of impressive solemnity, of patrician elegance and simplicity. At that moment it seemed to me the old church smiled. Her cup of happiness was full, her pride was justified. I saw her raise her arms as in benediction. I heard her murmur, "God bless you, my children."

---

rate rental facilities available. And above all, don't forget to cultivate your own garden—if it works, your parents' or grandparents' backyard, farm, or ranch may make the most moving, relevant spot for you to be married in.

Whether you're married at a religious or secular site, it is important to visit at the proposed time of your wedding to get a sense of light, traffic flow, and so on. Especially for secular weddings, it's crucial to schedule an on-site appointment with all the professionals involved in the ceremony—photographers, musicians, florists. Be mindful of your guests and how far they have

Couples may decide on virtually any secular site for a wedding ceremony. A backyard or garden at the height of spring may make a moving spot. MARTIN

to walk, the location of rest rooms, parking, and so on. And, of course, for all outdoor weddings, don't fail to have a contingency plan for foul weather. At their wedding in the New Orleans Botanical Garden, landscape architects Marianne and Alan Mumford provided guests with white umbrellas adorned with flowers and ribbons in case of rain.

Deciding on a Wedding Ceremony and Site

*L*ike every other aspect of a wedding, the choice of altar defines the bride and groom. Player Butler, for example, knew from the outset that she wanted to be outside for her wedding. She describes her own religion as more pantheistic than anything else, and knew that she was after a more secular setting than a church. "I care about the earth," she says, "and about things that are natural. I'd always dreamed of being married in a garden, under great trees, with a summery, Southern feeling." For her, Evelynton Plantation's boxwood garden with its rose pergola was the perfect spot for a

St. Mary's on the Highlands, Birmingham, Alabama. Whether you're married in a church or at a secular site, it's important to visit the site at the proposed time of your wedding to get a sense of light, traffic flow, and so on. DURHAM

Above: The bishop of the Greek Orthodox Church performed the Greek double-ring ceremony at the wedding of John Georges and Dathel Coleman. GIBBONS

Right: The interior of the Greek Orthodox Cathedral of the Holy Trinity in New Orleans, site of Dathel Coleman and John Georges' ceremony. GIBBONS

traditional Christian ceremony performed lovingly and with great sentiment by her stepgrandfather. For Gail Satterwhite and Thomas Hawkins, the crisp whiteness of Seaside, Florida, with its dramatic ocean backdrop was a natural expression of their own philosophies. And Nancy Powell recently told me of her daughter's unforgettable wedding on their ranch in Fort McKavitt, Texas, about an hour outside San Angelo. The ceremony took place at 6:00 P.M. on top of the fort, as "Taps" was played by soldiers in period costume.

One Victorian ceremony I would love to see updated is the tableau vivant. There is a wonderful account of a late-nineteenth-century Memphis wedding in which the bride, rather than walking in on her father's arm, simply posed the entire wedding party at a so-called altar in one parlor; then pocket doors were thrown open so that all the guests, seated in the adjacent parlor, could be treated to a finished wedding portrait.

A bride and groom should have a good sense of each other's religion and the part it will play in their lives together. One of the fundaments of the marriage ceremony itself, it will also have a good deal of bearing on the site they choose. If either has a longstanding affiliation with a particular church,

the choice of site may be an obvious one. But if they are looking for an alternative space, perhaps as a personal reflection of their lives and interests, they will need to have some discussion of their individual notions and do a little scouting for the appropriate spot.

In tailoring the service to suit their own needs, the same applies; the Christian prayer book or the traditional Catholic or Jewish ceremony may be the natural answer; they may, on the other hand, wish to examine more closely the traditional texts and orders and add to them meaningful stanzas of poetry or lines of prose or make substitutions for language they find archaic or a weak reflection of their own ethics. They may even choose to write their own vows. They may also have the

otherwise conventional ceremony often makes the moment. I'll never forget Gigi Gunther's wedding, when Father Tim Thomas of Trinity Episcopal Church in New Orleans said, "Now, Eric and Gigi, turn around and see the people who love you and who will support you throughout the rest of your lives." A truly sterling moment.

And once you've settled on the ceremony and its details, you might think about building a new tradition around it, thus making it a memory not only for yourself but also for other family members. Marlene Kreinin lovingly put together a wedding heritage book for her daughter Elana when she married Dennis Markovitz; part family tree for both sides, it also included snippets of favorite poetry, personal memories and thoughts, and special prayers and songs all contributed by family members and close friends. A wonderful keepsake and personal record. Molly Pritchett of Creative Stenciling in the Washington, D.C., area, designed a ninety-six-foot canvas aisle runner for a nephew's wedding. With roses and lovely marbleized squares as a dramatic decorative motif, it featured the name and wedding date of the couple, and will be used again for future weddings

challenge of synthesizing the best, most personally significant elements of two different faiths, at the same time making certain the marriage is legally binding and a satisfying portrayal of their views of the marriage covenant. Many Christian wedding ceremonies have borrowed generously from the lovely Jewish processional, in which both bride and groom are escorted to the altar by their parents. Successful

interfaith weddings have produced quite touching hybrids with rabbis canting and Episcopal ministers reading, all under a gorgeous floral chuppah. Episcopalian Marley Meyer, of Little Rock, Arkansas, for example, was married in her family church under a chuppah simply because she loved the symbolism and aesthetics of it.

Remember, too, that the slightly unorthodox touch in the midst of an

Defining and Planning Your Wedding Ceremony: A Checklist for Creating the Most Appropriate Service for You

1. Spend a good deal of time talking to your fiancé about what marriage means to you. Examine your own religion (both if they're different), and start with the traditional marriage ceremonies of each. Make a note of the sections you find particularly meaningful, and of anything you find outmoded or offensive. If you conclude you are not entirely comfortable with the traditional text, begin making notes about what should be deleted, changed, or merged. Think about special poetry and prose you might like to substitute or about writing your own vows, either from scratch or by tailoring what's there. Above all, establish firmly how important the religious aspect of the ceremony is to you.

2. Talk about your nonreligious desires for the ceremony. Do you like the idea of a big wedding party? What about children participants? How do you feel about where family members who are not in the wedding party will sit? Are there any controversial family situations? What about printed programs with names and relationships of the wedding party (frowned on by etiquette pushers as commercial and secular, but gaining acceptability and popularity nevertheless)? Jewish couples might consider an artistic ketubah as an exquisite legal keepsake. (The ketubah is the marriage contract read by the rabbi as part of the ceremony and later signed by the couple; recently ketubah illumination has undergone a vivid rebirth.) These are issues to be smoothed out and decided on now rather than getting caught by them later.

3. Schedule the officiant for your wedding. If you plan to write your own vows, let him know up front, and ask if perhaps he has copies of alternative services he has performed in the past. He will undoubtedly have suggestions for additional prayers or readings you might incorporate into the traditional service. Check to see if he has any restrictions: Is he comfortable performing the ceremony with another officiant? What about an officiant of a different faith? Does he have a problem with your reading or reciting your own vows? Ask about prenuptial counseling. How many sessions, how far in advance?

4. Consider the musical portion of the ceremony. Ask friends and family for suggestions for the processional, recessional, and special hymns or solos during the ceremony. Discuss nonsecular music with your fiancé and how best to incorporate it. Perhaps a friend or family member might sing or play an instrument, or you may wish to hire a professional vocalist or musician to accompany the organist, or even a children's choir.

5. Check with the officiant or director of the secular site about costs and about policy on photography and flowers. Can a flash be used during the ceremony? Is an altar guild responsible for flowers? If not, are there guidelines or restrictions?

For Gail and Thomas Hawkins, there could not have been a more ideal site than Seaside, Florida.

in the family, adding new names and dates as needed.

Rehearsals

*U*nless yours is a small, casual wedding ceremony, it's a wise idea to schedule a rehearsal the day before. This thirty-minute to one-hour exercise can make or break a good ceremony. The bride and groom, the wedding party, and parents all attend, and with the officiant's guiding, go through the paces of the actual service. Usually the minister will make opening comments and perhaps say a prayer to start the proceedings. Then he and a mistress of ceremonies or family member in charge of coordinating the ceremony will discuss the processional, the altar procedures, and the recessional. Officiants have their own personal methods for rehearsing wedding ceremonies, but I've found that the most successful—and least confusing—technique is to start in the middle of the ceremony, positioning everyone at the altar, with bridesmaids and groomsmen lined up—usually according to height—then honor attendants, children, bride, and groom. This gives the bride a chance to preview the total tableau and make her adjustments. The officiant will at this point go through an abbreviated version of the service, giving everyone their cues. Then the whole wedding party, led by the bride and groom, recesses.

Without breaking rank, they then practice the processional. Any questions can be answered at this point.

Selecting Music

*I*n the melee of decision making, it's regrettable that wedding ceremony music is often shunted aside until the last minute. Nancy Slaughter, director of music for St. Mark's United Methodist Church in Charleston, West Virginia, says, "Be sure that you have qualified musicians. You don't want to spend money for a beautiful dress and flowers and have a mediocre soloist. The Protestant service is so short anyway, it seems as if you spend months planning it, and it's over in ten min-

utes. A program of music and musicians in addition to the organist can add so much to the service."

In fact, music is a prime player in the very personal score of your wedding service. The joyful strains of the various pieces you choose will stick with you forever, long after wedding cake has been eaten and lush flowers have withered. If you're being married in a church, a good start is to listen to the resident organist at regular services and at weddings to get a feel for his or her talents, the power of the instrument, and the acoustics of the space. If your ceremony will be at a secular site, check with the director

Christ Church on St. Simon's Island, Georgia.

Rehearsal Caveats: Let the Bride Beware

1. DON'T plan the service at the rehearsal. The time for planning is months before, with your fiancé and your parents and your officiant. By rehearsal time, your choice of processional and recessional music should be set, and a good bit of thought should have been given to how you see the wedding party positioned at the altar, how they enter and exit, where children fit in, and where parents and grandparents will sit. Remember that the rehearsal is a highly charged moment, full of excitement and anticipation; regrettably, more than a little hesitation or indecision at this eleventh hour often invites chaotic intervention by mothers, maids of honor, and well-meaning relatives. Have your basic plan firmly established in your head and make the rehearsal a dry run rather than a brainstorming session.

2. DO remember that even the best-laid plans can go awry. Sometimes what you've sketched out in your mind or on paper flops in the flesh. Be flexible and ready to consider appropriate alternatives. Keep an open mind about the officiant's suggestions; his past experience in such matters is invaluable and may smooth out snags in short order.

3. DO let the officiant run the procedure. You'll have discussed your basic ideas with him ahead of time, so let him put your plan into action. Remember, he's used to herding people, calming them, and giving directions, so let him do the corralling.

4. DON'T forget to spend a little extra time with children in the ceremony. Younger participants need to feel the confidence a few additional practice runs can give. Take a moment to tell them how proud you are to have them in your wedding, and that you know they'll perform their very important, special roles beautifully. Remember to have children's mothers or someone close to them seated on an aisle near the front (if they're not at the altar with the wedding party); point out where that person will be and tell the children that they can expect to see him or her throughout the service.

5. DO remember to go over any speaking parts or special participation in the service. Make certain that anyone who's singing, reading, lighting candles, moving your train, and so on, feels more than comfortable with the whens and wheres of the situation.

6. DON'T forget to give the necessary seating instructions to ushers: who is permitted to sit within the ribbons (if any), where and when grandparents are to be seated, exactly when the mothers are to be seated and who will escort them, if you're sticking to a traditional Christian bride's and groom's side (left and right respectively) or a Jewish procedure (the reverse), or if it's immaterial because the wedding is in a garden and therefore unorthodox anyway.

7. DO use the occasion of the rehearsal to make appropriate announcements regarding pre- and postwedding procedures; it may be the last chance you'll have the wedding party captive to underscore final instructions. Even if you've been thoughtful enough to print up and distribute an itinerary of the weekend and pertinent ceremony instructions, it doesn't hurt to go through this little exercise again.

8. DO take this opportunity to thank everyone for being with you and your fiancé on this special occasion, and to underline how important their presence is to both of you.

about auditing another wedding or two there to gather your thoughts.

Wedding music falls into four basic categories: the prelude, or pieces that will be played during the thirty minutes before the service actually begins, when guests are being seated (special selections can be played for the mothers); the processional, usually a trumpet fanfare, played for the groomsmen and bridesmaids and the bride—who may prefer to have a separate piece played for her walk down the aisle; the ceremony music, or pieces performed as part of the service by either vocalists or a choir, or hymns sung by the congregation; and finally, the recessional, to which the wedding party exits.

There is an infinite number of heavenly choices, but before getting your heart set on them, schedule a meeting with your minister or the church organist and see if there are restrictions.

Research your music by listening to tapes and records; your local library is a good source for appropriate pieces, as are professional musicians. Then think about the nature of your particular ceremony, the size of the wedding party, the site, and the time of day. Keep the music appropriate; no matter how much you've imagined yourself walking down the aisle to a symphony orchestra's rendition of Vivaldi's *Four Seasons*, your country church's small organ may make a mockery of it; trendy secular music in a cathedral may be regretted years later. Frank

Hoadley of New Orleans recently told me of his youngest daughter's unforgettable wedding ceremony, which took place on a cliff on the rocky shore of Cape Elizabeth, Maine, overlooking the Atlantic. The bride's whole family came up from North Carolina, and there were also friends from New England. A friend from Boston performed the outdoor ceremony, a cousin whistled a tune, a folk singer sang and played guitar, and a nephew played violin.

You might also consider the intimacy of a choral wedding. Coles Jackson's two daughters were married within three years of each other, one in a little Episcopal mountain chapel in North Carolina, the other in a South Carolina cathedral. Despite the difference in the size of the sites, both brides had a choral wedding in which the congregation sang the processional, the gradual, and the recessional. They both selected "Praise to the Lord, the Almighty, the King of Creation," "Lead Us Heavenly Father, Lead Us," and "Joyful, Joyful We Adore Thee." In both cases, the bride and wedding party were preceded by a crucifer, acolytes, and a minister in the fashion of a regular church service.

For the New Year's Eve wedding of real estate developer and artist Denise Chenel and Mobile news anchorman David Daughtry, Faith, Hope and Charity Church of God was electrified with gospel singing. The groom sang a gripping solo of the Lord's Prayer,

additional soloists sang "Yes, Lord," and the Faith, Hope and Charity Church choir sang the recessional, "Oh Happy Day."

Wedding Photography

You should begin scouting for a good wedding photographer early on in the planning stages. Comments from friends may steer you in the right direction, but in the final analysis, nothing beats looking at wedding albums, so leave yourself enough time for a thorough sampling of the local talent. It's there that you'll discover whether you see eye to eye with a photographer, whether he's technician and artist enough for you, or whether his photos seem blurred or otherwise amateurish, missing close friends and family by taking too many impersonal crowd scenes. Like all of your other wedding decisions, your choice of photographer is crucial; after all, your wedding pictures are the most concrete reminder of the joys of the day; they form a pictorial collage that re-creates a younger you your children and grandchildren might otherwise never know.

Start interviewing photographers early; the best ones are booked well in advance. Once you've made your decision, establish price and package inclusions firmly. Then begin to communicate the overall feeling you're

after—standard poses or lots of candids and odd angles. Give the photographer all the pertinent information—size of the wedding party, size of your family, anticipated shots—so he'll have a handle on the job. The more communication you have with him, the better.

It's always a good idea to arrange for the photographer to meet you at both the ceremony and reception sites; that way, he'll have a feel for the terrain, the light, and so on, and you'll save time on wedding day. Help your photographer not to overlook his subjects by reminding your wedding party and family when and where they are to be photographed; once they've dispersed, it's often impossible to round them up again. You might even consider asking a good friend who's not in the wedding party to accompany the photographer part of the time to point out good photo opportunities.

Videographers are more and more a part of wedding proceedings these days, and you may wish to consider hiring one for the ceremony or reception. As a bride, you'll be swept from one well-wisher to the next most of the reception, and often a videotape viewed after the wedding is like being there for the first time. Videography is still relatively new, however, so be mindful of quality, which varies greatly among practitioners, and check your best sources for references. Remember to ask questions. Do they have editing capabilities? Are they willing to come out and preview the site? Will they be

using a hand-held camera or more advanced equipment? If the wedding is at night, will they be forced to use umbrellas and harsh strobes that may interfere with the gracious running of the event?

Above all, photography shouldn't interfere with your wedding; it shouldn't take the joy out of the day for you or your guests. As much as you'd like a complete record of the event, you must remember that you're the hostess and honoree, not a Tinseltown director. I've seen too many brides lose the sacredness of the occasion by trying to run the event like a

At the wedding site of Trudy Caldwell and William Byrd, Jr., Teenie Buchtel of Simply Perfect Parties created the atmosphere of an early-nineteenth-century garden. SCHILLING

movie set; if you're too busy trying to capture every moment on film, you can't be a participant in any real sense.

Heading for the Hills: A Highlands, North Carolina, Wedding

*J*anet Mosely had been living in Florida, far away from home, for eight years when Tom McMahan proposed to her. Tom's family was still in Illinois, and getting both families and friends, scattered virtually to the four winds, all together for the wedding might have proved a stumbling block for some. For Janet, however, there was never a moment's hesitation. The natural, and only, choice for her was the captivating mountaintop community of Highlands, North Carolina, where she had spent so many summers and where her parents had recently

Above: The wedding party, led by Tom and Janet, begins the procession down Main Street. A warm welcome note awaits them at the Highlands Inn, a historic landmark completely restored by Pat and Rip Benton.

Left: Reverend Charles A. Bryan, minister of the church, converses with Janet's bridesmaids after the ceremony.

moved. "I suppose I made my peace with being away [from home] physically," Janet says, "but I always know that Mom and Dad and [sister] Lisa are there if I need them. I guess security is a large part of what home and family are. Knowing that we always have our sanctuary—that's what Mom calls it—in Highlands, I feel like I always have a home to come back to if I need it or want it. It's been like a sec-

the priest who would marry me." Moreover, Janet's parents have become regular members of the congregation, and her grandmother is on the altar guild. Even with her career far away in Tallahassee, Florida, Janet's heart seemed permanently anchored to the quiet, unpretentious western North Carolina town; she was comfortable with the simple beauty of the historic Episcopal church with its deep, patined pecan boiserie and stained-glass windows immortalizing the natural treasures of the area—mountains, piney woods, native animals, birds, and the wonderful wild hydrangea and galax that are synonymous with the region.

Somehow, the simple Episcopal service with the Reverend Bryan at the

helm and family, college friends, and old high school pals at her side, was an evocation of Janet's own sensitive, caring personality. A refreshing lack of artifice peeked through every aspect of the ceremony, from the altar guild–designed flower arrangements of galax, wild hydrangea, spider mums, and Queen Anne's lace to the singing of old favorite hymns to the newlyweds' joyous walk with the whole congregation from the church to the reception at the warm, homespun Highlands Inn. There was something touchingly real, tangibly Southern about the whole affair; it possessed an ineffable quality often missing from more grandiose proceedings.

Father Bryan likes to meet with a couple at least three times before the

ond home to my family; it has meant so much to me that it seemed the obvious place to get married."

Janet had attended the Episcopal Church of the Incarnation during her summers in Highlands and knew the minister, the Very Reverend Charles A. Bryan, well. "I'd always enjoyed his services," she notes. "He's a wonderful and learned man. His philosophies and manner are just what I'd [wanted] in

Above: The Episcopal Church of the Incarnation, built in 1895, was the site of Tom and Janet's wedding.

Right: The wedding party waits to accompany Janet and Tom to the reception at the Highlands Inn.

being shoulder to shoulder, helping each other to carry the load.

"We ask them," he continues, "to sign a marriage booklet that they keep, which says, 'We understand that marriage is to be the union of heart, body and mind.' It's not just ethereal, it's not just physical, it's not just intellectual; it's the culmination of all three, intended by God for their mutual joy, to give help and comfort to each other."

Bryan takes full advantage of the rehearsal to bring a certain level of comfort and understanding of the Christian wedding ceremony to all the members of the wedding party and to the parents. He explains the symbolism of the three-part ceremony: the recognition and acknowledgment, the joining of right hands, and the exchange of rings. "It goes back to the days of chivalry," he explains. "A person's

wedding. That gives him three to four opportunities in which to get to know them and be certain they know each other on a proper level. He puts them through their paces in a sense, probing and clarifying, but in a tender, fatherly manner. "I usually use the diagram of the wooden wheel, hub, spokes, the arcs of the wood," he explains. "My focus is on the arcs of the wood. They are set corner to corner and are bound by a steel tire. The tire is heated and shrunk on. My analogy is that God is the steel tire, God holds us together. The arcs are called, in old English, 'felloe.' Fellowship," he continues, "is

❦

Above: Molly Craven decorated the moose and the mantel at the inn with white statice, mountain laurel, doghobble, and a simple bow of wired moiré ribbon.

Right: Against the backdrop of Pat Benton's country antiques, Highlands Inn chef Bryant Withers created a cheese and fruit table as well as a crudité table with a variety of dips.

Above: Chef Withers also orchestrated a dessert table with black forest cake, pecan squares, lemon tartlets, petits fours, chocolate-dipped strawberries, sugar cookies, and peppermints.

Right: The best man toasts the bride and groom.

❦

word was absolute. I ask, 'Is this the person you intend to marry?' They recognize each other, and answer yes. Will they take them for richer or poorer, etc.? That's recognition of the future.

"The reason they hold right hands is because the right hand is the sword hand. When you give someone your right hand, you've encumbered your shield or left hand and can no longer defend yourself. So that when I say, 'Hi, how are you today?' you've got a clean shot at my heart. That's what it means. I'm giving you my life by encumbering my defense.

"Then," he continues, "they exchange rings. The diamond isn't important, and the gold isn't either. What this stems from is the signet ring, the family crest, the signature, in fact. This seal given to her bestows upon her the right to buy and sell in his name! All she's got to do is plop the ring in wax, and she's signed [her husband's] name and bought a dozen alligators for the moat. Today, frankly, people ought to exchange credit cards," he notes with a laugh. "But seriously, the exchange means, 'With all that I have and all that I am, I honor you, I give you all that I've got.' So now I've given you my word, recognized who you are, given you my life by giving you my right hand, and now I give you my property." Each to the other.

The Reception

Revelry and Rejoicing: A Celebration of Personal Style

*S*ince well before the golden age of Greece, the more sacred aspects of the marriage ceremony have been the inseparable prelude to a big party. And not surprisingly—after all, the age-old rituals of eating, drinking, and dancing have long been expressions of blessing and of celebration in almost every known culture. From history's earliest moments, marriage was the critical answer to the problem of perpetuation. It was good for everybody. The joining of marital properties strengthened political and familial muscle, and pro-

Opposite: The Philbrook Museum's stately interior was a striking backdrop for Leslie and Bobby Lorton's reception in Tulsa.

Right: The Philbrook Museum's sculpture garden is a regal setting for a wedding reception.

creation itself meant endurance. The very concepts of fertility and prosperity, then, were soon bound up together under the banner of something known rather unacademically as good luck—neither scientific nor ascertainable, but plenty powerful. The perceived luck that attended a bride and groom was something precious to be shared with friends and family, and the most symbolic, and coincidentally sociable, means to that end was the joyous act of breaking bread and quaffing wine together.

The wedding feast became a kind of social stage for spreading the wealth, spiritual and otherwise. Sometimes it played out for days or weeks, in a splendid display of epicurean delights, dancing, and gaming. Other times, it was a simpler affair of passing around marriage mead and showering the bride and groom with grains of wheat. Throughout, though, there was the important sense of celebration and of the communal sanctioning of a new marriage bond.

The seventeenth-century at-home ceremony in the South was usually a short one, held in the morning or at noon to leave the rest of the day clear for a variety of festivities. A banquet followed, frequently with seating enough for but a portion of the guests. Interestingly, buffet service didn't save the day until well into the next century; for the moment, seating was a rotational affair, with the elderly enjoying the earlier service, and children relegated to third or even fourth

159

seatings. On the frontier especially, the menu was composed in great part of game, the elaborateness of the spread directly proportional to the luck of the kill.

A French visitor to Virginia in 1686 left an enlightening account of an overseer's wedding he was fortunate enough to attend. More than a hundred guests were present, he wrote, a number of so-called good estate with the ladies quite respectably appointed and pleasurable to look upon. He was particularly impressed by the feast, spread out magnificently in an orchard under the trees, despite the November wedding date. Eighty people sat down at the first table and were served so excessively he estimated there must have been enough for five hundred. It was the custom of the country, the foreign traveler observed, to serve the wedding banquet at two in the afternoon. Most of the guests stayed one or several nights, having come from afar, but the available beds were monopolized by the women and young girls.

With the gargantuan repast out of the way, dancing held sway, often until midnight. Unlike today, everyone danced at weddings, and, more importantly, the gentry all knew how, having been instructed rigorously as part of their social education. There was considerable emphasis on gaming—stealing the bride's shoes, for example, gambling, cards, and dice, as well as such curiously named parlor games as the Minister's Cat. One current ritual

An Eighteenth-Century Wedding Reception in South Carolina

Eliza Pinckney, née Lucas, a notable English belle who arrived in South Carolina about 1737, kept a telling record of the day by assiduously making copies of her letters to family and friends; for today's social historians, they provide a wealth of interesting background on planter pastimes and entertainments.

On [the occasion of] a reception for the young bride who had just come from her own stately home of Ashley Hall, a few miles down the river, the guests . . . had come perhaps from twenty miles around to do honor to the occasion. Gay would be the feast. . . . Miss Lucas has already told us something of what the country could furnish in the way of good cheer, and we may be sure that venison and turkey from the forest, ducks from the rice fields, and fish from the river at their doors, were there. The English style of cookery prevailed in pasties and rounds of beef, but modified by the country

and its products. Turtle came from the West Indies with "saffron and negroe pepper, very delicate for dressing it." Rice and vegetables were in plenty—terrapins in every pond, and Carolina hams proverbially fine. The desserts were custards and creams (at a wedding always bride cake, and floating island), jellies, syllabubs, puddings, and pastries.

The old silver, damask and India china still remaining show how these feasts were set out; with the "plateau" in the centre of the table, of silver, glass, or china, the tall branching candlesticks, the two handled loving cups, the heavy salvers with Queen Anne borders, and a shield or crest in the middle. Plenty of spoons they had, and two-pronged forks. . . .

The dinner over, the ladies withdrew, and before very long the scraping of the fiddlers would call the gentlemen to the dance,—pretty, graceful dances, the minuet, stately and gracious, which opened the ball, and the country dance, fore-runner of our Virginia reel, in which every one old and young joined.

—from *Eliza Pinckney* by Harriett Horry Ravenel (Charles Scribner's Sons, 1896)

For the more formal nineteenth-century Southern wedding, the finest silver, glass, and china were used.

Nineteenth-century weddings grew less restrictive in terms of the appointed hour of day, with afternoon and early evening weddings gaining in popularity well before the end of the century. The most formal remained the wedding breakfast, but be it breakfast, luncheon, or supper, it was the nineteenth-century reception that really saw the establishment of the buffet service. A commodious answer to the vexing problem of feeding and entertaining large extended families and wide circles of friends, it quickly became the mode and has remained a distinctly integral part of the Southern wedding ritual as it exists today. The relative disappearance of the formal seated meal from the Southern wedding did two things, after all: it allowed the hostess to feed everyone gradually, concentrating food in one place and leaving the rest of her house intact, free of makeshift tables and row upon row of chairs; and it virtually created the groaning board, giving the Southern hostess what she most desired—a blank canvas on which to paint a picture of hospitality as only a Southerner understood it. Her dining room, then, along with libraries and morning rooms and sun porches, became the foundation for a cornucopic still life of

missing from the weddings of yore was the tossing of the bouquet. And rather than departing with great fanfare, the bride and groom were expected to make a quiet exit well in advance of the guests at large; the bride was accompanied by her mother, sisters, and close friends to her nuptial chamber, where she was undressed and suited up in proper nocturnal toilette to receive the groom, who, after similar treatment by his own friends and family, was tucked intimately into bed beside her. Then, observing a custom that some consider a precursor of today's garter throwing, bedside onlookers pilfered the newlyweds' stockings—the girls stealing the

groom's and the young men the bride's—and tossed them over their shoulders at the young couple, with a promise of next-to-marry status for the one who came closest to hitting the targets squarely on the head.

In the next century, with farms and plantations more firmly established, the wedding-reception board became more lavish still, with fruits and vegetables in season, fish, turkey, hams, game of all description, and table after table of cakes and confections, jellies and ices. Still, the emphasis was on quantity rather than quality; there were no fancy sauces or delicate preparations, but rather a hearty spread of many items quite plainly prepared.

fruits, vegetables, meats, and endless desserts, all of which underscored the image of graciousness and plenty that Southerners sought to perpetuate and believe in. Interestingly, in a time when television and travel have all but erased some forms of regionalism, the traditional cocktail buffet reception, still overwhelmingly preferred in the South, remains the most distinguishing factor of Southern weddings as they are compared to those of their Northern sisters.

Although some Southern brides do opt for a more formal seated luncheon or dinner reception, better than 75 percent prefer a stand-up reception with occasional seating, creating the sense of movement and mobility, the lack of regiment, and the plentiful party atmosphere that has long characterized Southern wedding receptions. There's a sense of real exuberance as people mingle, mix, dance, and eat. It's a party with no apologies—and none of the stuffiness that sometimes haunts lengthy seated dinners. Caroline Rennolds Milbank, a native of Richmond, Virginia, and author of *Couture* and *New York Fashion*, notes, "It's certainly

not always the case, but there frequently is something sober and serious about Northern wedding receptions. They seem to do their best to seat you

between two people you've never met and will never meet again and as far away as possible from anybody you do know. And, of course, there you sit for

For a spring at-home wedding in King's Mountain, North Carolina, the lavish spread, catered by Lee Epting and styled by Gary Coley, featured rack of lamb, grilled chicken, and seafood salad. Ryan Gainey's lush arrangement of oak leaf and Anabelle hydrangeas provided an opulent floral counterpart to this groaning board. SCHILLING

hours of ultrasophisticated course after sophisticated course and endless toasts. In the South, we have a feeling we've done all that the night before at the rehearsal dinner; the reception in the South is much more relaxed; you're still moving through a series of wedding rituals like a first dance and cake cutting and bouquet throwing, but the format is essentially a party."

Planning Your Wedding Reception

*T*he reception is unquestionably the biggest single expense of the total wedding portfolio, and even small ones require a good deal of reflection and careful planning. Whether your reception is being given in your honor (and underwritten) by your parents, or whether it is strictly your groom's and your creation (and financial obligation), it remains consonant with the other elements of your wedding in its tendency to reflect your personal style. It is, after all, your first official party as husband and wife. Whereas the at-home wedding and reception once ruled the day, the 1990s offer a blazing galaxy of choices for wedding sites, music, food, and decoration. True, the family church ceremony and country club reception may still be the standard-bearer, but it is increasingly common to find brides and grooms looking beyond the obvious for a one-of-a-kind

reception site that redefines them, if only for a day.

Weddings tend to develop in curious ways. No decisions are made in a vacuum and each affects all the others. Major practical commitments like size of the guest list and time of year—rarely budget—are usually the first elements to be nailed down. After that, mood and dream come into play, giving a general shape to all the constituent

Charlotte Anderson's reception in Little Rock, Arkansas. Though punctuated by a series of wedding rituals, the format of the reception is essentially a party. HAYNESWORTH

pieces that eventually make up the big picture. Budget merely brings that picture into reasonable proportion.

A big Christmas wedding, for example, seems to suggest a spellbind-

ing candlelit cathedral with reception following at a local historic estate, decked in high style for the holidays. Small and casual at the same time of year might mean a hearthside gathering at the bride's parents' mountain cabin with wassail and plum pudding and Christmas carols sung by the fire. For spring, when the flowering fruit trees are in their glory, nothing beats a grassy backyard garden wedding and reception for a small group; for larger crowds, what could equal the family church with gorgeous bulbs planted in sun-drenched window boxes, Easter lilies at the altar, and a reception at the local botanical gardens with a billowy tent and bushels of cut flowers?

Some brides work almost backward, or from inside out, starting with a particular element they've always had a craving for: love for a grandmother's heirloom wedding dress, for example, may be behind the selection of a quirky Victorian house/museum for ceremony and reception; an animal rights activist might find the local zoo an irresistible backdrop for tying the knot. Some, on the other hand, begin with a bona fide blank slate, and just start looking at reception sites. The point is that deciding on reception sites, like all other aspects of the wed-

ding, is interdependent on other decisions. It's a package, after all, and must be considered as a whole.

But that's not to suggest that the package might not include attractive opposites. Carol Gross, for example, who married in Dallas in the early 1980s, had always had a fear of public speaking, so when it came to the thought of reciting her vows in front of a packed congregation, she positively clutched. Yet she didn't want just to slip off to a justice of the peace and thereby pass up the chance to wear a serious wedding dress and have a big reception. Finally, she opted for an at-home wedding with immediate family only, followed by a knock-out reception at the Dallas Country Club, satisfying both the urge for intimacy and for major merrymaking. And I've known brides who held rather grand church ceremonies followed by modest receptions but a few paces away at the parish house.

Liz Carpenter wrote up the unforgettable wedding of Texans Sarah Goettsche and Scott Fletcher, held on the bride's family's ranch in the Texas

Hill Country. "It was by design a scene of contrasts and contradictions," she wrote, "a wedding in the country but not a country wedding. The rural setting of the Hill Country landscape contrasted with the black-and-white tablecloths, a dance floor of black-and-white squares, violin ensembles, and rock bands. . . . It was plain and it was fancy: black-tie, boots, seven bridesmaids in black and white, five hundred guests dressed to the nines dining at the flower bedecked white carts of caterer Don Strange of San Antonio." Says Sarah, "When we started planning, we had the church and [a country club in Houston], but it was too ho-hum. Scott wanted it all outside." It made more sense for them to be married in the spot where they had passed so many languid hours picnicking and riding horses and spending weekends full of outdoor fun. And yet, their flair for the high-style and glamorous was completely in evidence. It was a wedding reception that perfectly paraphrased them.

One of the most appropriate wedding receptions in my recent memory was Miles Hamby's. An instructional technologist by trade, an eighteenth-century living history reenactor by passion, the Alexandria, Virginia, scholar met his future bride, Eleanor Hermann, at the Maryland Renaissance Festival. Their wedding was authentically eighteenth-century Virginia from start to finish. Miles designed and sewed Eleanor's spell-

binding café au lait raw silk gown and embellished her 72-inch train—the bows were later removed and presented as favors to the wedding party. All 150 guests, friends and fellow reenactors, arrived for the ceremony at Williamsburg's historic Bruton Parish fully decked out in eighteenth-century costumes, most of them handmade. There was an honor guard, an arch of swords, train girls, and plenty of cheering and huzzah-ing. The bride and groom arrived by carriage at Eve-

Above: At Jill Shoffner's reception the wedding cake, created by Lori Bonsma, was housed in a dramatic twelve-foot-high gazebo decorated with fresh wisteria. SCHILLING/VERANDA

Right: At the Swan House, a popular reception site in Atlanta, the Chattanooga Tent Company created a wonderful setting with white-and-blue-striped bar tents. The main tent, in the background, provided ample space for dining tables and a dance floor. SCHILLING

lynton Plantation, where they were met by another honor guard, a musket salute, and a trumpet fanfare. Following the receiving line, toasts were made and the buffet opened. A variety of authentic diversions and entertainments were available for the guests: lawn bowls, fortune-telling, blindman's buff, musical chairs, cards, and the usual attempts to steal the bride's shoes, only to have her purchase them back with a bottle of wine. Minuets and country dances preceded a dessert collation and cake presentation. Finally a Scottish wedding dance and kissing dance signaled the close of

events. Guests sang "Auld Lang Syne" as the couple departed.

Deborah Sloan and her fiancé, Richard, had a more contemporary gaming reception right at their club. To entertain their guests and spark conversation between those who might not have known each other beforehand, they provided a variety of lawn diversions, including horseshoes and croquet. For these canoeing enthusiasts, it was only fitting that their bar was an iced-filled canoe stocked with beers and soft drinks and adorned with sprays of fresh flowers.

Certainly the ultimate pull-out-the

stops wedding reception of my recent memory was that of Al Copeland and LuAn Hunter. The Valentine's Day nuptials took place at the New Orleans Museum in the great hall beneath the portrait of Marie Antoinette. The ceremony over, four hundred guests were treated outside to champagne, a fireworks display, and a helicopter dropping rose petals from on high. Meanwhile the great hall was silently transformed for a reception featuring Kool and the Gang and two other bands.

Narrowing the Field

There are innumerable choices to consider for the reception of your dreams—from the most casual beachfront or farm settings for picnic suppers to elegant, high-style gatherings in museums and historic houses to sophisticated soirees in venerable old hotels to any number of alternative affairs on riverboats and barges, in hot-air balloons, or in the local arboretum, science museum, or even aquarium. The first step to bringing the scattered images in your mind into a focused picture is brainstorming with your fiancé. Talk about all the weddings you've been to and what you liked and disliked about them. Comb the bridal magazines for suggestions. Think about the kind of people you really are and what kind of reception

feels comfortable for you both. Are you looking for something unique and ethereal, something totally unstuffy and casual, or are you in the market for black-tie tradition? Even if you think you know exactly what you want, don't be 100 percent sure there's not a better idea—or a way to improve on your own—out there. Ask questions and listen.

There are a number of elements that make up a reception, and depending on where you decide to hold the affair and whether or not you're taking advantage of the services of a wedding coordinator, you may find yourself booking services and dealing with several subcontractors yourself. As always, good planning and organizing make the event a success and propel you through the many trials and tribulations without costing you your sanity. Some brides may prefer a country club or hotel that provides a complete package, including food and beverage service and flowers, perhaps leaving them a simple choice of music. Others may opt for a more unusual site, and find themselves searching for and settling on each element individually, from selecting a caterer and devising a menu and banquet plan to hiring musicians to planning flowers and other decoration with a floral designer to reserving all rentals (tables, chairs, dance floors, linens, tenting, and so on). Particularly in this case, it's wise to keep a notebook for the reception alone, a kind of miniature wedding

planner, in which you organize all the names, phone numbers, decisions, literature, contracts, and so on pertaining to every element of the reception.

Selecting the Site

After settling on the size of your guest list, wedding date, and ceremony location, reception site is the next critical commitment. It may come as a surprise to learn that popular sites are booked up to and sometimes more than a year in advance, so it pays to get started on this one as early as you can. As you inspect each site, keep a checklist in mind of all the requirements both you and the site have. Look for size and space capacities, parking facilities, restrictions on hours of ingress and egress, distance from your ceremony site, restrictions on other services, and so on—all the elements that will affect the success and ease of your reception, for both you and your guests.

But, while keeping the practical considerations at your fingertips, it may be most important not to underestimate your first impressions; they will tell you more than anything else about how suitable the site is to your dream, however nebulous it may be in these early stages.

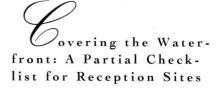

Covering the Waterfront: A Partial Checklist for Reception Sites

It may be helpful to keep these questions in mind as you look at possible reception sites:

• Rental fee and standard inclusions: What does the fee cover? What will you have to bring to the site at additional cost? Are there any discounts for off-season, off-nights, or off-days? Is there a deposit? Is it refundable if you cancel?

• Maximum capacities, flow: Can the space easily hold your guests? Does it work for a receiving line and cocktail buffet? Will the flow help generate dancing, talking, and eating?

• Privacy, exclusivity: Will your wedding be the only function in progress? If not, how will the facility be divided and still offer privacy?

• Rental hours: If the rental fee covers a four-hour event, can your caterer and other services arrive earlier to set up? If your ceremony is at the same site, can you and the wedding party arrive earlier to dress? If you are running late, are there additional fees?

• Parking: Is the parking area convenient to the site? Is valet parking available? Are there parking attendants or may you bring your own? What about courtesy vans in case of rain?

• Catering: Is there on-site food and beverage service? Can you bring your own caterer and/or choose from their approved list? What are the kitchen facilities like and when may they be made available to your caterer? Does the facility provide tables, chairs, linens, plates, glassware, and so on, or must you or your caterer provide them? Are there restrictions as to where food may be placed and served? Are there any restrictions on liquor? Is there a suitable changing room for catering staff? If you are to provide liquor or other items, when can you bring them?

• Flowers, decorations: Does the site handle this service in-house, or can you bring your own designer or florist in? Are there restrictions on floral and other decoration? When can your florist arrive to install the arrangements?

• Music, entertainment: Are there any restrictions on type of music, size of bands, and so on? Is a piano (or other instruments) included as part of the site rental? When can the musicians arrive and where can they dress? Is dancing allowed? Is a dance floor provided? Is there ample electrical power?

• Photography: When can the photographer arrive? May he or she preview the site in advance? Does the site permit scheduled photo sessions for your formal portrait? How early might the wedding party be photographed? Are there any restrictions on use of flash?

• Additional services: Are there adequate powder rooms? Are there attendants to service them? Are there changing rooms for the wedding party? How early or late are you permitted to use them? Is there air-conditioning, proper heating? Are there sufficient coat racks? What special services does the site provide, if any?

• Weather: If the reception is to be held outdoors, what alternatives are there for inclement weather? Are rented tents permitted? Will the site work in a sudden cold snap, a thunderstorm, an unexpected snow? Is it at its best in the early or late afternoon or evening? Do you "lose" it when the sun goes down?

• Insurance: Does the site have liability insurance in case guests are injured? If catering is on-site, does the site have enough liability to cover food- and liquor-related catastrophes? Will it hold you harmless for damages inflicted by your guests? Does it require a certificate of insurance from you to cover liability for accidents that result through no fault or negligence on its part?

• Cleanup: What is expected of you, the caterer, other professionals? What about accidental damages? Is there a damage deposit? Is it refundable?

Accent on Elegance: High-Style Hotel Wedding in Atlanta

*T*here's an interesting paradox that surrounds hotel wedding receptions: they're both easier and harder to commandeer because of where they're held. On the easy end of the spectrum, a bride has the benefit of a one-stop-shopping effect when she selects a landmark hotel; she will find that food and beverage service, rentals, and often music, flowers, and decoration all reside under the same roof, leaving her the luxury of coordinating all reception decisions through one person. It is the hotel's special events or banquet manager, then, who shoulders

A b o v e : Sandra Carling decorated the five-tiered lemon cake with lemon butter-cream frosting in a lacy pattern resembling dotted Swiss, as well as with pale pink sugar roses, tuberoses, and calla lilies.

L e f t : Jim White and his crew completed break-down of the ceremony and creation of the reception site in less than one hour, while guests enjoyed champagne and hors d'oeuvres in an adjacent room.

the responsibility for follow through, for running interference between all the services that make up the finished product, and for implementing the bride's changes of heart. The down-side, of course, is the sometimes difficult task of making the site come off as individual rather than packaged. The best hotels build in enough flexibility to give a bride plenty of latitude.

Kathy Levenson and her mother,

Above: Dr. and Mrs. Arnold Rubenstein, parents of the groom, and Renay Levenson, mother of the bride.

Right: The orchestra introduces Mr. and Mrs. David Rubenstein to guests, and the reception begins.

Renay, had always loved the stately grace of the Ritz-Carlton in the Buckhead area of Atlanta. The established elegance of its lobby and ballrooms offered just the atmosphere they had in mind for Kathy's wedding reception — a formal seated dinner. And the convenience of housing most out-of-town guests there gave rise to the idea of making the hotel, rather than Kathy's synagogue, the ceremony site as well. The final selling point was the hotel's catering director, Helene Adler Popowski — a polished, efficient party planner whose vocabulary does not include the term "nearly right."

To Helene and her impeccably trained staff they added Glorious Events' Jim White, a highly touted Atlanta florist/party planner and, coincidentally, a frequent working partner of Helene's. Jim would use the hotel's exquisite ornamentation as a foundation for a lavish, one-of-a-kind installation. Thanks to his handiwork, guests would leave behind the comfortable confines of the hotel lobby and enter a classical, otherworldly garden temple for the ceremony.

together until she was in college, their families had been friends for years, and they had a number of friends in common. There was no doubt, therefore, that the wedding was to be a big one with twelve bridesmaids, eleven groomsmen, his rabbi and her rabbi (hers, Rabbi Harry H. Epstein, had married her parents and grandparents), and four hundred guests. Renay's concern was not so much the logistics of the event—she knew the hotel, with Helene at the helm, could deal with the numbers handily—but how to make it warm, how to keep the whole affair from seeming a chaotic mob scene.

Kathy finished college with an undergraduate business degree from Georgia State Business School, but her first three years at the University of Texas meant she had two sets of college friends, as well as high school friends and family to include in the wedding. Although she and her groom, David Rubenstein, who works for a real estate developer, had not gone

❧

Above: On dining tables at the reception, thirty-inch silver candelabra epergnes were filled with roses and white dendrobium orchids, then draped with ivy. The candles were covered with sheer shades to cast a warm glow.

Right: Kathy's grandmother, Mrs. Simon Rosenblum, dances with Alan Levenson, father of the bride.

In her first conversations with Jim, therefore, the notion of softness was foremost. She and Kathy were interested in something sophisticated, rather formal, and very traditional. They wanted a European garden effect, and they wanted the garden filled with roses.

Ringing the cavernous room with ficus trees all softly lit with white lights, Jim created the effect of an outdoor sanctuary. Columned arches with lushly planted pedestals framed the aisle and were repeated both in the chuppah design and around the stage supporting the chuppah, giving the space a legitimate interior architecture.

The full length of the aisle was punctuated by a series of topiaries, created by crowning lovely harp-shaped pedestals with bountiful bouquets of mixed open roses in white, pink, and yellow. Interestingly, these arrangements were removed after the ceremony and used as tabletop centerpieces.

For the chuppah itself, Jim fashioned an unusual square arbor by positioning four ivy-festooned lucite columns beneath a round canopy edged magnificently with garlands of ivy, roses, lilies, dendrobium orchids, and other greenery.

What took place directly after the ceremony should perhaps put Helene and Jim on twin pedestals. Between the hotel banquet staff and Jim's crew, there were fifty worker bees on site; while Helene masterminded the prereception site, the two teams managed to

*For the rehearsal dinner, hosted by the Ruben-
steins at the New Swiss Hôtel, Darva Stapleton
of Forget-Me-Not Flowers created table arrangements of kale, forsythia, and roses.*

The transformation of the ballroom
took place without the guests' slightest
knowledge. In the prereception plaza,
they sampled cheeses, crudités, assorted
breads, smoked salmon, and finally
vodka and caviar, served lavishly from
their own station, which was dominated
by a garden urn ice sculpture spewing
roses and trailing ivy. Grilled baby
lamb chops, ravioli marinara, tempura
vegetables with plum sauce, and kosher
knockwurst en croute were passed
around intermittently.

Within the hour, a tuxedoed butler
sounded the dinner chime and guests
assembled in the magically revamped
ballroom for a first dance. Alan Levenson, Kathy's father, welcomed everyone with a champagne toast, followed
by a blessing of the traditional challah
by Rabbi Philip Kranz.

An elegant dinner of tenderloin with
morel brandy sauce and chicken stuffed
with spinach, artichokes, and sundried
tomatoes was finished off by a simple
but quite lovely five-tiered cake, the
creation of Sandra Carling. And dancing to two bands—the Ritz-Carlton
Orchestra directed by William Noll and
the Fabulous Emeralds, which alter-
nated sets—did not abate for a moment
during dinner and continued apace
until the bouquet was tossed at 1:30 A.M.

transform the ceremony setting—the
partitioned half of the total ballroom
space—into a dramatic reception site in
less than one hour. Tables, of course,
had been set prior to the ceremony and
were waiting behind the partition to be
carted into place. All ceremony chairs
were swiftly dispatched into service as
dining chairs, while the columned
arches were moved to form the four
corners of a dance floor. The chuppah
then became home to the wedding cake
in a symbolic interpretation of its ceremonial use as God's sanctioned covering of the marriage and the new home

resulting from it. Valerie Leven of Creative Tables in Atlanta draped the cake
table with an ivory lace overlay caught
up in rosettes.

A reception dinner plan was final-
ized after a series of meetings with
Helene. "You have to get to know a
family," she says, "to understand what
feeling they want for a wedding reception; you need to ask questions that
bring out their likes and dislikes and
their basic personalities. You find out
what they're comfortable with, offering suggestions for things that are first
quality and that suit their own tastes."

Choosing the Caterer/ Making Menu Selections

*B*ooking your caterer is the next hurdle in reception planning. Once site is decided and, along with it, the tenor of the reception, selecting a caterer may be an obvious decision. A country wedding at a ranch or family farm may call for a local barbecuemeister. A Chesapeake Bay dockfront reception may demand a fabulous raw bar and assorted grilling stations for serving up the local catch. A country club or hotel wedding reception will most likely offer its own menu selections from which you may craft special combinations. While small receptions at home or in a parish house are often beautifully handled by diminutive outfits or even family members, complicated affairs at alternative sites—historic houses or gardens or museums or municipal buildings—more than likely will require a skilled professional caterer with plenty of staff, extra presentation capabilities, and, above all, the ability to cook and produce an outstanding end result in difficult kitchen situations.

Word of mouth is probably your best resource for caterers, beyond actually sampling their wares at weddings and parties you've attended. Remember to get input not only from individuals but from corporate clients as well; they entertain routinely, often lavishly, at a variety of local facilities and can give you a good prospectus on

performance. Try radio and television stations, law firms, museums, art galleries, and so on. It pays to do some telephoning to establish caterers' basics: whether or not they're available on your date, how they operate in general, how flexible they are, whether they've had any experience catering at the site you've selected. You'll either develop a rapport this way or realize you're not seeing eye to eye up front, before spending time at a scheduled appointment.

Then schedule a meeting with several caterers. It's crucial to meet them at the facility you've selected for the

At the Swan House in Atlanta, Chattanooga Tent Company created an elegant tent for a seated dinner. The placemats were made from real salal leaves. SCHILLING

reception, rather than at their own place of business or at your house, although this may occur on a second meeting. If you're completely unfamiliar with a caterer's work and are just going on recommendations, ask him if he has any specialties or signature designs or dishes. Ask to see proposals and menus he's put together for other clients' weddings. Discuss all the par-

ing pieces, linens, and additional tables and chairs, and if not, can he rent them for you? How much staff will he provide? How do they dress? Can he do any on-site cooking, such as pasta bars, crepe and omelette preparation, grills, or sauté stations? Does he have liability insurance and a liquor license? What about the possibility of preparing some of your favorite menus? Don't be afraid to ask for a tasting; many caterers are agreeable.

When you've arrived at the contract stage, remember to find out what sort of deposit is necessary and when you need to give him a final count.

The wedding cake may come from your caterer or you may have a cake specialist design and provide one for you; be certain that you specify all the distinguishing features by looking at pictures and pointing them out, and that you discuss delivery and setup with your reception manager.

Flowers and Decorations

*F*or an at-home wedding or a country club or hotel wedding reception, you may have little to provide in the way of decorative landscaping, while alternative sites may require elaborate installations to achieve the effect you're after. But it can just as easily be the other way around. A divine alternative site—the lavish Anderson House, headquarters of the

At Jill Shoffner's reception, the bridesmaids' bouquets were placed on an antique French garden bench, creating a brilliant kaleidoscope of colors.
SCHILLING/VERANDA

ticulars of your wedding reception: the time of day and year, the mood you're after, the setting, whether it's formal or informal, whether you want a full seated meal, either served or buffet, a buffet with enough seating for everybody but no seat assignments, a cocktail buffet with plates and forks and occasional seating, or a cocktail buffet with only pickup foods. Discuss the pros and cons of different services and their impact on cost.

Don't forget to ask the caterer what his price—whether flat fee or per person—includes. Does he provide serv-

Society of the Cincinnati in Washington, D.C., and the legendary Jefferson Hotel in Richmond, Virginia, for example—may stand quite dramatically on its own with no embellishment needed, whereas the country club or hotel ballroom—the site of countless weddings attended in the past—may present the biggest challenge. A bride may want to put her individual stamp on the affair by creating dramatic stage sets.

Interview several floral designers whose work you've seen and liked, or at least heard about, and again, don't make the mistake of not meeting them at your reception site. Offer your general thoughts about the feeling you want to create, and let them use their own ideas in making it come alive for you. If the site offers a blank canvas, come up with a theme that's full and effective without being contrived. But above all, keep decoration appropriate, no matter how imaginative, and follow it through to a natural conclusion, so that it's understandable and readable. Lindsey Coleman's cherubic motif—played out in her bridesmaids' white dresses, on the reception tabletops, and spotlit in overhanging trees—was charming without being heavy-handed. Lee Rutherford's family plantation, Chasley, was trimmed to perfection, from the grouped torches

Florist Ron Barrett of Mobile prepares to set up Lee Rutherford's reception.

leading up to the manor house to the simple green and white foliage centerpieces and white tablecloths. Atlanta designer and antiques shop owner Jan Shoffner brought her whole house into the picture for the Christmas reception of her daughter Jan, filling her kitchen sink with lush strawberries, replacing her living room furniture with a heart-stopping seventeen-foot Christmas tree trimmed with peach bows and angels, spicing up a circular drive outside with a dozen six-foot Christmas trees twinkling with tiny lights, and furnishing a tented dance floor with camouflaged heaters.

As with all your subcontracted services, you may expect a contract or agreement from your florist. Be certain you're in accordance on what it includes and that the florist has coordinated his setup and his plan carefully with the reception site manager. If your reception is at an outdoor site, you may be in the market for rented tenting to guard against a rained-out event or just to create a fanciful space and atmosphere. Although white tents are still the color of choice, according to Andy Nolan of Chattanooga Tents, the latest trend is clear tents decorated to a twinkling glimmer with candlelight and tiny white string lights. He also notes the popularity of alternative dance floors—black and white tile-look or painted floors with marbleized and other faux-finishing effects. And, of course, sophisticated ambient and spot lighting.

Music: Selecting the Big (or Little) Band

There are countless choices for wedding-reception music and many brides don't feel the need to stick to just one, preferring instead to lead off with the quiet elegance of a chamber group and segue later in the program into a more danceable sound. Music should be in keeping with the general mood of the reception and ceremony, but there is really no wrong choice, save a band that is too loud or otherwise too much for the space. For Cindy Brennan's Jackson Square reception, the big band sound of Jimmy Maxwell's twelve-piece orchestra was the right touch, while Player Butler—who was after a big-band feel, but found it would have deafened her guests at Evelynton Plantation—settled on a five-piece portion of the Kings of Swing and concentrated less on the driving downbeat of Glenn Miller and more on the lightness of Gershwin and Cole Porter. Kathleen Turner, who also married in New Orleans, hired Chuck Easterling's impressive fourteen-piece group to play Duke Ellington, Count Basie, and other jazz dynamos; she had a marvelous surprise performance by Al Hirt, a guest at the wedding, who serenaded her first dance. For Gail Hawkins's Seaside wedding, a close friend and concert pianist played favorite movie themes and popular songs.

At Gail and Thomas Hawkins's beachfront wedding, Richard Raphael plays favorite tunes on the piano. Gail's father, Ralph Satterwhite, looks on.

If word of mouth fails you in your search for good reception music, check again with professionals who will have had occasion to hear a variety of good entertainment. Try agents and local entertainment and music associations for suggestions as well. If you're unable to preview a band at a local club or at another event, insist that they provide demo tapes for you to listen to. At the least, they should provide a list of the pieces they play so you can get a feel for their specialties.

In settling on a fee and a contract, be sure to specify how many pieces will be played, how long they will play and when they will schedule breaks, cost of overtime, what the musicians will wear, what their electrical needs are, and whether or not they've played at your reception site (if not, insist they talk directly to the reception manager, or better, visit the site). Discuss in as much detail as you can exactly what you want them to play. You may find it helpful to give them a list of what not to play—absolutely no top 40, for example. You may want a pleasant mix of pop music, jazz, classics, and show tunes, or perhaps special ethnic tunes that are meaningful. Discuss any special instructions: estimated time of first dance, cake cutting, bouquet and garter toss, and departure so that breaks won't interfere; whether or not you expect the band to make any announcements; whether you expect any musically inclined guests to take over the microphone, and so on.

Photography

*Y*ou will have taken steps to reserve a photographer for your ceremony and formal shots, but the candid shots at a reception require some further thinking. Atlanta photographer Denis Reggie, who covers more than fifty weddings a year, offers several tips on selecting a good photographer for the day.

• Don't be tempted to have an amateur—friend or family member—shoot your wedding. You have only one chance to capture the day on film; leave it to a professional.

• Ask friends for references and look at albums to assess quality and proper coverage.

• Hire early; the best photographers are sometimes booked up to a year in advance.

• Don't skimp on discussing what you want. Decide whether you're after artsy candids, crowd scenes, a real sense of the site. How many posed shots, how many candids?

• Establish how early the photographer may arrive at the site and work up a schedule for the formal poses. Consider asking a friend to accompany the photographer and point out good subjects.

• Don't forget the intimate moments: you with your mother, father, brothers, or sisters, preparing your toilette, distributing flowers, showing off your ring, looking at the guest book, flower girls talking, and so on.

Blueprint of a Reception

*N*ormally, the reception begins with a receiving line, which may include bride and groom, both sets of parents, and the whole wedding party. An abbreviated and more manageable receiving line would consist of bride, groom, and both sets of parents. Formally de rigueur, receiving lines are often axed in the effort to minimize waiting lines that tie up the festivities; just as often nowadays, the bride and groom will simply make the rounds. If you do have a receiving line, make cer-

A group picture at the wedding of John Georges and Dathel Coleman. Help your photographer by reminding your wedding party and family when and where they are to be photographed. GIBBONS

By the end of the second hour, the cake-cutting ceremony should have taken place. At this point, you will cut the cake, exchange bites with the groom, and toast each other with champagne. Traditionally, this is the moment for appropriate toasts; the best man, in theory, makes the first toast, followed by the father of the bride, who often winds it up by thanking everyone for being there. If the rehearsal dinner has been the scene of lengthy toasting, it's a very good idea to limit toasting at the reception. Normally, your caterer will cut the rest of the cake and distribute it or allow

❧

L e f t : At Cindy Brennan's reception, waiters get the party going by serving champagne to the guests prior to the arrival of the wedding party. SCHERMAN

B e l o w : Mark Michelsen prepares to toss Player's garter to his bachelor friends. CASTON'S

tain it doesn't block the entrance to the facility, and consider offering champagne to those in line.

If there is a guest book, it is usually the charge of a close friend or young niece or cousin not in the wedding party. Guests sign the book as they enter the reception, either before or after the receiving line.

It is important to make certain the party seems to be well under way when guests arrive. That is to say, bars open, food being passed or buffets laid, music full tilt. Nothing makes a drearier impression than holding back the festivities until the bride and groom arrive; it inevitably leaves guests shuffling around, uncertain and aimless, as they wait for a cue. Remember, this is a big celebration; don't give the appearance of being stingy with the good cheer.

Wedding receptions generally run from three to four hours, ample time in most cases for progressing through the various rituals and for taking plenty of pictures. By the end of the first hour, a first dance will have taken place, allowing the other guests to dance. If you're a stickler for tradition, establish a prescribed order for these momentous dances: you and the groom, you and your father, your groom and his mother, you and your new father-in-law, your groom and your mother, the wedding party. Some brides and grooms enjoy making quite a production of the whole affair by having the band announce the proceedings piecemeal.

guests to serve themselves. M. I. Scoggin, a New Orleans wedding coordinator, cautions brides to be certain not to cut the cake too late; older guests and children look forward to this part of the festivities and hate to depart before it takes place.

About thirty to forty-five minutes before your scheduled departure, you will toss the bouquet and garter, if you decide to include this bit of latter-day tradition in your reception program. The bouquet is tossed first, customarily backward over the shoulder in the direction of all the single women at the reception; the one who catches it is predicted to be the next to marry. The garter is then removed by the groom and tossed in similar fashion; the gent who makes the lucky catch is also supposed to be the next to marry. Some traditions then have him place the garter on the leg of the girl who caught the bouquet.

If you're changing into going-away

clothes, now is the moment for you to disappear upstairs or to whatever quarters are reserved for you. Your mother, bridesmaids, close friends, and family will likely accompany you for last pearls of wisdom and encouragement and congratulations as the groom

❧

Above: Ann Wilson catches the bouquet at the wedding of Lisa Ruffin and Jimmy Harrison. The single woman who catches the bouquet is predicted to be the next to marry. DEMENTI-FOSTER

Left: The bachelor who caught the garter slips it on the leg of the happy bridesmaid who caught the bouquet. CASTON'S

repairs to his quarters with his father and groomsmen. Let your bridesmaids carry any luggage or other items that need to go into the getaway vehicle, and send all other wedding-party members down ahead of you to announce your imminent departure. If you're having something festive thrown at you as you depart, it will have been distributed by this point, leaving you the exciting moment of saying final good-byes and tearing through the crowd.

Passport to Perfection: A Franco-Mexican Marriage in Houston

*F*or some brides and their mothers, planning a complicated wedding reception is an incurable headache, with an endless stream of impossible decisions, logistical nightmares, and technological short circuits. Others absolutely thrive on the challenge. The more irksome the process, the more riddled with insurmountable problems, the more fun they seem to have, and the greater the personal pride in the finished product. One mother of a recent Houston bride is the very embodiment of this rather Southern phenomenon. She is equal parts orga-

Above: The menu, a delicious synthesis of Mexican and French specialities, included everything from lamb chops in fresh mint to chicken fajitas.

Left: The flower girl and a guest enjoy the music of Ned Battista's nineteen-piece orchestra.

nizer, artist, inventor, and troubleshooter. Possessed of remarkable energy and a vivid imagination, she interacts with a wide, responsive network of amateurs and experts to get the job done with enviable results every time.

Even though she had just masterminded one daughter's wedding that summer, a second daughter's November wedding simply revved up her creative engines. Both mother and daughter were interested in creating a totally different feeling from the earlier wedding—a moonlit summer evening affair—by slating the event at high noon, an appropriately religious hour for bride and groom, she of French descent, he of Mexican. For the reception, to be held at a landmark private club in Houston, an altogether new look was needed, a daunting prospect since the club was known to be vigilant in its enforcement of decorating restrictions. And both mother and daughter were emphatic about capitalizing on the strong cultural and family traditions on both sides. Expecting a significant number of international guests, they knew it would be critical to make everyone feel comfortably at home and yet energized by the foreign and the new. Where to begin?

Oddly enough, with a local architect. The bride's family had recently discovered that architects, with their particular blend of skills, make fine general contractors on such projects as weddings and debuts, especially architects who are also trusted friends. So it was that Edwin Eubanks, of Eubanks/Bohnn Associates, stepped in to influence the end result. "The organization of a wedding," he comments, "is actually very much like building a house. It's detail work, once you have a plan. There's a lot of applied method, and the process and follow-through are critical." Edwin worked with the bride's mother to assemble a professional project team. The bride and

groom were included in all design decisions, playing an integral and creative role in the planning phases.

"What makes this wedding so special to me," says the mother, "is that like my first daughter's wedding this past summer it was inspired from the heart one hundred percent. There was so much personal research. We had tastings at the club, we went to San Antonio to hear the mariachis . . . we even called my daughter's fiancé long

Above: The clam ice sculpture featured chunks of crabmeat and lobster, accompanied by several sauces.

Left: The music began with a mariachi greeting as margaritas and hors d'oeuvres were served.

distance and held the phone out so he could hear them. Those little things are what make the whole thing so memorable."

The family's orientation has long been toward arts, architecture, and gardening, and the reception was certainly a monument to all three, with no shortcuts and no stones left unturned. For starters, the reception was to have the feeling of a sun-drenched garden. Lighting expert Richard Hernandez therefore installed special yellow filters in all the fixtures to bathe the room in wonderful afternoon sunshine. (For the bride's sister, he had done just the opposite, creating a dazzling nighttime effect, with moonlight made possible by blue filters and a ceilingscape of tree shadows and twinkling stars.) The bride and her mother loved the idea of cool marble to further enhance the garden effect, but knew the club wouldn't tolerate any sort of permanent alterations; momentarily stumped, they resolved the problem by hiring

The cake, a quatrefoil shape designed by the bride and created by Patrice Ramain of the French Gourmet Bakery, was a wonderful complement to the crocquembouche, *or French wedding cake.*

artist Suzanne Morriss to paint faux-marble canvas sleeves for all the columns, a perfect complement to the marbleized pedestals that would support lush flower arrangements.

Which brings us to the flowers: a true Provençal kaleidoscope of brilliant color, including great bursts of lilies, tulips, peonies, roses, and hydrangeas. The bride's mother is considered an accomplished rosarian, and violets are grown near their property in the south of France, so both blooms were prominently featured. Bobb Wirfel and Scott McCool of Houston's In Bloom have worked with the family over the years, considering it both a privilege and a challenge to create floral works of art for such horticulturally knowledgeable clients. The bride was particularly partial to violets, to grapes, and to the injection of the color blue—a typically French touch—and Wirfel, whose talents are legendary in Houston, responded sensitively, working up tiny violet nosegays to decorate the cake, binding the bride's and groom's chairs together with blue and white ribbons accented with grapes and violets, creating bases of grapes for the topiary centerpieces, and incorporating the electric jolt of blue hydrangea at every turn.

Friends of the bride's mother generously contributed their personal talents and time; they decorated the bride's table with swags and bows, ravaged their own rose gardens in order to fill silvered doily flutes with fresh rose petals to throw, and answered the non-stop telephone calls.

The bride and groom departed under a shower of rose petals in an antique Rolls Royce, bound for a honeymoon in Anguilla and a new residence in Atlanta, where she has an art consulting firm and he handles Hispanic accounts for a notable advertising agency. They would look back at their wedding reception as a one-of-a-kind special occasion, full of poignant personal memories and a renewed sense of family pride.

The Fare

Across the Board: Elements of the Southern Wedding Feast

*W*edding feasts in the South evolved in the same way as most Southern social rituals and customs, with humble beginnings being replaced gradually by more refined substitutes as the centuries progressed. The rather immodest display of plenty as the physical expression of hospitality and celebration made an appearance early on in the South, even when availability of everything from foodstuffs to dressmaking materials

❦

Opposite: At a recent Nashville wedding, Charles Cates set up a kitchen under a tent and fed the four hundred guests a supper of artichokes with French dressing, rare beef tenderloin with bearnaise sauce, baby squash, and haricots verts.

Right: Sylvia Weinstock of New York worked with florist Ryan Gainey to create this elaborate yet delicate cake for Robin Robinson. SCHILLING

was scarce. An enormous array of food was offered guests at wedding celebrations, in a kind of frontier version of the Roman bacchanal, with turkeys, hams, beef of some description, wild game, and oysters or other fresh fish complemented by endless tables of sweets, jellies, and ices. And yet, even into the eighteenth century, when plantations had geared up into high productivity, the emphasis remained on quantity rather than quality, as Joe Gray Taylor notes in his definitive *Eating, Drinking, and Visiting in the South.* "The food at such gatherings was not gourmet style," he writes, "in fact, with the exception of New Orleans and possibly Charleston and Baltimore, the concept of fine food in the European sense hardly existed in the Old South. From the British yeoman, from the Indian, and from the frontier the Southerner had inherited a preference for large amounts of different kinds of good food rather than a few dishes of presumably superb food."

The early Southern wedding ceremony was usually a morning or midday affair, with a formal breakfast immediately following or a less formal luncheon some hours later, at about two o'clock in the afternoon. Guest lists were large because families were large, and the mother and father of the bride routinely fed as many as one hundred invitees even in the late seventeenth and early eighteenth centuries. This feat was accomplished by rotational seatings and serving

Left: Lee Rutherford chose a very traditional seven-layer white cake with lemon filling. Silver swans were filled with white sweetheart roses.

Opposite: For her wedding in 1924, Cornelia Vanderbilt had a formal brunch following the ceremony.

partially why [in the South] you still don't have the situation you have everyplace else in the country where you have a sit-down meal."

Wedding ceremonies were frequently scheduled at night in the nineteenth century, and evening suppers with music and dancing that went on past midnight became more and more the norm. As part of its extensive store of primary sources, the Hermann-Grima House offers a telling account written in 1846 by Mrs. Louis-Albert Cazenove on the subject of her niece Annie Gardner's wedding. She writes, "Annie was married at home [Alexandria, Virginia] at 8 o'clock Wednesday evening, 15th April [1846]. There were present only the connections and intimate friends of both sides and I assure you they formed a considerable party. Mr. Lee [C. F. Lee, the groom] having a host of cousins, brothers, etc., in Washington and Virginia, and the bride, you know, has not a few. . . .

"As is the fashion here," she continues, "refreshments were handed around upon waiters [trays]; consisting of two very handsomely frosted large cakes, plain and fruit; pyramids

family-style, aided by the presence of servants.

In the nineteenth century, however, the guest list expanded more dramatically still, and the buffet breakfast, luncheon, or supper became the wedding entertaining formats of choice. Charlie Mackie, former director of the Hermann-Grima House in New Orleans, says, "The New Orleans tradition of not having a sit-down meal at the wedding reception really goes back a long way, and it [was established] for the same reason you do it today: you've just got too many people you've got to invite. If both the mother and father of the bride had eight or nine brothers and sisters in their families and so did the groom, you had fifty people right there that you had to cram in; for big Catholic families, you just couldn't squeeze them in. I think that's

of ice cream, jellies, pyramids of grapes and oranges fastened together with sugar; pickled oysters and chicken salad, and as a finale coffee and chocolate. We got home about twelve."

Perhaps more interesting is Mrs. Cazenove's description of the edibles offered at a party she hosted the following week for the bride and groom—to which, incidentally, the bride wore her wedding gown. "First," she records, "came around an immense cake, consisting of three in a pyramidal form; the under one was fruit, on top of that was a pound cake, on that again a sponge. The whole was most splendidly iced by the confectioner here. I never saw anything more beautiful. There were about 2 inches outside of each cake which was frosted, and round the edge of each was what they

call a fence of the sugar, consisting of little drops an inch in height and joined together by a delicate network of the sugar. On the top were doves, these were Frenchy, two with their bills together, perched on a quiver of arrows, which was also in a wreath of white silver roses. There were two ornaments of this kind on the top and they quivered and trembled in fine style; they were of sugar also. After the cake came these pyramids of ice; after, calf's foot jelly, charlotte russe; after them the ice cream in the shape of two large doves . . . accompanied by macaroon and coconut cakes. After the doves came chicken salad and tongue sandwiches. After that frozen Roman punch, which was the signal there was to be nothing more."

Marilyn Van Eynde, assistant director of the Woodruff-Fontaine House in Memphis, agrees: "At Victorian wedding receptions, they served real food, not the little mints and cakes you might expect. They believed in seven-course meals, usually served buffet-style: roast beef, turkey, corn puddings, pies and cakes."

The turn of the century ushered in much of the diversity we see today in wedding reception menus, with a simple punch, wine, wedding cake, and assorted mints and confections for smaller occasions, all the way to the opposite end of the spectrum, with veritable groaning boards reminiscent of a century earlier but, in gentry circles, with considerably more refined preparations.

Nowadays, of course, there are nearly endless variations on the basic Southern wedding reception, as brides more and more often select months other than June and moments other than eight o'clock Saturday night in which to tie the knot. Career, school, and family conflicts have made the entire calendar year viable for engaged couples, and the traditional hours of noon, six o'clock P.M., and eight o'clock P.M. have relaxed to include morning, mid-afternoon, and early evening as desirable alternatives. This broader wedding time etiquette has quite naturally opened the door to a panoply of

For a Christmastime tea reception, Lori Bonsma creeated these elegant hatbox cakes and confections decorated like presents.

Right: Many brides in the South do opt for the formality and ceremony of the seated dinner. At the Peabody Hotel in Memphis, one menu included a carousel of lamb, accompanied by a salad of mixed greens and edible flowers, served with a walnut dressing. RISS/VERANDA

Below: Wonderful confections and candies can be served in addition to the wedding cake. Anne Hodges of Crystaflower decorates petits fours with crystallized flowers.

interesting and entertaining menu ideas for today's wedding receptions. The seasons, the site, and the personalities of bride and groom all have a bearing on what winds up on wedding tables, and, frankly, nothing is beyond the pale. At a Christmastime tea reception, elegant bonbons and other confections all decorated to look like presents might shore up a tabletop Christmas tree, with wassail and eggnog as refreshments and a wonderful seafood presentation of pickled

shrimp, marinated scallops, raw oysters, and herbed dipping sauces nestled beneath a Christmas tree ice sculpture. In the spring, Southern brides might consider a delectable wedding breakfast of gravlax with fresh dill and black breads, shrimp warmed in a sherried tarragon mustard sauce with miniature corn muffins, hot curried fruit, and featherlight blini with Smithfield ham and apple-raisin sour cream.

Although the cocktail buffet still remains the popular choice in the South, there are brides who opt for the formality and ceremony of a seated meal, and, perhaps just as often, those

who prefer the other extreme, finding their most natural expressions of hospitality in toothsome barbecues, game cookouts, and fish fries in the country, at the river, or on the beach. And even the cocktail buffet itself has myriad shades of interpretation, running the gamut from straight passed and pickup foods to a number of different food stations offering hot and cold items with plates and forks. There may be occasional seating to accommodate guests who want to savor the edibles as they talk and watch the dancing; just as often, tables may provide casual seating for all the guests. Jordan Westenhaver of Catered Occasions in

For Lee Rutherford's country-themed luncheon menu, Homer McClure presented a striking menu: red caviar and sour cream canapés shaped like barnyard animals, curried pumpkin soup served in jelly jars, and a pasta dish, garnished with alstroemeria blossoms.

lighter grilled version with a simple herbed vinaigrette. Ethnic predilections and passions, too, have crept into old Southern menus, giving birth to divine hybrids like phyllo pastry bundles of roasted quail and onion confit, tiny pizzettas topped with chèvre and Smithfield ham, and old-fashioned North Carolina pork barbecue spiced with fresh cilantro, roasted corn, and a dollop of guacamole and wrapped in a warm flour tortilla.

Homer McClure of the Silver Ladle in Mobile notes a distinctive Southern interest in family traditions and food ways, even when the guest list is large. "People in the South like to use their own game—venison, goose, duck, dove, and quail—and interpret their own recipes," he says. "Food is so important to them. They seem to be looking for more nostalgic foods for wedding receptions, foods that fit the time of day and year. The whole presentation is key." Homer loves old-fashioned afternoon tea weddings with open-faced finger sandwiches, tiny caviar tartlets, and sweet tea breads. But he also enjoys blue-jeans-and-boots weddings, as he calls them, with homespun menus of barbecue,

Williamsburg, Virginia, notes, "In the South, it's not as important to have five different kinds of forks and three different kinds of knives and spoons at each place as it is to have that sense of conviviality, of people talking to each other and laughing and dancing and enjoying delicious, well-seasoned food—fresh, regional, recognizable food, and plenty of it."

The influences of California and New York have given Southern chefs and caterers a new outlook on old favorites, updating rare beef tenderloin, for example, with a vidalia onion marmalade rather than the expected horseradish, or sautéed-on-site backfin lump crab cakes with a pureed watercress and basil vinaigrette instead of tartar sauce, or even faithful chicken salad with red pepper pesto mayonnaise or reconsidered altogether in a

Brunswick stew, potato salad, and, as an elite afterthought, tiny fruit- and nut-shaped ice cream bonbons passed in silver ice buckets with sterling tongs.

For Lee Rutherford's wedding reception at Chasley Plantation, Homer worked closely with the bride and her mother to create an early fall country supper of predominantly cold, room temperature, and cooked-on-site foods. Says Laura Rutherford, mother of the bride, "Since we were outdoors in the country with sunflowers and almost a woodsy feeling, we didn't want fancy food; we just wanted it to taste good. We wanted to have a fairly healthy quantity of a few selected items, rather than a little of a lot. Most people had come a long way, and when you're in the country, you tend to find an appetite you never knew you had." Some items were passed, some were meant to be picked up, and some—such as a friend's home-cured ham, shrimp remoulade, backfin lump crabmeat in a homemade caper mayonnaise, and pasta with mesquite-grilled chicken—required a small plate. Delectable Southern cheese straws were passed in baskets.

Donn Franklin of Cuisine & Company in Virginia Beach says, "Even

For Janet Mosely and Tom McMahan, chef Bryant Withers served fresh mountain trout with dill, a speciality of the Highlands Inn, as well as smoked salmon with apples and cream cheese, and Beluga caviar.

though people are more health conscious these days, food at Southern weddings tends to be filling, if not heavy. Even though most receptions are cocktail buffets, the bride usually intends her guests to be well fed. Regional items are still very important," he continues. "It makes the most sense from every standpoint to go with what's local and what's in season. And we're seeing a lot less pretension in the

types of foods and the presentation—both are becoming earthier and more natural, in keeping with the site, of course. We've been doing Viennese tables lately with a dramatic *croquembouche* as a centerpiece, but with wonderful whole Southern desserts around it: pecan pies, coconut cakes, apple dumplings, and bread puddings, that sort of thing. But then on the fancier end, we're doing strawberry trees with

different dipping sauces for the fruit, and truffle trees with lemon leaf underneath and candied violets stuck in between the chocolates and spun sugar at the bottom. Just luscious."

Of course, place is everything in putting a menu together; alternative sites that make their own strong statements may guide food and menu choices, while more neutral rented spaces often offer the bride a real carte blanche in the catering arena. The two—food and facility—should make sense together, working as a team rather than canceling each other out with a lot of mismatched virtuosity. For Player Butler's late summer afternoon reception at Evelynton Plantation, guests were treated to an old-fashioned, unpretentious country supper. Jordan Westenhaver of Catered Occasions did what she does best by incorporating particular client favorites—homemade peach ice cream in frosty silver bowls, cooked-to-order crab cakes, Smithfield ham biscuits—into a lush, lovely collation with a residential, rather than a commercial, air. No number seven silver-plated chafing dishes here. Instead, Jordan's beautiful collection of old silver and copper serving pieces created an appealingly familiar feeling at various food stations, all serving up flavorful summer salads, fruits, and cheeses to go along with the grilled and sautéed items— very much as if an old family collection had been pulled down from the shelves for the occasion. In this particular set-

Fabulous Food Favors

Send your wedding reception guests home with an edible memento of the occasion. Here are some updates on venerable old traditions:

• Old-fashioned cake boxes with your names or initials and the wedding date printed on them. Guests love to take home an extra slice to sleep on or just to savor later.

• Love knots in herbed wheat bread: An earthy update on the old tradition of silk knot favors, often used to symbolize the early sacred rite of tying bride's and groom's clothes together—a metaphor for marriage. Wheat, of course, has long meant fruitfulness and prosperity.

• Eggs in dark or white chocolate: Age-old symbols of fertility and new beginnings, edible eggs make lovely favors. Try a chocolate-dipped coconut nest filled with tiny white chocolate eggs and candied violets or a larger champagne truffle egg with piped-on initials and date.

• Chocolate coins: An old Victorian courting custom makes a comeback with gorgeous Godivas or the best work of a local chocolatier. Often a date can be inscribed on foil or other paper covering.

• Miniature champagne in special editions: Let your guests drink a toast to your new union after you've tossed the bouquet. Lots of local vineyards are willing to produce a private label for a special bottle in appropriate favor sizes.

• Dragées in tulle bundles or tied paper packages: Sugar-coated almonds spread good luck and prosperity from bride and groom to all the guests. Very much in the French tradition.

• Chocolate sweetheart roses: An edible interpretation of the most potent declaration in the language of flowers: "I love you." As the ultimate thank-you to your guests, make up miniature nosegays of white and dark chocolate sweetheart roses in dramatic clear boxes.

Buffets allow guests to sample an array of different textures and flavors. For Dathel Coleman, Michaels Catering provided a tantalizing display of fresh fruit, pâté, and New Orleans sauces.

ting, she notes, it would have been ridiculous to take the food-as-high-art approach; the poached salmon, for example, was served with a refreshing cucumber *concasse* instead of being covered still-life-style in cucumber scales, food pairings were real rather than contrived, garnishes made sense.

For Gail and Thomas Hawkins's beachfront wedding reception in Seaside, Florida, Dave Rauschkolb and Scott Witcoski of Bud and Alley's Restaurant put together a mouthwatering menu based on their continuing research in classic Northern Italian, country French, and regional American cuisines—all strong, assertive styles particularly well suited to a dose of sunshine and fresh air. Here, a medley of flavors redolent of the restaurant's own herb garden combined in a menu featuring rabbit terrine with tomato *concasse*, country pâté with roasted sweet peppers, fish terrine with tapenade, grilled radicchio with blue crab and wild rice, grilled zucchini with gorgonzola, pancetta and white beans, pepper-charred tenderloin with horseradish, smoked salmon crostini with grilled red onion and fresh dill aioli, plus assorted cheeses and fruits.

The cocktail buffet so typical of Southern wedding receptions has done nothing if not give birth to the concept of food stations, in which the proverbial board magically divides and reproduces itself into myriad miniboards, creating an interesting staccato effect in food landscaping, as well as eliminating nightmarish lines. The whole ethic of eating at a Southern wedding, then, has remained somewhat apart from traditions elsewhere in the country in that guests rarely expect to create a multicourse meal on a plate and eat it in one fell swoop. Rather, by sampling the tantalizing array of different textures and flavors degustation-style, guests graze their way through the evening in a leisurely manner, mingling chatter and congratulations, dancing and toasting with a kind of evolving meal. Lines are a rarity because guests don't all eat at the same time, and the old-fashioned sense of plenty ensures they'll be well nourished both physically and visually. As Robert Lupo, clubhouse manager of the Southern Hills Country Club in Tulsa, Oklahoma, notes, "Things are still very different in the South, because wedding receptions tend to be larger, often 500 to 800 people. Brides want a lot of wonderful items with plenty of interest. To serve that number, we tend to have more buffets, more food stations with a tremendous variety." Robert enjoys the grand gesture and frequently uses ice sculptures and carvings that make a dramatic statement in the spaces he manages. Recent favorites have been a treasure chest brimming with shrimp, lobster, oysters, clams, and other seafood with a variety of sauces, an ice reindeer sculpture presiding over a mixed salad of *mâche, frisé*, red-tipped oak leaf and other lettuces, and an ice crystal vase spewing a profusion of cut blooms as a centerpiece.

Susan Gage, a noted Washington, D.C., caterer, doesn't believe in food stations per se, nor does she like to see one overwhelming groaning board. Rather, she landscapes a space with a series of buffet tables, using a combination of rounds and oversized ovals. Each table is a finished statement incorporating food and flowers in a grand scheme. Since she doesn't want to have guests interrupting their conversational flow by bobbing up and down to hit another station, she essentially creates a complete repast on each

Grilled chicken garnished with artichokes and edible flowers was one of the mouth-watering dishes served at a wedding reception in King's Mountain, North Carolina. SCHILLING

table, pairing unusual and interesting tastes in a tempting medley. A chef cooks at least one item at each table, and her impeccably trained staff, skilled in French service, passes seconds to guests on silver platters. Each area is staffed with a captain for cocktails and hors d'oeuvres, for the buffet, for the dessert, and for the breakdown.

For Courtney Banks's January wedding at the National Museum of Women in the Arts, the bride and her mother had originally envisioned a seated buffet, taking full advantage of Susan's celebrated adroitness in the tablescape department. But when acceptances came in at nearly a third higher than expected, space wouldn't permit the buffet tables; one week prior to the wedding, an undaunted Susan changed the entire plan to a seated dinner with ultra-elegant French service for 240 guests.

On the mezzanine level, there were open bars and champagne was passed around against a lush backdrop of deep green–skirted, tapestry-topped round tables. An elegant raw bar beckoned with old copper serving pieces draped in inky seaweed, and delectable hors d'oeuvres—cheese heart puffs, herbed brie tartlets, cherry tomatoes stuffed with mozzarella and pesto, marinated cilantro lime shrimp on tostadas with fresh guacamole, grilled beef *bruschetta* with basil cream, and smoked salmon *bruschetta* with dill mustard—were passed on silver trays.

The dinner itself was a still-life medley of French-cut veal chops with Calvados and caramelized apples, baby squash, haricots verts, and lacy potato pancakes, all served from gorgeous old silver platters. A sinfully rich first course of lobster ravioli lightly napped in lobster cream sauce was the perfect prelude. After the magnificent cake was cut on the dance floor, guests found their way to various dessert tables, tantalized by the unbelievably delicate specialties of Marilyn Mueller's Criollo Chocolates, featuring Marilyn's signature chocolate jewel box of couverture chocolate with chocolate flowers and foliage on top and a cache of homemade truffles inside. The groom's mother, Helen Pappas, added wonderful Greek desserts to one table as well, with tiny silver leaf pears, elegant cookies, and baklava.

Working with a Caterer

*N*o matter how small your wedding reception is, the food is likely to be catered. Depending on your knowledge of and interest in food and cooking, you may have a pivotal role in developing the menu and presentation. Or you may decide you have other fish to fry—what with invitations, music, photographers, bridesmaids' dresses, presents for the wedding party, and so on—and give a caterer plenty of slack in interpreting your basic desires with his or her own brand of creativity.

As is the case with so many wedding professionals, one of your best sources of advertising for caterers is word of mouth. The very best, of course, is your own mouth tasting rather than talking. Be on the lookout, when you attend wedding receptions and parties, for bright new lights on the catering horizon, whether they be aggressive young establishments looking to make a name for themselves or tried-and-true legends in the business who seem to have revamped their menus and their mood. Take time to notice linens, serving pieces, and presentation and make sure to sample the wares on other people's tables for good leads.

But while you're digesting the victuals and the visuals, remember that choices must be made, often difficult ones. It's critical that you never lose sight of your site; the effete edibles and eye-popping installation you've just waxed poetic over might well be the ticket for a gilded old downtown hotel, but outdoors on your grandfather's rustic ranch . . . a ridiculous notion. What's manna in one setting, after all, may be poison in another. And though most good caterers aim to be flexible enough to do many things well, most have a bent; it's best to choose one for what he does best—and then let him do it. In other words, figure out which caterer comes closest to what you want to accomplish, and then try to work with him from there. Forcing an old-school family caterer to produce a lot of rarified menu items will make you just as

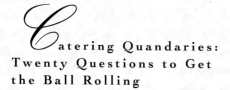

Catering Quandaries: Twenty Questions to Get the Ball Rolling

1. Have you worked at my wedding reception site before? What kind of party was it? Seated, plated meal, seated buffet, cocktail buffet, other?

2. What are your specialties or signature dishes? Signature styles or looks?

3. Do you have a list of passed and stationary hors d'oeuvres? Entrees? Desserts? Do you have pictures of your work?

4. Do you have the capability of on-site cooking such as pasta bars, sauté and grilling stations, and so on? Are you able to work outdoors or in limited kitchen facilities?

5. For my reception site, what do you recommend for a lovely presentation that minimizes lines and bottlenecks? Can you provide a comfortable blend of butlered and stationary hors d'oeuvres, buffet tables or food stations, and on-site cooking stations?

6. Would you recommend a cocktail buffet, seated buffet, or plated meal for my particular site? How is price affected by each? Can you suggest some alternatives that might be less expensive? A wedding breakfast? An ethnically themed menu? A tea menu?

7. Are you willing to produce some of my own recipes?

8. May I preview another wedding reception or similar party you're catering to get a sense of your staffing, flow of the party, look and presentation, and so on? Will you provide a tasting of some of the items I'm considering?

9. Does your staff bake wedding cakes? If not, can you recommend someone?

10. Do you have your own rental items: tables, chairs, linens, tableware, barware, and so on? Do you have samples or pictures of the types of wares you use? If you don't have your own rentals, will you arrange to lease them and coordinate quantities?

11. What sort of staffing do you have? What is the ratio of staff members to guests? What does your staff wear?

12. Do you have a liquor license? Do you handle complete bar service with bartenders, setups, and alcohol? May I provide my own liquor?

13. How much setup do you customarily do? Tables, linens, flowers, other? What about cleanup?

14. Do you charge a flat fee or by the head? Can you guarantee your price and if so, how far in advance? What does your price include? Food and beverage? Rentals? Labor? Tax? Gratuity? Miscellaneous? Will there be any additional charges? Is there a minimum guest count to hold the price?

15. Do you have liability insurance?

16. How do you expect payment? Is there a deposit or down payment? Is it refundable? When do you need a guaranteed head count?

17. Will you send me written confirmation detailing the discussed date and time of the reception (hours of service from start to finish), menu, layout, the rentals, bar plan, labor, required advance time for setup, cost?

18. Can you give me a firm ceiling on food cost increases?

19. Are you willing to feed photographers, videographers, musicians, and other professionals? Can you come up with a substantially reduced-rate menu for them? Can you suggest an unobtrusive spot for them to grab a bite during their breaks?

20. Will you pack a going-away basket for my groom and me? Will we be able to keep extra leftover food? If I'm considering donating leftover food to a charitable organization, can you handle the coordination of it for me?

unhappy as paying for a carriage-trade caterer's highly trained staff and inventory of elegant serving pieces when all you're really after is a ranch-style breakfast buffet. And, incidentally, they'll be less than enthusiastic, too.

Once you narrow the field to one or two caterers whose look and taste you're impressed with, make contact. Ask for references and don't be afraid to call them. You'll want to schedule meetings with caterers before you make a final decision; if you haven't seen or tried their handiwork firsthand, portfolios and pictures are helpful, and many caterers will agree to tastings. Ask to see their linen samples and serving pieces, and try to establish a staff-to-guest ratio. You'll want to establish how much a caterer is able to coordinate on top of the menu: rentals, flowers, special decorations. And you'll want to find out whether the caterer has experience at the site you've chosen for your reception.

Wedding Cakes

*W*edding cake has been around for eons, although not in its present form. It's said that the ancient Romans practiced a ritual of pelting bride and groom with wheat grains to guarantee fertility and prosperity. Later Roman bakers began fashioning the wheat into small cakes presumably to be eaten by the bride and groom, with any left-

overs to be crumbled over their heads. The Greek version was similar, although honey and sesame seed were added. The custom caught on in Western Europe and continued until the Dark Ages pulled in the reins on everything, including wedding traditions, reducing the once lovely little cakes to pedestrian biscuits. The custom in England was to pile the biscuits or scones in a tall pyramid, the higher

Patrice Ramain of Houston worked with the bride to create this quatrefoil-shaped wedding cake. The butter-cream icing was decorated with a special beading technique and covered with nosegays of violets and lilies of the valley.

🌿

the better, and gather round as the bride and groom attempted quite comically to buss each other over the top of the stack. Legend insists that a sneer-

the traditional round shape has seen newer company of hearts, ovals, squares, and diamonds—even novelty shapes that send a message about the bride's or groom's particular passions or hobbies.

Icings are just as varied, with everything from melt-in-the-mouth butter cream to smooth-as-glass rolled fondant to architectural marzipan. And decoration runs the gamut from a cascade of fresh flowers to photo-real pastillage blooms to spun-sugar ribbons and piped-on trimmings of Fortuny pleats, basketweave, and lacy sugar fencing over linen-look pink or coffee tones.

A number of traditions are still associated with wedding cakes, not the least of which is that the bride's and groom's giving each other a bite symbolizes their first domestic act as man and wife, a sort of pledge to support and love each other from that moment forward. This century has invented the belief in saving the top layer of the cake for the newlyweds' first anniversary. Nowadays it is customarily frozen, taking the gamble out of the original tradition, in which the cake that crumbled before year's end signaled the death knell of a good marriage. And wedding cake is still believed to have prophetic powers; a slice under the pillow is quaintly thought to forecast the future intended for unmarried maidens. Ring pulls are still a fairly common practice in the South, especially for younger brides.

ing French chef who witnessed the odd rite firsthand determined to turn the haphazard heap into a proper cake by icing the whole. The French *croquembouche*—an impressive obelisk of *pâte à chou* puffs held together by a delicate web of spun sugar—was born this way, as was the first iced, multilayered cake.

In Colonial America fruitcake was favored for its ability to last, although when refined flour made its way into the colonies, white wedding cakes bumped the fruitcake into second position as a groom's cake. For many years, the butter cream–iced yellow pound cake was the predominant wedding cake. Now, of course, brides choose all manner of cakes and flavors, often alternating layers for interest. Layers may be stacked or separated by pillars or columns, and

In this novel tradition, various charms are baked into the cake and attached to long ribbons for all single bridesmaids and female guests to pull. Not unexpectedly, each charm makes its appropriate augury for the future: a heart signals that love will soon follow; a horseshoe promises good luck; a ring indicates the next to marry; a button or a thimble regrettably means its new owner will be an old maid.

Unquestionably, one of the most well-known names in wedding cakes throughout the South is Ida Mae's Cakes of Distinction of Jacksboro, Texas. Ida Mae Stark started the company by accident about 1950, when she found she was baking more and more wedding and specialty cakes for friends. Self-taught and dedicated to creating good-tasting, all-edible cakes, she experimented with the gamut of gum-paste flowers and royal icing lacework, making forays into unusual shapes and silhouettes decades before many of today's front-runners. Today the company is owned and run by Becky Sikes, who worked for Ida Mae when she was in high school. Becky has maintained the same high standards that made Ida Mae's name a household word. "Ida Mae came up with a recipe forty years ago," she says. "We can put a cake out on the table in the heat of the summer and it will still be good a week later because we don't use anything that goes rancid. I can't give away all my secrets, but I will say there's a slight hint of lemon and orange in my cakes, even the peel, to keep it fresh. We've come up with lots of different cakes in the last years," she continues, "but that's the mainstay and the one that Ida Mae is known for. The icing is handmade and all the icings turn a different shade of white, so you never look at a cake and see it all one color."

Becky usually shows a portfolio of pictures to prospective brides to give them ideas, but when they begin to formulate a notion, she produces a series of sketches or renderings to come closer to what they want. Ida Mae originally developed many of her lace designs by combing through old silver patterns and style books, and the backlog of accomplishments is staggering; although the annals of Ida Mae's client history offer enormous inspiration, Becky stands by Ida Mae's dedication to never repeating a wedding cake exactly—she'll produce anything the client wants, and have it delivered just about anywhere, too.

A Taste of Europe by Gisela, a Fort Worth concern that has made its mark in Texas over the years, excels in making realistic edible flowers on basic butter cream–iced cakes. Says Gisela Techt, "I love to create a sense of pastel shading with the flowers, especially if it's an all-white cake. Even in the shapes of flowers, you sense a soft, subtle difference. We do lilies, orchids,

tulips, callas, cherry blossoms, stephanotis, all sorts. They're all handmade candy sugar flowers that are hand colored. I learned the techniques, but you really have to develop your own style to make your decoration unique." In some cases the flowers become cake-table decoration for Gisela. She finds that making up tiny bouquets of the sugar flowers to scatter around the cake or weave into a

Above: Matt and Kelly Strange's traditional butter-cream white cake with lemon filling was simply decorated with fresh flowers and served in the old barn on the Strange family's ranch in the Texas Hill Country.

Opposite: Leslie Daubenberger's cake was decorated with ariana and Lady Di roses, pink and white bouvardia, pink peonies, tulips, lavender and white freesia, pink and white astilbe, sweet peas, delphinium, white campanula, and ivy.

candelabra arrangement on either side of the wedding cake makes a stunning effect. Gisela, unlike some wedding cake makers, also enjoys creating rather elaborate table skirting for the cake table, often incorporating a bride's own piece of openwork or lace for an overlay. Bow draping, alternating bows with pockets, French pleats, box pleats, and regular pleats trimmed with lace are among the finishing touches in her repertoire. Although she takes obvious pride in the careful re-creation of candy sugar flowers, Gisela feels certain it's really the taste of her cakes that keeps customers coming back. All her cakes are filled with fresh mousse cream, often a different one between each tier.

Rolled fondant, the smooth-as-silk icing that has become popular in recent years, makes a particularly nice alternative to butter cream, especially in the hot summer months of the South. Ellen Divers, a Richmond, Vir-

ginia, wedding cake maker who created a luscious pale pink cake for Player Butler, notes, "It has a very clean finish to it, and it holds up beautifully, even if the wedding is outside at the height of summertime."

Kathleen Short of Lafayette's Kathleen's Short and Sweet experimented with fondant recipes from South Africa and Australia for six months until she could adapt them to the types of wedding baking she was doing, most of it learned from her mother. She rolls the fondant out, smoothing it with the palm of the hand for a gorgeous satin finish, then decorates each tier with hand-molded gum-paste flowers of all types. Fresh flowers may be substituted for the sugar ones, in which case Kathleen prefers to work with the client's florist so that the cake will coordinate with the rest of the wedding flowers.

Suzan Schatz built up Tulsa's Soigné Sweets in her home and is now renowned for her delicious and unusual wedding and specialty cakes. They are made entirely from scratch with fresh butter, whole eggs, fresh-squeezed lemon, Belgian chocolate, vanilla bean, and various liqueurs. Her icing is a European-style butter cream that must be made at the last minute and refrigerated. "It's more expensive," she says, "and it's harder to decorate with, but it's worth it." Most of her clients tend to ask her to decorate the tops of her cakes with fresh flowers. For Leslie Dauben-

berger and Bobby Lorton, Suzan created a spellbinding five-tiered torte wedding cake with fresh lemon curd and champagne in the batter for extra moisture. The icing was an Italian meringue butter cream flavored with Grand Marnier. The groom's cake was a two-tiered torte chocolate sour cream cake with chocolate truffle filling. The icing was a poured smooth bittersweet chocolate ganache topped with chocolate bows.

The cake that Jan Funk of Ft. Walton Beach, Florida, created for Gail and Thomas Hawkins captured the spirit of their wedding perfectly. Its three tiers—the bottom two stacked, the top one elevated by columns—were iced in a hexagonal latticework pattern, a graceful echo of the gazebo ceremony site. The cake's piña colada flavoring with pineapple torte was fittingly appropriate for the oceanfront affair.

Marilyn Mueller, a Washington chocolatier who as a rule dislikes doing wedding cakes—and will do them only for Susan Gage—created a dramatic design for Courtney Banks by shoring up the whole with a kind of solar system of five round cakes at the base—two chocolate, one almond (so the bride wouldn't get chocolate on her dress when she cut it), and two pound cakes. The top three layers of the cake were made up of luscious combinations of different kinds of chocolate. The whole creation was iced with French meringue butter cream and decorated with elegant pastillage flowers.

Getting Hitched in the Texas Hill Country

To most Texans, the name Don Strange is synonymous with barbecue; when they're looking to kill the fatted calf, Texas-style, they just phone up Don down in the Hill Country and start talking business. So, while all the usual wheels of wedding preparation began to spin after Don's son Matt, business manager for the legendary third-generation enterprise, announced his engagement to Kelly Howell of Dripping Springs, Texas, there was one notable exception: there would certainly be no sleepless nights agonizing over who would cater the big event. Nor was there a moment's hesitation as to where it would all take place. Don's well-known ranch in

Welfare, Texas, had been home to Matt, after all, and Kelly had come to know it as the warmest kind of home away from home. The placid rolling hills and gurgling streams, the rocky outcroppings and drifts of bluebonnets and Indian paintbrush, the idly wandering livestock, and the big Texas sky all seemed the ideal altar for Kelly and Matt. And to celebrate the celebration? Few party planners have a better sense of what belongs to that special

✣

Above: The sign for Don Strange's ranch let guests know they had come to the right place for Kelly and Matt's wedding.

Left: A wagonload of thirst-quenching iced tea and lemonade awaits the guests.

atmosphere than Don Strange. He's not only made a career of it, he's given it his heart.

Resisting the impulse to take over the event, as well and capably as they might have, Don and his wife, Frances, took a round-table approach to the reception, trading ideas with Kelly, Matt, and Kelly's parents, Billie and Jack Howell, adding special touches and flourishes to stock-in-trade Strange effects. Says Frances, "We all sat down and really talked out what they wanted the reception to be like. Kelly and her mother didn't want it to be extravagant; they wanted to keep it simple, just like the country setting. We all sat around talking and brainstorming about what we liked and the ideas started coming. Somebody's favorite thing was tenderloin, everybody loved shrimp, Kelly was dying for pasta, and then somehow we thought about lamb chops, and finally Don thought about something light like a poached salmon with a nice dilled mayonnaise. Basically we did what we liked."

In the final hours, the menu also wound up including such Texas novelties as venison crepes, heart-healthy chicken tacos, and grilled chicken wings, as well as Don's signature Garden of Eden fresh fruit and vegetable stands—Connestoga wagons banked with potted plants and cut flowers, foliage and flowering kale, and full to overflowing with ripe fruits and vegetables. Don even invented a special drink for the occasion: to make a Longhorn Sparkler, place a ripe strawberry in the bottom of a champagne

flute; add half an ounce of fresh lime juice, half an ounce of Triple Sec, and top with iced champagne.

The wedding weekend was predictably relaxed, full of friends, family, and, of course, food at every turn. Much like the bride and groom themselves, all the parties and events were marked by a refreshing lack of pretense. From start to finish, the emphasis was away from false appearances and trumped-up effects and anchored instead in honest hospitality and high spirits. This was an event, after all, that was intended by the hosts to be

Above: The groom's "cake" was a Boston cream pie, one of twenty-seven prepared by his grandmother. Don garnished them with galax leaves, fresh fruit, and baskets of strawberries.

Left: At the rehearsal dinner, cooks prepared a Mexican feast on the spot. The specialities included gorditas served with guacamole and corn relish.

The rehearsal dinner was vintage Don Strange. Held at an old storefront he had purchased some years ago in nearby Waring, the casual Tex-Mex evening was a festival of two-stepping, Tequila, and nonstop tasting. Lone Star beef barbecue, fajitas, gorditas, and a tantalizing array of other Mexican specialties were cooked on-site, and old Coke machines overflowed with fresh fruit and raw vegetables and dips; guests wandered from one tempting arena to another, hard-pressed to make a choice between shimmying and shaking to a 1950s-style band, heading out under the stars with an icy longneck beer, or relaxing with a strong cup of Columbian coffee and a slice of one of dozens of homemade fruit pies and tarts.

The ceremony took place in front of the farmhouse, with four hundred white chairs facing an impressive stand of live oaks and a babbling brook beyond. Kelly and her father arrived at

Above: Kelly and her father arrived at the ceremony in a horse-drawn carriage.

Right: Don used the ranch's old well as a backdrop for a wonderful fruit and vegetable display.

Below: Some guests hung their hats in the farmhouse, which is surrounded by a bed of zinnias and an old-fashioned vegetable garden.

guzzled greedily by the gallon rather than sipped daintily by the thimbleful.

So rather than a forced march through a lot of tired traditions, the whole sojourn turned into a refreshing holiday for bride and groom, wedding party, parents, and all their guests. Bachelor and bachelorette parties kicked off the ceremonies Thursday night, making way the next day for a pampering poolside luncheon for played-out bridesmaids at the Howells' home. "The Polishing" was hosted by Frances, who insisted that the leisurely pace of the afternoon—a delectable lunch of rare tenderloin with hot sweet mustard, roasted pepper pasta salad, fresh fruits, and miniature desserts plus intermittent swimming, manicures, and pedicures—was just the antidote for the girls.

Right: A beaming Kelly and Matt after the ceremony. JENNINGS

Below: Don and Frances enjoy a dance during the rehearsal dinner.

the ceremony site in a bridal-white horse-drawn carriage. Afterward, the wedding party and guests wandered over to the reception area in and around the big barn, where, amid grapevine-wrapped posts, muslin-draped tables offered up an array of victuals. An iced tea and lemonade stand was set up outside near the meadow, as was the wedding book, and wonderful fruit and vegetable presentations took up residence near an

old well. Additionally, old doctors' buggies were drawn up close; lined with ginger, red berries, African protea, and still-life arrangements of fresh fruit, they also served up steamed shrimp with cocktail sauce.

Kelly's traditional tiered cake had a wonderful fresh strawberry filling and butter-cream icing, while the groom's cake was, in fact, twenty-seven cakes—all Boston cream pies (Matt's longtime favorite) baked by his grandmother Mary Singleton. An oil derrick was placed beside the principal groom's cake. A fitting salute to a Texas tradition.

The Trimmings

In putting together this compendium of Southern weddings, I've had the pleasure of making friends with brides of all ages and interests, meeting their parents and their grooms, and working with and learning from the talented professionals who've created the fabulous effects at their ceremonies and receptions. They've graciously let me rummage around backstage before and during the performance to see how the production made it to opening night and why it earned unanimous bravos from family and friends. Ideas, I've learned, are everywhere—and two good heads can turn out more than three times as

Opposite: Roxana Lorton of Tulsa makes final adjustments to a table at her son Bobby's rehearsal dinner. The centerpieces were designed by Anything Grows of New Orleans.

Right: Floral-patterned and striped linens enhance the tables being set up for Player Butler's reception at Evelynton Plantation. CROSS

many ideas as one. The remarkable ability of client and expert to brainstorm together, of professionals to collaborate in cooperative ventures, has produced special events that are both inspiring and touchingly personal.

The weddings in this book are unique in every aspect—from size to site to solemnity. And yet each one speaks with a decidedly Southern accent. Many of the unexpected effects and creative twists on solid traditions are signature touches of the professionals who have created them. Others are riveting in their relative simplicity; they're small projects that are entirely manageable even for the uninitiated. Following is a roundup of but a few of the clever, inventive looks I've run into along the journey. Some come from brides and their mothers, others from seasoned professionals, and still others are favorites from my own repertoire. Try them out at your own wedding or that of a good friend or family member. Don't be afraid to experiment with materials and techniques to give

these effects your own personal stamp, and remember them as well when planning all types of creative parties.

Flower Island or Garden

News of an engagement brings with it wonderful opportunities for one-of-a-kind entertaining, and often, with today's hectic schedules, settings outside the home are the least taxing

The portable flower island, or garden, centerpiece adds a personal touch to parties held in restaurants.

on the hostess. The neutral ground of a favorite restaurant makes an especially nice choice for bringing families together for the first time, but the hostess may want to make the public setting private and individual by adding special decorative touches. When I'm entertaining at a restaurant, I like to do away with the rather ordinary bud vases usually in place and add an exotic flower island or garden as a centerpiece.

Unlike so many large, dramatic centerpieces, the flower island is completely portable on its convenient flat styrofoam base; the whole creation can be completed a day ahead, tossed in the back of your car, and transported with relative ease to the restaurant just moments before your reservation hour. And, too, the high-style impact that comes from combining fresh and potted blooms gives you a lot of extra mileage for your money; you wind up with a big look that's also a bargain, since you'll be able to take the potted plants home to your garden afterward. Or you might consider wrapping the small, lush pots in moss tied with raffia and presenting them to your guests at the end of the occasion.

Materials

Yield: One flower island or garden
1 15" x 25" sheet green styrofoam
    (1½" thickness)
Living sheet moss
A good knife
5 to 6 potted plants: pansies, ivy,
    petunias, begonias, for example
5 to 6 single-flower vases (small bud
    vases, or even perfume bottles will do)

2 to 5 bouvardia*
5 or 6 roses*
3 or 4 dendrobium orchids*
Lemon leaf

* Any nice combination of fresh cut flowers works well. Gerbera daisies, peony and parrot tulips, and a mix of Asiatic lilies, for example, are a great point of departure. Select whatever is in season that suits your theme.

Method

1. Cut a wavy, interesting base out of the sheet of styrofoam. You can create a modified figure eight or any amorphous rectangular shape that suits your fancy, as long as you keep in mind the dimensions of the table.

2. Cover the entire piece of styrofoam with living sheet moss, patching pieces together tightly.

3. Surveying the moss bed, devise a plan for the potted plants, spacing them pleasingly throughout the bed with height, color, and density in mind. Place the plants directly on top of the moss and shift them until you have the desired scheme.

4. Once you've settled on a plan, begin carving niches in the styrofoam to hold each pot. To do this, remove each pot and gently lift the moss underneath it. Place the pot directly on the styrofoam and trace the base with a pencil. Remove it again, and, following the outlines of the base, cut a one-inch-deep niche in the styrofoam. Place the pot in the hole and bank its sides with the pieces of the moss you've removed, camouflaging the pot almost entirely.

5. Repeat this procedure until all the pots are installed and covered.

6. Use the small bud vases to fill in spaces between the pots. Follow the same procedure of removing moss, making a slight indentation in the styrofoam with a knife, and nestling the bud vase—with water in it—in the hole. Again, bank with moss.

7. Fill bud vases with single stems or small groups of specimen stems until you have a pleasing distribution of color, height, and mass, much as you might in an English cutting garden.

8. To finish the design, fill in lightly throughout with lemon leaf.

Note: The flower island is wonderfully versatile and can be adapted quite easily to any theme or season. You may use any combination that strikes your fancy: vegetables and herbs; evergreens and berried branches; tropical exotics; spring bulbs such as hyacinth and iris blended deftly with cut tulips, jonquils, and tiny muscari. I've even made wonderful rose gardens with breathtaking tea roses, climbing roses, and camellia foliage with a rain shower of rose petals to fill in.

Floral Chair-Back Place Cards

*I*solating your small party from the rest of the madding crowd at a popular restaurant can be perplexing. I like to set imaginary boundaries by decorating all my chair backs with sweeping, beribboned bouquets; aside from the floral punch, they can also do double duty as place cards.

While I've always been dazzled by beautiful chair-back bouquets, I have found that the ones that make the best magazine layouts are often both unfea-

sible and uncomfortable in practice. I prefer a more manageable bouquet, no larger than a hand-held nosegay, really. It rests on the chair back at a natural diagonal, as might a sheaf of wheat, and is caught up gracefully with a luscious wired French ribbon. Perhaps even more than a dramatic centerpiece or wonderful place favors, chair-back bouquets immediately create a private-party atmosphere, no matter how imposing the rest of the space. The bouquet is easily turned into a place card, either by slipping a small card into the arrangement or by writing names directly onto foliage with a Pilot gold pen.

Materials

Yield: One floral chair-back place card
Assorted greenery (aspidistra, galax, lemon leaf, huckleberry)
3 tulips
3 bouvardia
3 roses
1 orchid
#22-gauge florist wire
Wired French ribbon
Pilot gold or silver pen (available at hobby or art supply stores)
Blank place cards (optional)
1 roll double-sided tape

Method

1. Assemble assorted greens in one hand. Place broad, tall leaves at the back of the arrangement, making sure

they stand about six inches higher than the other foliage.

2. Begin adding tulips, bouvardia, and roses to the foliage. Slip the orchid into the center of the arrangement, or artistically off-center if you're so inclined.

3. Secure the bouquet with the florist wire, and cover the wire with the wired French ribbon, making a six- or eight-loop bow and leaving tails to dangle.

4. Tie the bouquet to the back of the chair with the wire.

5. Take a second length of the French ribbon, loop it through the bowknot and bring it around to create a second bow on the front side of the chair back. This creates a lovely effect on the front of the chair and hides your mechanics in the process; when a guest is seated, he or she can lean back easily against the bow without damaging it and without feeling prickly stems or wire.

6. Using the gold or silver pen, write guests' names on small white place cards. They should nestle into the arrangement easily and visibly, but if they slip, you may secure them with double-sided tape.

7. You may elect to write guests' names directly onto the tall foliage at the back of the bouquet. Galax and aspidistra leaves take well to this. Practice first on a piece of paper, shaking the pen for a minute to increase the ink flow. Then try a leaf or two until you feel comfortable with the process. Leaves should be inscribed and left to dry completely before assembling the bouquet.

Note: You can create chair-back bouquets with a variety of materials that fit your mood or the season. A simple sheaf of magnolia leaves with a fragrant blossom in the center makes a delicious summer statement. For Christmas, try berried holly and heather with rich torch ginger as a focal point. If you need the bouquet to last longer than the duration of the average party, put each stem into a water vial covered with moss.

Floral chair-back place cards transform even the most ordinary of party spaces into a festive setting.

Darva Stapleton's Flower-Wreath Headpiece

The bridal ensemble offers so many stages for special effects: beautiful silk garters can be monogrammed and handed down from generation to generation; a piece of your grandmother's antique lace can be transformed into an elegant collar to set apart a new dress; tiny water vials to hold orchids or lily of the valley can be stitched into dress hems; even lovely wedding slippers can be further enhanced by seed pearls and special braiding. One of my favorite looks is the showstopping flower-wreath headpiece that Darva Stapleton of Forget-Me-Not Flowers in Atlanta showed me how to do. A lush and lavish tribute to Mother Nature and a crowning glory for the bride, this headpiece is adaptable to all sorts of faces and figures; a tall, willowy bride can carry off a serious and rather weighty crown of flowers and ivy, whereas for the bride of slighter figure, the wreath can easily be trimmed down to more wispy proportions.

The full floral headpiece is attached directly to a tulle veil and secured by hairpins. If you're wearing heirloom lace, you'll want to take the extra precaution of attaching the wreath onto a piece of tulle first, and then affixing the whole with corsage pins to your own lace veil. This is a look that, because of its fullness, does not work well with a blusher.

The floral-wreath headpiece offers a refreshing alternative to more traditional headpieces.

Materials

Yield: One flower-wreath headpiece
Tree ivy (heavy-stemmed variety)
#22-gauge florist wire
Hot glue gun and glue sticks (available at any Woolworth or K Mart)
Ranunculus
White princess spray roses
Euphorbia
Variegated sage
Green periwinkle
Green Lady's Mantle

Method

1. After measuring the bride's head, create a circlet of the proper dimensions with several strands of tree ivy, securing ends with wire. Continue to add ivy until you reach the desired fullness. This forms the base of the wreath.

2. Cut stems off of ranunculus and spray roses, leaving only the blossoms.

3. Using the hot glue gun, begin affixing flowers to the wreath. Start at the top of the wreath, or the 12 o'clock position, and begin pasting ranunculus and spray roses in clusters. Add sprigs of greenery—sage, periwinkle, and Lady's Mantle. Repeat the procedure at the bottom of the wreath, or the 6 o'clock position. Since the top and bottom of the wreath are focal points during the ceremony, it is important to concentrate flowers and greenery in these spots.

4. Continue to add ranunculus, roses, euphorbia, periwinkle, sage, and Lady's Mantle to the rest of the wreath until you reach a pleasing fullness.

5. Attach wreath to the band of the veil with hairpins or corsage pins. Be sure that the pins are not visible.

6. You may elect to put fresh flowers on the rest of the veil by hot-gluing them directly onto the tulle in an intermittent design or in a garland effect at the hem of the veil.

7. Keep the finished wreath in a cool spot; mist lightly to insure freshness.

Invitation Ideas for Small Parties

Undisputedly, the key ingredient to a great party is the guest list; good food and a festive, relaxed atmosphere—no matter how formal or casual the occasion—simply complete the picture. While themes are certainly not a prerequisite for party success, I still find they appeal to my sense of logic, offering me a firm decorative foothold and a format to follow, from invitations to table settings to coffee and dessert. I'm such a devotee of unusual invitations—they jumpstart the whole party into high gear with an air of excitement and anticipation—that I tend to incorporate them into most of the parties I give. I've developed a system for smaller parties, say fewer than fifty people, that works beautifully for me. First I invite guests by telephone about two to three weeks before the party. The calling goes quicker than you might imagine, and by the end of the process I have a firm guest list without the anxiety of waiting for responses. Then, with my smaller confirmed list, I set about creating special invitations that announce the theme of the party. For parties of this size, I always hand deliver invitations—children are usually happy to take on this project for reasonable remuneration—so confirming my list in advance allows me to stretch my limits on the type of invitation and not waste delivery on guests who won't be able to make the date.

Nothing is beneath consideration in devising a clever invitation: I've used small potted plants in little terra-cotta pots with a lovely watercolor invitation attached by ribbon; a split of champagne with the original label replaced by a calligraphied label giving party particulars; a wonderful farmer's basket of red and green apples with an invitation stuck in on a long price tag–type skewer; colorful coated-plastic Chinese food containers lined with bright tissue paper to hold pralines, cookies, and so on, and with the invitation printed out on elongated fortune-cookie paper; whole watermelons girdled by a fat ribbon and a summery invitation; even miniature cakes iced with the names of the bride and groom and delivered in tiny cake boxes with a small invitation pasted on the inside of the boxtop. Then, without being too heavy-handed, I carry the theme through the occasion—on my tables, in the menu, and even in thoughtful favors for guests to take home.

Hand-Painted Glassware

I particularly love to use hand-painted wineglasses or glass salad plates as place cards. I'll repeat the decorative theme of the glass on napkins at each place, and then offer each guest a shiny personalized bag with festive tissue paper and ribbon to put them in as take-home favors.

Materials

Washing soda (available at most grocery stores)
24 inexpensive wineglasses or glass plates
Vogart paint pens (available at art supply stores)
Cardboard
White tissue paper
Paper towels

Method

1. Put the washing soda in your dishwasher soap dispenser and wash glasses or plates; let them dry thoroughly in the dishwasher.
2. Meanwhile, choose a simple design for your plates or glasses. Flowers, butterflies, watermelons, and sprigs of holly, for example, are all manageable choices. Practice your design on cardboard first until you're comfortable with the paint pens. Depress the tip of the pen in order to get ink flowing freely. And test all the colors to get a feel for relative values. When you're satisfied you have a good workable sample, reserve it as your primary pattern.
3. When plates or glasses have dried, remove them from dishwasher using tissue paper (or surgical gloves, if you prefer) to keep them entirely free of oils from your hands and fingertips.

Spread them out on a clean dish towel until ready to use.

4. Note that you'll be painting the outside of a wineglass but the underside of a plate to keep chipping to a minimum. With your pattern in front of you, begin by painting the outline of the design. Fill in any areas that require the same color paint, and let dry completely. Then select another color and paint any areas that require that particular hue, as indicated by your pattern. Repeat for all colors, letting each dry completely before going on to the next, until your design is complete. Your paint strokes should be thick and full, and a light impressionistic touch is probably more important than absolute accuracy.

5. It's helpful to keep a paper towel close at hand for blotting the pens and cleaning up any smears or slips as quickly as possible.

6. Finally, paint the name or monogram of each guest on the glass or plate. For lettering on the underside of the plate, you'll be writing in reverse; a template is very helpful. Just draw a good sample on construction paper, and tape it to the top side of the plate; flip the plate over and loosely trace it. (If you have a larger guest list and this task seems overwhelming, you can simply execute the name or monogram on the front of the plate along the rim at the top or bottom center.)

7. To set the paint, place glasses or plates upside down on cookie sheets, and bake in a 275-degree oven for twenty to thirty minutes. Let cool at room temperature. (For plastic glasses or plates, let dry at room temperature for at least twenty-four hours.)

Note: If you have a hankering for fancier designs, you may opt to use a commercial stencil or cut out a picture for inspiration. Remember to affix it to the upper side of a plate and the inside of a wineglass before painting in the pattern.

The author painting a floral design on a glass plate.

Tim Trapolin's Hand-painted Camellia Napkins

*T*im Trapolin, a master artist and floral designer for Anything Grows in New Orleans, showed me how to make the elegant hand-painted napkins and tablecloth he created for Bobby Lorton's rehearsal dinner, a sophisticated summer soiree held in Bobby's parents' lush backyard in Tulsa, Oklahoma, the night before his storybook marriage to Leslie Daubenberger.

Tim often varies the design of his hand-painted napkins slightly for each guest, using a wide range of free-form or stylized flowers, abstract images, or even hobby-related insignias. "It's important not to make it complicated," he notes. "Keep it loose. You don't want to overkill on the paint, because the beauty of this is the interaction of the design and the textile." Tim uses bright metallic golds and silvers as well as various shades of different matte colors, and he prefers working with pale fabrics in the cream, white, even pale peach, pink, and yellow ranges—all soft grounds that are a pleasing foil for the paint colors. Stark white is too glaring, he notes, and dark colors like plum or burgundy or deep blues tend to turn paint colors muddy. Natural fabrics such as cotton and linen are a must; synthetics don't pick up the paint effectively.

Tim prefers a small design, usually executed on the quarter fold of the napkin, rather than an overall pattern, which dilutes the impact of the hand-painting. His camellia is perfect for its lyrical Southern flavor as well as for its relative ease of execution. It is created with a medley of soft, deep colors and applied with two types of brushes: a #575 Chinese bamboo paintbrush for flowing outlines and lettering, and a Grumbacher-Gainsboro #6 paintbrush for the broader strokes used to shade in a design. He uses Deka fabric paints, all of which can be hand-mixed on the job. To achieve a pleasing modulation of hues, Tim regulates translucency and opacity by adding either a colorless extender or a covering white or pearl white to his paints. See illustrations on pages 88 and 89.

Materials

Linen or cotton napkins (preferably large European size)
Newspaper
Black Magic Marker
Deka fabric paints (red, blue, yellow, green, and metallic gold or silver, #400 colorless extender for translucency and #419 covering white or #420 pearl white for opacity)
#575 Chinese bamboo paintbrush
Grumbacher-Gainsboro #6 flat paintbrush

Method

1. Wash napkins to remove sizing. Be sure not to use fabrics treated with water repellent. Dry napkins, iron, and fold in quarters.
2. Clear a large table surface and give yourself plenty of room to work on. Spread out several thicknesses of newspaper to protect your work surface. You may also wish to wear an apron.
3. Cut a double thickness of newspaper the size of the folded napkin and slip underneath the top fold of the napkin to keep paint from bleeding through to other layers. You may wish to repeat this for several napkins so you can move quickly from one to the next while painted napkins are drying.
4. Before starting to paint, practice the camellia design (or whatever design you select) by using a black Magic Marker on a piece of paper. Experiment until you feel comfortable with the outline and veining of leaves, etc. (You may also wish to use colored pencils or colored felt-tip pens to experiment with colors, remembering that hand-painting is an inexact art; the more spontaneous, the more appealing.)
5. Begin by painting the outlines of the camellia in gold using the Chinese bamboo paintbrush. Hold the brush about one inch from the end, and try to keep strokes fluid. The brush has a fine point and will create a nice lyrical line, no matter how amateur your calligraphy skills.
6. Still using the bamboo brush, sketch the bride's and groom's initials. (For Bobby Lorton and Leslie Dauben-

tone, be sure to dip the brush in water to rinse it before going on to a different color. Use painterly strokes, but avoid a thick buildup of paint; it's important to feature the texture of the fabric as well as the paint.

8. Finish the flower by using green tones to fill in foliage.

9. Once paint is thoroughly dry, set by ironing on the wrong side for one minute at hot setting, two minutes at medium, or four minutes at warm. Or put in a commercial dryer on hot for thirty minutes.

David LaVoy's Glass-top Garden

*D*avid LaVoy of Atlanta is known for his lush, horticulturally savvy floral interpretations and installations. For small, special dinner parties such as an engagement dinner, he loves quite theatrical effects; one such favorite tabletop treatment is his earthy moss garden, a natural full-table foundation for one-of-a-kind place settings. Although the mechanics of the installation tend to call for a glass-top table, either round or rectangular, it's possible to execute the moss garden on a wooden table by first covering the surface with protective canvas or plastic. I had a piece of mirror cut to fit the top of my dining room table for treatments of this sort; it's handy for protecting the table as well

Artist Tim Trapolin painting his camellia design on linen napkins.

berger's rehearsal dinner, the napkins and a special coordinating tablecloth were presented to the bride and groom by Bobby's parents as a wonderful keepsake. However, the same hand-painting format can be successfully used for all types of entertaining; just monogram napkins with guests' initials, rather than those of the bride and groom, and offer them as special favors.)

7. Using the Grumbacher-Gainsboro brush, fill in the camellia with loosely modulated tones of blue, pink, and red to create a delicately shaded flower. You may mix colors to suit your tastes, but, if you want a clear, undiluted

Potted plants:
    Small bird's-nest palm
    2 peach begonias
    1 pocketbook plant
    3 primrose
    Ivy plant with strands 12"-36" long
1½ bunches iris (Hildegard and
    Japanese)
3 bunches ranunculus
1 bunch each of:
    Joy spray roses
    Ivy plant with long streamers
    White, pink, and yellow freesia
    Lavender
    Peach perfection tulips
    Daffodils
    Mixed gerbera daisies
    Champagne roses
    Lady Ioca roses
    Heather
    Majolica spray roses
    Tonja roses

as for giving my dining room a new look for a special party.

David covers the entire surface of the table with soaked Oasis and moss, then landscapes it as he might a cutting garden, with potted plants and a brilliant mix of fresh cut flowers. The flatware, china, and crystal are set right onto the moss bed, so that guests are treated to a kind of Mad Hatter's alfresco fantasy. See illustration on page 80.

Materials

60" round glass-top table*
35 blocks of Oasis foam (available at
    any floral supply store), soaked in
    water
2 boxes living sheet moss

* As noted, you can create this look on any table that's not size-prohibitive simply by covering it with canvas or plastic.

Note: Your selection of flowers and plants will depend on the color scheme of your table. The design can be complex, as is David's, or quite simple, such as a medley of interesting foliage.

Method

1. After soaking the Oasis, cut each piece in half lengthwise, keeping as straight an edge as possible.
2. Cover the entire table with the Oasis blocks. Make sure that the pieces fit together snugly, leaving no gaps. Upon completion, trim the Oasis back, leaving roughly a two-inch glass border at the edge of the table.
3. Wet the sheet moss and squeeze out the excess moisture. Break it apart gently into smaller pieces. (This will facilitate inserting fresh flowers later.)
4. Cover the entire Oasis surface with the moss.
5. Set the table with flatware, crystal, china, candlesticks, and any other dinner accoutrements desired.
6. Begin landscaping with the potted plants. First place the pots on top of the moss, shifting them until you've developed a pleasing layout that incorporates the whole table. To position the pots firmly, lift pieces of moss underneath them and nestle pots into soaked Oasis until well entrenched. Then wedge pieces of moss back around pots to camouflage.
7. Fill in the area around the pots with cut flowers. For flimsier stems, use a pencil to poke holes into the moss before inserting the flower. Group flowers singly and in odd-numbered clumps to create the haphazard appeal of an English garden. Stems should be cut at different heights and flowers should be turned at various slants, in imitation of the loose rhythm of nature.

Hand-Painted Canvas Leaf Table-scape

*W*eddings provide endless opportunities for giving—to and from the bride and the groom, to and from the hosts and hostesses who have honored the couple with their hospitality and entertaining spirit, to and from family and friends who have supported the enterprise with their time, love, and creativity. Favors of all description cement the moment in guests' memories, whether it's a keepsake from the reception, a wedding shower, or a prewedding party. And, as always, new slants and interesting approaches to presentation make giving all the more special.

I have always loved the notion of the pull-apart table, in which the governing theme's elements break down into portable party favors. Nothing quite beats the impact of creating a festive one-of-a-kind table-scape for the honorees, but sending them home with a piece of the tableau, especially when it can be used again, makes the whole gesture unforgettable. The hand-painted wineglasses, plates, and napkins described on pages 212-215 make wonderful favors as well as creative entertaining devices. The canvas leaf table-scape, another effect I love, is an update on the Ronaldo Maia galax tablecloth that hit entertaining circles a decade ago.

I used to give my tables a woodsy feel by scattering real leaves about with a free hand. But I discovered that hand-painting the leaves on canvas gave me a permanent tabletop decoration with numerous applications. By first draping tables with a white to-the-floor cloth as an underlay and a smart black-and-white striped, checked, or zebra-patterned overlay, I get a smashing look for both buffet and dining tables. You can use any sort of cloth, as long as it is uncomplicated and in bold contrast to the leaves. At the close of the party, you can offer the whole set to the bride (or other honoree) as a handmade present for her to entertain with later. Or, for smaller parties—a bridesmaids' luncheon, for example, or a wedding shower—divide the canvas leaves up among the guests; four or six smaller leaves make a fun set of coasters, while larger specimens form creative place mats. For a more structured seated dinner or luncheon, you can stick to larger-sized leaves and create individual place mats; the mixed or matched set makes a nice favor afterward for the bride.

Materials

6' x 6' canvas, backed with gesso
   (available at art supply stores)
1 pair of scissors
Selected leaves*:
   Bird's-nest palm
   Fatsia

The author demonstrates how to paint the veining on a canvas leaf place mat.

❧

Elephant ear
Galax
Paint: a mixture of fabric paint, such as
 Deka or Jacquard, and acrylic paint in
 jewel tones, such as magenta, green,
 red, and purple
Paintbrush: 1" to 1½" wide with stiff
 bristles (inexpensive)
Satin-finish polyurethane

*You may select any leaves you wish. Your resulting table may be entirely tropical, richly autumnal, or lush and summery.

Note: The materials will yield about fifteen to twenty-five leaves, depending on size. This should be sufficient for a seventy-two-inch round table.

Method

1. Lay canvas out on the floor and begin tracing the leaves you've selected. Try to fit them together as closely as possible so as not to waste canvas.
2. Using scissors, cut out each leaf.
3. To paint the leaves, start with the outline of the leaf, filling in the center section next. Use obvious, bold brushstrokes to give the leaves a spontaneous, nonstylized look.
4. Use the edge of your brush or your finger to trace in veining.
5. Let the entire canvas dry thoroughly, and then polyurethane the surface.
6. Let the polyurethane dry; it may take as long as three full days.

Note: You can add to your collection at any time, and use the set in a variety of ways for different parties.

Frances Rodgers's Linen Hatbox Gift Wrap

*F*rances Rodgers of Cache Pot Interiors in New Orleans not only has an eye for fabulous merchandise, but also comes up with inventive packaging that elevates the object and its wrapping to an art form. Her present within a present offers a bride a wonderful decorative hatbox to use for storing treasured items or for flower arrangements—it's a great way to hide a plastic container for potted plants, but it can also be packed with bright tissue paper and individual Botticelli bottles to showcase specimen stems. Meanwhile, the wrapping and bow are actually beautiful table linens, either antique or new, to start off the bride's collection.

Materials

1 hand-painted or fabric-covered
 decorative hatbox
8 matching Battenburg napkins*
1 36" Battenburg lace cloth (bridge-
 tablecloth size)*
Covered wire or rubber band
2 rolls each of 1"-wide gold and 2"-wide
 white wired French ribbon

*You may, of course, use linens of any description, including antique heirloom pieces you wish to pass down.

Method

1. Pack the hatbox with colorful tissue paper. Add four of the eight napkins and replace lid.
2. Center the box on the lace cloth and gently gather the ends to create a "fountain" at top center. If the box is hexagonal, bring up one panel at a time, lapping and tucking around the edges as you go.
3. Secure fountain with the covered wire or rubber band.

4. Roll each of the four remaining napkins and crease in the center. Cinch each with a length of the gold and the white ribbon, letting tails dangle.

5. Tie one napkin onto the linen fountain at the 12 o'clock position. Then continue adding napkins in the same manner at the 3 o'clock, 6 o'clock, and 9 o'clock positions, creating a flower effect with a tangle of thin ribbons dangling.

6. Make a six-loop bow with the gold

and/or white ribbon and tie it onto the top of the fountain. Twist and shape the wired ribbon and bow into wavy, natural forms. Leave tails dangling at varying lengths.

Ron Barrett's Flower Hoop

*F*lower hoops are an old English tradition, and florist Ron Barrett of Zimlich Brothers in Mobile frequently suggests them for brides who have lots of children as attendants. Charming as part of the ceremony, the hoops also keep children occupied at the reception, since all manner of games can be devised with them. At Lee Rutherford's wedding reception, the children swung them, peered through them as if through pictures frames, and even twirled them around their waists like so many hula hoops. Bearing in mind this wear and tear, Ron builds the hoop with a base of hardy English ivy and adds a variety of fresh, paper, and silk flowers to create a garden-fresh look with a fraction of the fragility. The idea is to capitalize on both aesthetics and practicality; children are expected to be less than gentle with the hoops, so it's best to avoid delicate blossoms and make the most of tougher stock that can stand up to their antics. See illustrations on pages 42 and 67.

Materials

Yield: One flower hoop

18" embroidery hoop

2"-wide strips of cotton batting (about 6)

1 small bolt of inexpensive #9 satin florist ribbon

4' to 6' of #10 double-faced satin ribbon

2 24"-long strands of English ivy

9 to 11 daisies, silk flowers, paper flowers*

18" of #3 picot ribbon

*If you want to use all fresh flowers, choose sturdy ones, such as dendrobium orchids and Asiatic lilies. While

Filled with and wrapped in fine linens, Frances Rodgers's hatbox makes a visually dazzling wedding gift.

carnations are not my favorites, it must be admitted that mini, or pixie, carnations are resilient.

Method

1. Cover the embroidery hoop with cotton batting. Start at the top and twist around the hoop until it is completely padded.
2. Wrap the hoop evenly with florist ribbon.
3. Knot one end of the double-faced satin ribbon at the 12 o'clock position (the top of the hoop). Cut, leaving a three-to-seven-inch length of ribbon as a streamer. With the remaining ribbon, make a knot in the same place and begin wrapping the hoop in a clockwise direction, twisting as you go to show both sides of the ribbon. At random intervals, knot the ribbon and cut, leaving streamers of varying length (from three to seven inches).
4. Keep twisting and knotting until the hoop is completely covered. The intermittent knots and streamers will create a sporadic and interesting effect.
5. Tie the ivy and the silk, paper, and fresh flowers on approximately one-third of the hoop with the picot ribbon.

David LaVoy's Petit Bouquet

Atlanta florist David LaVoy specializes in all types of bouquets, both arm- and hand-held, from over-sized cascades to diminutive nosegays. He's especially fond of the French-style petit bouquet for its ability to showcase a variety of specimens in a controlled, picture-perfect format. See illustration on page 117.

Materials

Yield: One French-style petit bouquet
1 bunch white freesia
2 bags white stephanotis
7 sprays ivory princess spray roses
#24-gauge florist wire (18"-long pieces)
1 roll green floral tape
Satin ribbon, varying widths (¼" to 2")
Corsage pins, one for each bouquet
Wired French ribbon, varying widths (¼" to 2")
Tissue paper
Large plastic bag

Method

1. Condition flowers to desired openness. For this type of bouquet, you'll want some flowers fully open and others tightly closed. To open flowers, cut stems at an angle and let them soak up water for several hours or even overnight. To retain flowers tight and closed, keep them in cool water in a cool environment. Leave flowers in water until ready to use.
2. Cut off the blossom of each flower, leaving a one-half inch stem. Take a piece of straight florist wire and stick it horizontally through the bulb of the blossom. Then take a second piece of florist wire and insert it through the bulb at a right angle to the first wire. Bring the four ends of the wires down, twisting as you go, to create a stem. Wrap the wire stem with green floral tape. Repeat this procedure for every stem.
3. Create four clusters of three wired flowers each. You may group the flowers in each cluster as you see fit: a spray rose, a stephanotis, and a freesia, for example; or three spray roses; or two freesia and one spray rose. To secure the cluster, wrap the three stems together with floral tape.
4. To begin assembly of the bouquet, place one of the flower clusters at the center. Then add individual stems around it. Odd numbers (ones and threes) create a more interesting rhythm than even numbers. Continue to add clusters to the bouquet, filling in around the clusters with the individually wrapped flowers. Keep adding the flowers until your bouquet has reached a round, full shape.
5. Now wrap the stems of the entire bouquet with floral tape to secure them.
6. To finish the bouquet, make a collar out of the discarded rose leaves. Remove the best leaves from each discarded rose stem. Twist a piece of florist wire, bent into a U-shape, around the base of the leaves. Wrap the wire with floral tape for a smooth finish. Repeat for the leaves of twelve

to twenty stems, depending on how many you will need to make a foliage collar around the base of the bouquet.

7. Place the leaves around the base of the bouquet to form the collar, and secure with tape. Cover the tape with satin ribbon, leaving streamers to dangle. Secure the satin ribbon with a corsage pin.

8. Make a bow using the wired French ribbon and tie it onto the stem of the bouquet.

9. Mist the bouquet with water. Nestle it in tissue paper and wrap in a roomy plastic bag. Seal the bag with a twist and store in a cooler or refrigerator to keep crisp.

Evelynton Plantation Larkspur-Sheaf Centerpiece

*F*loral designer Annie B. Black coordinates manor house flowers and floral installations for the many special events held every year at Evelynton Plantation in Charles City, Virginia. She works with brides on their one-of-a-kind weddings, helping them to bring their visions into reality, while playing to the strong architectural lines of the

Floral designer Annie Black making the larkspur-sheaf centerpieces for Player Butler's reception at Evelynton Plantation. CROSS

house. Annie specializes in treatments that are loose, full, and English in feeling, always varying heights, densities, and colors to a natural turn. For the garden-party atmosphere created by Evelynton's formal Italianate terrace, she loves capping off lavish wedding buffet tables with containerless sheaf arrangements. With no visible means of support, these striking compositions make eye-catching centerpieces that

insinuate themselves into the surrounding flora. Annie finds that for a spring wedding, the brilliant lime green "vessel" created by winter wheat makes a smashing container for viburnum, tulips, iris, and dogwood; in the summer, she might opt for a sheaf of larkspur—as she did for Player Butler's July wedding—as a foundation for roses, delphinium, lilies, and Queen Anne's lace. See illustration on page 41.

Materials

1 plastic florist container (8" in diameter x 24" high)
2 large rubber bands
3 to 4 bunches of tall larkspur (36" tall)
Raffia or wired French ribbon
2 to 3 blocks Oasis, soaked
1 bunch each of:
   delphinium
   rubrum lilies
   Oriental lilies, cream
   Oriental lilies, pink
   Queen Anne's lace
   3 to 4 branches curly willow
10" terra-cotta or plastic saucer
Spanish moss or green moss
8 to 10 full-blown roses or gardenias

Method

1. Secure the two rubber bands around the container, one about two inches from the bottom, the other about two inches from the top.
2. Begin slipping stalks of larkspur under the rubber bands, one next to the other, until you have covered the entire container.
3. Cover the rubber bands with lengths of raffia or wired French ribbon, tying them in simple bows at front center. (You may place bows off-center for an asymmetrical effect if you wish.)
4. Stack blocks of soaked Oasis in the container to the rim. Fill container about three-fourths full with water.

5. Add and arrange flowers in the Oasis as you would in any other container. Make the arrangement loose but lush, using branches of curly willow or any available flowering branches for interest.
6. Place container in terra-cotta or plastic saucer and loosely cover the saucer with the Spanish or green moss.
7. Fill saucer with water and add full-blown rose blossoms or gardenias at base of arrangement. (If flowers are used, Spanish moss is optional.) Your open roses may spill onto the surrounding tabletop for a spectacular effect.

Tom Bailey's Daisy Pew Arrangement

*A*rguably the most intimate part of the wedding process, the ceremony is also the most intensely individual. Whatever the sanctuary, decorative touches are often surprises, but I've always felt the most effective looks are those that are the least contrived and the most in keeping with the site. Lee Rutherford, for example, felt strongly that she didn't want a trace of the effete at her ceremony in a historic chapel near Mobile—just open windows and full window boxes, simple altar arrangements, and uncomplicated pew markers. The choice of flowers? Also pure and simple—daisies, as if just plucked from the nearby fields.

In deciding upon suitable pew markers for the small chapel, Tom Bailey of Haertel's in Mobile wisely avoided the grand gesture of standing candelabra or massive topiaries, for fear they'd overwhelm the space. Instead he chose to use simple arched Oasis holders that clamp onto the pew with minimal fuss. A feathery combination of daisies, springeri fern, and smilax was earthy and down-home, utterly appropriate for the simple sanctuary. See illustration on page 66.

Materials

Yield: one pew marker
1 Oasis holder (available at florist supply stores)
3 sprays of wild smilax
9 strings of springeri fern
25 field daisies
4 yards #9 ivory satin ribbon
#22-gauge white-taped wire
1 4" wired wooden pick

Method

1. Thoroughly soak the Oasis holder with water.
2. Insert enough pieces of wild smilax into the Oasis holder to cover it.
3. Intersperse the springeri fern throughout.
4. Following the basic arched shape of the Oasis holder, concentrate shorter-length daisies in a mass at the top of it, gradually moving out to the ends with longer- and intermediate-length stems

to create a cascading effect. The resulting arrangement should be loose and
natural.

5. With the satin ribbon, make an
eight-loop bow with two cascading
streamers. Attach it to the wooden
pick with the white-taped wire and
insert the pick into the Oasis holder.

Wrapping Chairs

T love to wrap my chairs whenever I have the chance. It's a great way
to dress up ordinary rented metal
chairs or enhance ballroom or dining
chairs. You can use almost any cotton
or chintz, but I'm partial to sheets for
their finished edges and versatility.

Material

1 good-quality twin-size sheet

Method

1. Drape fabric over chair, bringing
the material just to the floor at the
back of the chair and generously skirting it over the sides and front.
2. Gather fabric at either side of the
chair and bring around to the center of

*These drawings (starting from the 10:00 position
and proceeding clockwise) illustrate how fabric is
draped over a chair, knotted at the back, and kept
smooth and tight along the floor.*

the back, tucking, as needed, as you go. Tie a simple knot at the center of the back, leaving short tails exposed. The edge along the floor should be tight and smooth.

The Basic Knotted Overlay

Wedding receptions come in all shapes and sizes, but from the pull-out-all-the-stops extravaganzas to the simplest of spreads I've found that the increasing attention to linens has elevated the wedding feast to quite another plane. The inventive use of overlays, underlays, and dressmaker table skirting has brought to most of the reception settings in this book wonderfully interesting pairings of color and texture and pattern. From the chaste look of bridal whites to subtle color studies in linen and damask to the upbeat edge of stripes and dots and florals masterfully combined, it's often the power of the cloth that transforms a setting from mediocre to magic. Bed linens are never beneath my consideration; decorative sheets are quite luscious these days, and if you can master the very basic techniques of drapery knotting, you'll find you don't have to cut or hem them at all; just wash or dry-clean them after the party, retire them to your linen closet, and watch your inventory grow.

Materials

(For 72" round table)
1 high-quality queen-size sheet
(Palais Royale, Bill Blass, and
Laura Ashley all offer fine choices)

Method

1. Center sheet over table.
2. Gather up fabric at each corner of the sheet and knot in a loop. Knots may fall at the hem of the fabric or midway up; you may leave the tails exposed or tuck them under for a more finished look.

The Rosette Overlay from Hands All Around

Such dressmaker detailing as pleats, swags, rosettes, shirring, and ruching make tables as much a feast for the eyes as the menu is a feast for the taste buds. Some of the most inspired table techniques I've seen have come from a small Washington, D.C., outfit called Hands All Around, which was hired by Marylin Bradley's Creative Parties to develop a concept for all the tables at Courtney Banks's reception.

Judy Partlow and Gail Griggs created Hands All Around in answer to the linen rental demand in Washington. As the business grew, they not only expanded their own smashing inventory of linen skirting, underlays, and overlays, but also began creating custom linens using a client's own fabric. They are masters at creative draping and knotting techniques, and bring a team of helpers to turn out tables at their larger parties. Their rosette overlay is a basic treatment that works with a number of fabrics. Point lace, polished chintz, damask, linen, and cotton all take well to the method, each giving an entirely different feeling to an installation.

Materials

(For a 72" round table)
120" square lace overlay
Rubber bands
Straight pins

Method

1. Drape the lace cloth on the table as an overlay. It should drop generously onto the floor, about one and a half feet at each of the four corners. Take precautions to center the overlay perfectly on the table.
2. Start at one of the overlay's four

Both the basic knotted overlay and the rosette overlay begin with a sheet or lace cloth draped over a table (middle row, left.) The top drawing illustrates the basic knotted overlay; the right and center drawings in the middle row show how to form a rosette; and the bottom drawing depicts a finished rosette overlay.

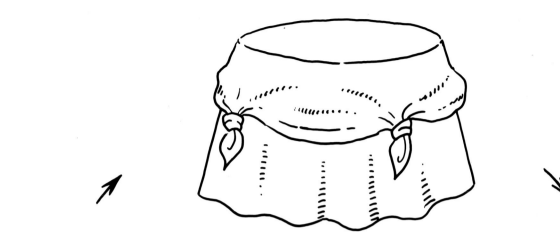

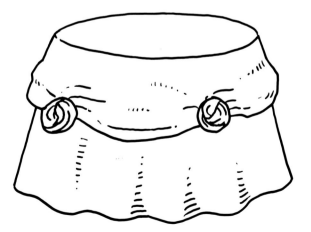

Bitsy Duggins demonstrates how bridesmaids'
bouquets are inserted into the pockets of her
trompe l'oeil cake tablecloth.

corners. Gathering the material in both
hands, work up from right and left of
the center point to a spot about six
inches from the edge of the tabletop.
This should create a tail center point,
with a graceful scallop of material on
each side leading to the next point.
3. Secure the gathered tail with a rubber band.
4. Twist the tail gently into a knot,
tucking the end under to complete the
rosette. Pin the tail under if necessary
to create a smooth finish.
5. Repeat this procedure with each of
the remaining corners of the overlay.
The finished overlay should have a
graceful swagged effect punctuated by
four rosettes.

Note: For a consistent look, Judy and
Gail recommend having each table
done from start to finish by only one
person rather than by a team.

Bitsy Duggins's Trompe l'Oeil Cake Tablecloth

New Orleans decorator Bitsy
Duggins's artistic cake tablecloth
treatment is a one-of-a-kind delight.

Both the underskirt and the overlay
are made of stiff canvas, painted and
molded to a billowy turn that would
make Michelangelo proud. Having the
rigidity of papier mâché, the cloths
nevertheless appear to be windblown.
Pockets, ingeniously created by crimp-
ing and pleating the material while the
paint is still wet, are tailor-made to
hold bridesmaids' bouquets. Here
Bitsy re-created simple bridesmaids'

bouquets of curly fern, jasmine, white
camellias, orchids, French tulips, and
montbretia, but she notes that simply
by changing the nature of the bouquet
and the colors of the cloths, you can
create a markedly different feeling.

Materials

12 yards artist's canvas
9½ yards jumbo cording

1 gallon latex paint (white or pastel color)
1 gallon wallpaper paste (available at any paint store)
2 9' x 12' plastic drop cloths
42" round table
3"–4"-wide paintbrush
36 clothespins, 2 for each bouquet, and the rest for the draping effect
Plastic cups, one for each bouquet

Method

1. It takes six yards of canvas to make the underskirt and six more for the overlay. Cut material into thirds to create two off-center seams, rather than one center seam. Sew together and put aside. Sew jumbo cording at the hem of the bottom skirt.
2. Dilute paint with prepared wallpaper paste. If paint is too thick, it tends to crack as it dries.
3. Place drop cloth over table. Center the bottom skirt over the drop cloth and paint it completely.
4. While the bottom skirt is still wet pull gently at the cording on the hem to form undulating folds, giving the illusion of graceful movement. Allow twenty-four hours to dry.
5. Next, place second drop cloth over bottom skirt. Then center overlay cloth on drop cloth and paint. While still wet, but after the underskirt has dried completely, begin gathering, pleating, and cinching up the fabric in big drapy folds using clothespins. As you go around, create pockets for the brides-

maids' bouquets at roughly equidistant intervals. To make the pockets, draw up the wet fabric, mold fabric around a plastic cup, and secure with two clothespins.
6. Repeat this technique for as many bouquet holders as needed.
7. Let the cloth dry completely; it should take about twenty-four hours. When dry, the overlay will be about twelve inches shorter than the bottom cloth, owing to the gathering.
8. Remove the plastic cups and clothespins. The cloth, complete with posy pockets, should be frozen in shape.
9. Make a small slit at the very bottom of each flower pocket, to keep bouquet in place once it's inserted.

Anne Hodges's Petits Fours with Crystallized Flowers

Anne Hodges of Crystaflower in Atlanta has parlayed a fascination with eighteenth-century entertaining and dessert embellishments into a successful commercial enterprise. The business she began in 1987 specializes in crystallizing fruits, flowers, and foliage—all of which she grows organically in her own garden—as edible ornamentation for miniature desserts. Her recipe for crystallizing flowers and foliage is a secret, based on her adaptations of eighteenth-century recipes. Often she decorates petits

fours with them as an accompaniment to wedding cake. I use a very simple crystallizing technique from *The Joy of Cooking* and high-quality store-bought iced petits fours. See illustration on page 189.

Materials

Petits fours
Crystallized flowers
    5 or more of the following flowers:
        Johnny-jump-ups
        Violet and borage blossoms
        Rose petals and tiny roses
        Pansies
        Zinnias
        Impatiens
        Forget-me-nots
        Cornflowers
    1 egg white
    ½ teaspoon cold water
    1 sable paintbrush
    Extra-fine granulated sugar
Screening rack (available at floral supply stores)
Airtight containers
Toothpicks
Canned white icing
Paper towels
Tweezers

Note: Do not use any bulb flowers.

Method

1. Pick flowers after the dew has evaporated, about 10:00 A.M., and put on

paper towels to dry completely.

2. Mix the egg white and water, and paint each flower with the mixture.

3. Before the mixture dries, dust the coated flowers thoroughly with granulated sugar, letting the excess fall onto the paper towel so you can reuse it.

4. Put the blossoms on screening rack to dry. When I'm in a hurry, I place the painted flowers on a bed of sugar, about one and a half cups spread evenly over the bottom of an eight to nine inch Pyrex pie plate and bake at 150–175 degrees for about an hour. Let cool.

5. When dry, store in airtight containers.

6. When ready to affix flowers, smear a bit of canned icing on top of each petit four with a toothpick. Then, using tweezers, place a crystallized flower or two onto the icing.

Note: Flowers are fragile, of course, and many will break during the crystallizing process as well as when you're embellishing the petits fours. Therefore it's important to start with a good number more than you will actually need.

Cutting Wedding Cake

*G*isela Techt of A Taste of Europe in Fort Worth has offered me a foolproof technique for cutting and serving a wedding cake without destroying its artistic silhouette. When the last guest is served, the cake looks as lovely as it did before bride and broom made the ceremonial cut.

Materials

2 large cutting knives
Glass of warm water
Small basket or bowl
Plates

Method

1. Start serving from the back of the bottom layer. (Depending on the size and shape of the cake, you can cut anywhere from one-third to one-half of it without affecting its appearance in front.)

2. Remove one-third of the flowers from the bottom tier and place in a bowl or basket.

3. Each serving should be cut two inches deep, one-half inch wide and four or more inches high (depending upon height of the tiers).

4. To keep cake from sticking to the bottom, insert a knife to the right of the slice and under it, then gently slide the knife toward the left side and leave it there. (Be sure to dip your knife in the glass of warm water occasionally in order to keep it clean and more effective.)

5. Insert another knife on the right side, and use both knives to move the cake forward for easier removal.

6. After removal of the outer portion of the bottom tier, you'll be removing the center pieces from the same tier.

7. Place a flower on every serving for garnish.

8. Repeat for upper layers.

Opposite: Once flowers have been removed from the portion of the cake to be cut, insert knife to the depth you wish the slices to be (top), then cut slices at the desired width and begin to remove them, using one knife or two (center). Decorate each slice with a flower (bottom).

Right: Maurice Delechelle of La Marquise in New Orleans created this three-tiered square genoise cake with butter-cream frosting. It is filled with fresh strawberries and a touch of Grand Marnier. Both the cake and the table are decorated with fresh camellias and antique tussy-mussies from Bitsy Duggins's collection.

Appendixes

*B*ride's Checklist

Courtesy of Andre de La Barre and Design Consultants, Inc., New Orleans

First Decisions

• Set the date.
• Book the ceremony site.
• Book the reception site.
• Begin drawing up guest list.
• Select the wedding party.
• Select wedding dress.
• Book the florist.
• Book the photographer.

At Least Two to Three Months Before

• Make sure your insurance policy covers your engagement and wedding rings.
• Select bridesmaids' dresses and all accessories.
• Book the caterer, sign contract, leave deposit.
• Book the church vocalist for the wedding ceremony, if necessary.
• Book the reception musicians, sign contract, leave deposit.
• Book video service, if needed.
• Reserve the limousines.
• Register china, crystal, and silver patterns.
• Order wedding invitations, announcements, informal and personal stationery.
• Select calligraphers.
• Finalize guest lists for all events and parties.
• Make honeymoon reservations.
• Update passport and obtain visas if necessary.
• Schedule wedding and honeymoon vacation time with employers.

Two Months Before

• Select type and flavor of cake and select bakery; same for groom's cake.
• Consult with florist to decide type and number of arrangements for ceremony and reception.
• Determine number of corsages, bouquets, boutonnieres.
• Have mothers of bride and groom select dresses; select apparel for fathers, too.
• Confirm delivery date of wedding dress with dressmaker.
• Have your engagement picture taken (5" x 7" or 8" x 10" black and white). Determine which newspapers it should be placed in; contact newspapers.
• Have gardeners prepare plants/bedding for reception area, if necessary.
• Order custom table skirting for reception.
• Decide on guest hotel favors and rehearsal dinner favors, if any.

One Month Before

• Buy groom's wedding ring; order engraving.
• Buy groom's gift.
• Buy gifts for maid/matron of honor and other attendants.
• Have final fittings for bridal gown, bridesmaids' dresses, flower children's attire, etc.
• Have color wedding portrait taken.
• Apply for marriage license; schedule blood tests, if necessary.
• Arrange lodging for out-of-town guests.
• Buy stamps for thank-you notes.
• Record and display gifts as received. Start thank-you notes immediately.
• Plan bridesmaids' luncheon (menu, flowers, favors, place settings, etc.); send bridesmaids' luncheon invitations.
• If involved, plan rehearsal dinner (menu, flowers, favors, place settings, etc.); send rehearsal dinner invitations.

- Order catering and refreshments for house on day of wedding.
- Schedule hairdresser for house on day of wedding.
- Order personalized wedding-reception napkins.
- Reconfirm transportation schedules.
- Make checklist and schedule for bridesmaids' luncheon, rehearsal dinner, and wedding.
- Reconfirm photographer and determine types of photos wanted and where they will be shot; insist that photographer visit site prior to wedding.
- If changing name, get forms for bank accounts, social security, etc.

Two Weeks Before

- Reconfirm dates, times, and schedules of the following in writing:
    photographer (times and schedule, including rehearsal dinner)
    caterer (wedding reception and food at house, if any)
    musicians/band (church and reception)
    flowers (house, bridesmaids' luncheon, rehearsal dinner, reception, wedding party)
    centerpieces
    clergymen
    limousines
    cake
    tenting
- Plan guest itinerary to be placed in hotel rooms.
- Obtain out-of-town-guest hotel list and arrival dates.
- Plan seating arrangement for rehearsal dinner.
- Have place cards and program prepared by calligrapher.
- Have church ceremony program printed.
- Give caterers estimated guest count.
- Arrange for refreshments/food at wedding suite.

One Week Before

- Confirm publication of wedding announcement in newspaper.
- Wrap gifts for bridesmaids and groomsmen, attendants.
- Have bridesmaids' luncheon.
- Give wedding trip itinerary to parents.
- Pack honeymoon clothes.
- Arrange for preserving of wedding gown after wedding (should be cleaned immediately following wedding).
- Buy film for personal cameras.
- Prepare wedding night overnight bag; arrange to have it delivered.
- Deliver guest packets to hotel rooms.
- Reconfirm all arrangements by phone or fax.

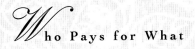

Who Pays for What

The following is the traditional breakdown of who should pay for what. Usually the major share of the wedding expenses is assumed by the bride's family, but this is by no means an absolute. Before you start making definite plans, sit down with all parties involved and clarify the financial arrangements.

The Groom and His Family

- Bride's rings
- Flowers (bridal bouquet, boutonnieres for groomsmen, corsages for mothers)
- Groomsmen's dinner or bachelor party (optional)
- Gifts for groomsmen
- Honeymoon
- Officiant fee
- Rehearsal dinner

The Bride and Her Family

- Gifts for maid/matron of honor, bridesmaids, and children attendants
- Bride's dress, accessories, and trousseau
- Bridesmaids' luncheon (optional)
- Ceremony (location rental, organist/soloist, other music, decoration)
- Flowers (Attendants' bouquets, flowers at church and reception)
- Gift for groom
- Groom's wedding ring
- Invitations, calligraphy, and stamps
- Photography
- Reception (location rental, caterer, beverages, wedding cakes, decorations, music)
- Thank-you gifts for hosts and hostesses of any parties
- Transportation to and from ceremony/reception for out-of-town guests and wedding party

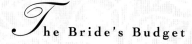

The Bride's Budget

Whether your wedding is big and extravagant or small and simple, it's important to establish a budget. Once you make your decisions about size, site, and so on, figure out how much you can spend on each phase. Be sure to think about which part of your wedding is the most important to you. If you have always dreamed of wearing a designer dress and serving French champagne, consider passing hors d'oeuvres rather than having a seated affair and forgoing the eighteen-piece symphony orchestra. Keep a record of your expenses and pad the budget a bit since unexpected costs always arise.

A simple guideline such as the one below should keep you on track. Again, write everything down!

Item/Expense	Plan #1	Plan #2
Bride's Dress		
Dress		
Veil		
Accessories		
Ceremony		
Charge for use of site		
Organist/Soloist		
Other Musicians		
Flowers		
Bridal bouquet		
Attendants' bouquets, corsages, boutonnieres		
Arrangements at the ceremony		
Arrangements at the reception		
Fresh flowers for wedding cake		
Invitations		
Invitations and envelopes		
Stamps		
Calligrapher or scribe		
Note cards with maiden and married monograms		
Presents		
Gifts for attendants		
Groom's wedding present		

Item/Expense	Plan #1	Plan #2
Photographer		
Daily/hourly rate		
Film and development		
Reprints		
Miscellaneous		
Reception		
Location rental		
Caterer		
Beverages		
Music		
Decoration besides flowers		
Rentals (tent, tables, chairs, linens, etc.)		
Wedding cakes		
Transportation (to and from ceremony and reception)		
Bride and groom		
Wedding party		
Parents		
Out-of-town guests		
Total		

Formal Invitation Etiquette

Along with most of her cohorts, Miss Manners is positively passionate when it comes to the sacrosanctity of traditional, formal wedding invitations. In my view individuality is fine; after all, the wedding invitation with an avant-garde veneer doesn't make the ceremony any more binding. However, I can't say I find any legitimate substitute for the genuine article, so here are a few rules of thumb for formal invitations:

Penning the Envelopes

- No abbreviations (streets, state, city, etc.) except for Dr., Mr., Ms., Mrs., and Jr.
- Avoid the wording "and family." (Use only in the case of complicated relationships, e.g., stepbrothers and stepsisters.)
- Send children over 13 (though some argue 18) a separate invitation.
- Use full names (spelling out everyone's middle name is optional).
- For a couple who are both doctors, use "The Doctors" (e.g., The Doctors Pritchard).
- Use a return address.
- Use first-class stamps.

An inner envelope is optional, but if you do use one bear in mind:
- Include only the names on the outer envelope.
  (Do *not* include first names for married couples, e.g., Mr. and Mrs. Lancaster.)
- For invitations addressed specifically to children under 13, use first names only.
- For invitations to both parents and children, use full names.
- For single friends with a date, add "and guest."

Sample Wording of Typical Wedding Invitations

Church Ceremony:

> Dr. and Mrs. Gene Redford Sanders
> request the honour of your presence
> at the marriage of their daughter
> Jessica Ann
> to
> Mr. George Samuel Thompson
> on Saturday, the seventh of October
> One thousand nine hundred and ninety
> at twelve o'clock
> St. John's Church
> Charleston

Separate Reception:

> Dr. and Mrs. Gene Redford Sanders
> request the pleasure of your company
> at the reception of their daughter
> Jessica Ann
> and
> Mr. George Samuel Thompson
> on Saturday, the seventh of October
> One thousand nine hundred and ninety
> at half after one o'clock
> Pine Ridge Country Club
> Charleston

Combined Church and Reception:

Dr. and Mrs. Gene Redford Sanders
request the honour of your presence
at the marriage of their daughter
Jessica Ann
to
Mr. George Samuel Thompson
on Saturday, the seventh of October
One thousand nine hundred and ninety
at twelve o'clock
St. John's Church
Charleston
and afterward at the reception
Pine Tree Country Club

Sample Wording of Not-So-Typical Wedding Invitations

Remarried mother:

Mr. and Mrs. William Hodges
request the honour of your presence
at the marriage of her daughter
Abigail Lane White

Remarried father:

Mr. and Mrs. Mark Clinton Whiteside
request the honour of your presence
at the marriage of his daughter
Katherine Lee Whiteside

Divorced parents together:

Mr. and Mrs. Curtis Perry
and
Mr. and Mrs. Jonathan Morris
request the honour of your presence
at the marriage of
Mary Foy Morris

Both sets of parents:

Mr. and Mrs. James Hilliard Watson
and
Mr. and Mrs. Charles Thomas Clark
request the honour of your presence
at the marriage of
Suzanne Watson
to
Mr. Lawrence Clark

Bride on her own:

The honour of your presence
is requested at the marriage of
Miss/Ms. Miranda Leigh Marks
to
Mr. Walter Harris Cummins

Woman with a professional title:
(A woman doctor or dentist should not use her professional title if
her parents issue the invitation, but she may use it if she issues the
invitation herself.)

The honour of your presence
is requested at the marriage of
Doctor Susan Lyle Carter
to
Mr. James Alcott Acker

Photography Checklist

Several weeks before the wedding, carefully review with your photographer the moments you want captured—this will make his or her job much easier.

Before the Ceremony

Bride alone in her wedding dress
Bride with father
Bride with mother
Bride with parents
Bride with family
Groom with father
Groom with mother
Groom with parents
Groom with family
Bride with bridesmaids
Groom with groomsmen
Wedding party getting ready
Bride leaving for ceremony
Groom leaving for ceremony

During the Ceremony

The groom and best man at altar (if Christian ceremony)
The wedding-party processional
Father and daughter walking down the aisle
Any other type of processional
Exchange of rings
The kiss
The departure

During the Reception

The receiving line
The wedding party
Bride and groom with parents
Bride and groom's first dance
Bride dancing with father
Groom dancing with mother
Cutting the cake
Various guests*
Bride throwing bouquet
Groom removing garter
Bride and groom departing

*Be sure to ask a good friend or close family member to stick close to the photographer for at least the first thirty minutes of the reception. This person should be able to point out the bride's and groom's closest friends and family who are not in the wedding party. This will eliminate the chance that you'll end up with lots of pictures of that distant cousin, three times removed, in your wedding album.

Wedding Flowers by Shade

An asterisk indicates various branches, herbs, or wildflowers that grow wild in the Southeast. Because they are readily available, I often use them in my arrangements. (The varieties differ, of course, in other parts of the country.) In any case, branches, herbs, and wildflowers must be picked in the early morning or late afternoon and immediately plunged into warm water. After five or six hours soaking time, they're ready.

White

Agapanthus
Alstroemeria
Amaryllis
Anemone
Anthurium
Aster
Astilbe
Auratum lily
Baby's breath
Bouvardia
Calla lily
Camellia
Candy tuft
Carnation
Cattleya orchid
Cherokee rose
Curly willow
   (bleached)
Daffodil
Dahlia
Daisy
Delphinium
Dogwood
Dropwort*
   (Meadowsweet)
Erasmus
Euphorbia
Floribunda, or spray
   rose

Foxglove*
Freesia
Gardenia
Gerbera daisy
Gladiolus
Grape hyacinth
Hollyhock*
Hyacinth
Hydrangea
Iris
Lilac
Lily of the valley
Lisianthus
Magnolia*
Marguerite daisy
Monte Cassino asters*
Narcissus
Oakwood hydrangea
Opium poppy
Pansy
Pear blossom
Peony
Pitcher plant*
Poinsettia
Poppy
Queen Anne's lace
Quince
Ranunculus
Rose
Snapdragon
Star of Bethlehem

Statice
Stephanotis
Stock
Tuberose
Tulip
White bedstraw*
Yarrow
Zinnia

Peach

Alstroemeria
Dahlia
Gerbera daisy
Lily
Parrot tulip
Pear blossom
Peach lily
Poppy
Protea
Sonia rose
Sweet William

Pink

Alstroemeria
Alum root*
Amaryllis
Amaryllis belladonna
Anemone

Anthurium
Azalea
Bougainvillea*
Bouvardia
Calla lily
Camellia
Cattleya orchid
Carnation
Cornflower
Dahlia
Dames rocket*
Dittany of Crete*
Flowering quince
Freesia
Gerbera daisy
Geranium*
Gladiolus
Hyacinth
Hydrangea
Hyssop*
Larkspur
Nerine lily
Peach blossom
Peony
Phlox
Poinsettia
Poppy
Protea
Ranunculus
Rose
Rubrum lily

Snapdragon
Stock
Tulip
Zinnia

Yellow

Acacia
Alstroemeria
Anemone
Black-eyed Susan
Calendula
Calla lily
Chrysanthemum
Cock's comb (Celosia)
Connecticut king lily
Daffodil
Dahlia
Eremerus
Euphorbia
Forsythia
Freesia
Gerbera daisy
Gladiolus
Goldenrod*
Indigo* (wild)
Iris
Marigold
Montbretia
Narcissus

Nasturtium
Oncidium orchid
Ornamental pepper
Poppy
Primrose*
Ranunculus
Rose (Lady Bankshire)
Snapdragon
Statice
Stock
Sunflower
Tulip
Yarrow
Yellow bedstraw*
Zinnia

Blue

Agapanthus
Anemone
Artichoke (Globe)
Brodiaca/Triteleia*
Chicory*
Cornflower
Delphinium
Globe thistle
Hyacinth
Hydrangea
Hyssop*
Iris
Larkspur
Monkshood*
Rosemary*
Sage* (meadow)
Speedwell
Spiderwort*
Statice
Wisteria*

Magenta

Anemone
Aster
Azalea
Carnation
Cock's comb (Celosia)
Dendrobium orchid
Gerbera daisy

Orange

Bird of paradise
Calendula
Chinese lantern
Enchantment lily
Euphorbia
Firecracker lily
Gerbera daisy
Gladiolus
Marigold
Monbretia
Nasturtium
Ornamental pepper
Poppy
Rose
Safflower
Torch lily
Tulip
Zinnia

Purple/Lavender

Allium Giganton
Alstroemeria
Anemone
Aster
Carnation
Cattleya orchid
Chinaberry*

Chrysanthemum
Cymbidium orchid
Delphinium
Dendrobium orchid
Freesia
Gladiolus
Heather
Iris
Ironweed*
Joe-pye weed*
Lavender*
Liatris
Lilac
Lisianthus
Phalaenopsis orchid
Poppy
Rose
Slipper orchid
Statice
Sterling silver rose
Stock
Tulip
Violet*
Wisteria*
Zinnia

Green

Bells of Ireland
Cymbidium orchid
Gladiolus
Hydrangea
Jack-in-the-pulpit*
Parrot tulips
Obaki Anotherium
Viburnum

Red

Amaryllis
Anemone
Anthurium
Camellia
Carnation
Cock's comb (Celosia)
Dahlia
Freesia
Gerbera daisy
Ginger
Gladiolus
Gloriosa lily
Holly berry
Nerine lily
Poppy
Quince (flowering)
Rose
Sweet William
Tulip
Zinnia

Tomato Red

Anthurium
Azalea
Bouvardia
Camellia
Carnation
Gerbera daisy
Gladiolus
Gloriosa lily
Nasturtium
Ornamental pepper
Poinsettia
Poppy
Rose
Tulip
Zinnia

Brick

Alstroemeria
Carnation
Chrysanthemum
Cock's comb (Celosia)
Cymbidium orchid
Freesia
Snapdragon

Brown

Cattail
Curly willow
Kangaroo paw
Pineapple with pink
    and green
Pussy willow with
    silver gray

$\mathscr{E}$quipping the Bar

Whether you're having an engagement party for seventy-five or a rehearsal dinner for two hundred, the following bar provisions guideline will assist you in deciding about quantities of liquor and mixers and the number of bartenders you'll need to serve your guests adequately. Be sure to think about the preferences of your guests; if they are big wine or beer drinkers, increase the wine and beer and decrease the hard liquor, and vice versa. Make note that Southerners are bourbon aficionados, so you might wish to decrease the amount if you reside north of the Mason-Dixon line.

Ratio of Bartenders to Number of Guests

2 : 75
4 : 200
6 : 300
8 : 400

Provisions for 75

3 cases champagne*
4 liters Scotch
3 liters vodka
4 liters bourbon
2 liters gin
1 liter rum
1 750 ml vermouth
1 750 ml sherry
1 750 Dubonnet or Campari
1 liter tequila (optional)
1 750 ml rye (optional)
2 cases dry white wine
6 bottles dry red wine
1/2 case regular beer (more in the summer)
1 case light beer (more in the summer)
24 bottles sparkling water (5-ounce bottles)
1 case tonic
3 cases club soda or seltzer
24 bottles of mixers (ginger ale, Coca-Cola, 7-Up, plus one diet kind)
1 quart juice (orange, tomato, etc.)
12 limes
12 lemons
Pitcher of ice water
Ice (1 pound per person)

Provisions for 200

8 cases champagne*
10 liters Scotch
10 liters vodka
10 liters bourbon
6 liters gin
3 liters rum
1 liter vermouth
1 liter sherry
1 750 Dubonnet or Campari
1 liter tequila
1 750 ml rye
6 cases dry white wine
1 case dry red wine
2 cases regular beer (more in the summer)
3 cases light beer (more in the summer)
5 cases sparkling water (5-ounce bottles)
2 cases tonic
5 cases club soda or seltzer
48 bottles of mixers (ginger ale, Coca-Cola, 7-Up, plus one diet kind)
3 quarts juice (orange, tomato, etc.)
18 limes
18 lemons
Pitcher of ice water
Ice (1 pound per person)

*John Roland of Southern Hospitality Systems, Inc., suggests stocking twice this amount of champagne.

*C*leaning and Storing a Wedding Veil

Courtesy of Bryce Reveley

Materials

Orvus-WA Paste (available at feed stores)
2 bed sheets (natural fiber)
1 cardboard tube or roller (from wrapping paper roll, fabric/
    carpet holder, or map/print container)
5 to 6 yards washed, unbleached muslin
String or ribbon

Preparation and Washing

1. Remove all of the combs, wires, etc., that are attached to the veil. (If the headpiece is particularly complicated, then drawings should be made or photographs taken.)
2. Wash the veil.
    A. Line the sink with an old towel.
    B. Mix up a solution of four tablespoons Ivory liquid or one tablespoon of Orvus-WA Paste per gallon of warm water.
    C. Let the veil soak for 45 minutes.
    D. Rinse well, letting the water run and drain at the same time until it is clear enough to drink.
3. Using the towel as a sling, cradle it around the textile and let it absorb the water, as textiles are in their most vulnerable state when they are wet.

Drying

1. Spread a sheet over a shower curtain (be sure to cover the rod and rings).
2. Spread the veil over the sheet and gently block it with your fingers.
3. Cover the veil with the other sheet. (This will absorb moisture and speed the drying process).
4. If the veil is very wide, fold it in half or thirds.
5. Let the veil dry for an hour (longer if needed).

Preparing for Storage

1. Using a cardboard roller, wrap prewashed muslin around the roller so that none of the cardboard is exposed, and then tuck in the ends. (You might need an extra pair of hands to help you with this.)
2. Place the veil on a dry, clean surface.
3. Fold the veil in half or thirds, to accommodate the width of the roller.
4. Place the roller at the end of the veil closest to you.
5. Start rolling, keeping the tension even, until you have rolled up the veil completely.
6. Wrap the roller with another sheet of prewashed muslin.
7. Tuck the excess into the ends of the roller.
8. Using string, ribbon, or even tear strips from the muslin, tie the roller in the middle and at both ends.
9. DO NOT WRAP IN PLASTIC.

Storage

1. Store the veil in a dry, cool place, preferably a closet.
2. Store horizontally, if you have the space.
3. If stored vertically, you must rotate the roller, end on end, at least once a year.
4. If folded, the veil must be refolded once a year. If folded in half, fold it the next year in thirds and reverse the order the following year.

$\mathcal{P}$reserving Your Wedding Dress

Undoubtedly, you will want to preserve your wedding dress, so be sure not to let too much time pass before you have it professionally cleaned. Find out which dry cleaners in your town specializes in wedding dresses—word of mouth is usually the best source. Talk to your mother, grandmother, or anyone else who has preserved her dress and has had the opportunity to use or look at it after a long period of time and can therefore attest to the work. If you live in a city, you can usually find a professional cleaner who will do the work by hand. Though the latter route is expensive, it is well worth it.

After removing the dress, take the following steps

• Fluff the different layers of the dress and place the dress on the original hanger.
• Hang in a cool, dry place, making sure the dress is not cramped.
• After at least one week but no later than three weeks, take the dress to your cleaners. If there are any champagne spills, it takes this amount of time for the spots to show up. Champagne left untreated will badly yellow the dress and may even erode the material.

At the cleaners

• Be sure to inspect the entire dress (and veil) with your cleaner carefully. Together you should locate any spots or stains.
• If you know the source of the stain, be sure to tell him—this will help him determine which cleaning process to use.
• Based on the fabric, stains, beading, and trim, the cleaner will establish a cleaning process.
• Unless you'll be wearing the dress again within the year, don't bother having it pressed—it's only a waste of money.
• After the dress has been cleaned it should be wrapped in acid-free tissue or preferably in a prewashed muslin sheet.
• The bodice and the sleeves should be stuffed with acid-free tissue paper or prewashed muslin as well.
• Make sure the cleaner uses a sealed acid-free storage box especially designed for wedding dresses. The veil can be stored in the same box in a separate compartment.
• Do not let the cleaner use plastic anywhere in the box—it emits fumes that spot.

Back at home

• Remove any decoration that could potentially stain fabric (anything metal, fabric-covered buttons or pins) and shoulder pads. You could have the cleaners do this for you.
• Store the box in a cool, dry place that is not subject to extreme temperature changes. Do not store in an attic, basement, or cedar closet or chest.
• If you do store the dress on a hanger, be sure to sew straps to the bodice of the dress to relieve stress on the shoulders. Also, securely wrap the dress in a prewashed muslin sheet.
• Take out your dress and veil once a year, let it air for twenty-four hours, and re-box or re-hang. At this point, be sure to to tend to any new stains that might have appeared.

Suggested Reading

Bruce, Philip Alexander. *Social Life of Virginia in the Seventeenth Century*. 1907. Reprint. Williamstown, Mass.: Corner House Publishers, 1968.

Burwell, Letitia M. *A Girl's Life before the War*. New York: F. A. Stokes, 1895.

Church, Beverly Reese, and Bethany Ewald Bultman. *The Joys of Entertaining*. New York: Abbeville Press, 1987.

Clinton, Catherine. *The Plantation Mistress: Woman's World in the Old South*. New York: Pantheon Books, 1982.

Davis, Richard Beale. *Intellectual Life in Jefferson's Virginia, 1790–1830*. Ann Arbor, Mich.: Books on Demand, 1964.

Eaton, Clement. *The Growth of a Southern Civilization, 1790–1860*. New York: Harper & Row, 1961.

Hill, Thomas E. *Never Give a Lady a Restive Horse: A Nineteenth-Century Handbook of Etiquette*. 1873. Reprint. New York: World Publishing Company, 1969.

Holiday, Carl. *Woman's Life in Colonial Days*. Williamstown, Mass.: Corner House Publishers, 1922.

Loring, John. *The Tiffany Wedding*. New York: Doubleday and Co., 1988.

Maia, Ronaldo. *More Decorating with Flowers*. New York: Harry N. Abrams, 1991.

O'Hara, Georgina. *The Bride's Book*. London: Michael Joseph, 1991.

Peacock, Virginia Tatnall. *Famous American Belles of the Nineteenth Century*. Philadelphia and London: J. B. Lippincott, 1901.

Rothman, Ellen K. *Hands and Hearts: A History of Courtship in America*. New York: Basic Books, 1984.

Scott, Anne Firor. *The Southern Lady: From Pedestal to Politics, 1830–1930*. Chicago: University of Chicago Press, 1970.

Spruill, Julia. *Women's Life and Work in the Southern Colonies*. Chapel Hill: University of North Carolina Press, 1938.

Stanard, Mary Newton. *Colonial Virginia: Its People and Customs*. Philadelphia and London: J. B. Lippincott, 1917.

Stewart, Martha. *Weddings*. New York: Clarkson N. Potter, 1987.

Taylor, Joe Gray. *Eating, Drinking and Visiting in the South: An Informal History*. Baton Rouge: Louisiana State University Press, 1982.

Taylor, William R. *Cavalier and Yankee: The Old South and American National Character*. New York: George Braziller, 1961.

Tharp, Leonard, and Lisa Ruffin. *Leonard Tharp: An American Style of Flower Arrangement*. Dallas, Tex.: Taylor Publishing Company, 1986.

Turner, Kenneth. *Flower Style*. New York: Weidenfeld and Nicolson, 1989.

Wilson, Charles Reagan, and William Ferris. *The Encyclopedia of Southern Culture*. Chapel Hill: University of North Carolina Press, 1989.

Winterthur Museum. *American Elegance: Classic and Contemporary Menus from Celebrated Hosts and Hostesses*. New York: Abbeville Press, 1988.

Wyatt-Brown, Bertram. *Southern Honor: Ethics and Behavior in the Old South*. New York: Oxford University Press, 1982.

Afterword

When Johnny and I got married twenty-seven years ago, I was barely twenty-one years old. Although I knew I would have a big wedding—800 guests as it turned out—and that it would most likely be at the New Orleans Country Club, I really had no specific ideas about what it should be. Of course, I wanted everything to be beautiful and great fun for our family and friends, but the details just weren't important to me at the time. I was swamped trying to finish up school, but even if I'd had more time, I'm not sure I would have known how to articulate my ideas in anything but the vaguest terms. Fortunately, I knew I could rely on my mother's wonderful taste to bring it all into focus, and that I could count on my good friends' help and input throughout.

The whole planning process is a blur to me now, and, looking back, there are funny little snippets of things that stick out in my memory: begging my favorite minister, Dr. Serex, to come out of retirement to officiate; my best friend Kathy Boylan's picking out the music for the ceremony when I was in such a quandary; musing over flowers and feeling confident that Rohm's florist would deliver something wonderful for the church and ceremony, as they always had for other milestones in my life. I remember trying on dresses and headpieces and thinking about bouquets. And I'll never forget stumbling on the unusual antique jewelry box that I would give to Johnny for a wedding present. But the endless details, the exhaustive checklists and choices of the organization phase, I must have somehow negotiated in an excited daze—and very much with my mother's help.

In working on this book, I've had the rare treat of being able to peek behind the scenes at weddings all over the South, of getting to know the brides and grooms and many of their relatives and friends, of feeling their excitement and sometimes their prewedding panic, and, above all, of coming to understand their very individual interpretations of the wedding process. I've been able to talk to the dozens of amateurs and experts, friends and professionals who've put the finishing touches on what finally occurred in front of the curtain, at ceremonies and receptions that run the gamut from the tiny and intimate to the bold and extravagant. Through Lisa's and my research, we've unearthed a whole compendium of special Southern traditions, all with historical precedents that add new meaning to more contemporary conventions. Now, armed with this wonderful new data, I find I'd love to get married to Johnny all over again. I'm enraptured by details and by the unlimited artistic options available to brides today. Wedding and party effects have never been more evocative.

I've tried to share as many of these creative, new ideas and designs as possible on the pages of this book. Some of them are age-old family traditions, some are the latest looks from professionals, and some are just favorite elements from my own repertoire, special entertaining effects that I use for myself and my clients. There's a new slant on everything from photography to fashion, from invitations to etiquette, from food to flowers to reception finery, from tying the knot to tossing the bouquet and all the entertaining in between. I hope you'll be inspired by *Weddings Southern Style* whether you're getting married or just giving a party for someone who is, and that you'll use the ideas you find here as a springboard for expressing yourself in all your entertaining.

Acknowledgments

I want to thank my husband, Johnny, who has encouraged, supported, and loved me throughout this project and all of my other endeavors for twenty-seven years of marriage; God, who continually watches over me and guides me; my two sons, John Mark and Ford, of whom I am extremely proud; and the rest of my family: my parents, Beverly and W. Ford Reese; my two sisters, Linda and Marianne, and their families; my brother, Thomas, and his family; my brother-in-law, Chris, and his family; and my in-laws, Kay and Noel Bailey—all of whom make up the best support system and source of inspiration that I could possibly have.

My thanks also to Jim Hayes, George Thompson, and all the people at Atticus Press without whom there would have been no book. To their managing editor, Amanda Adams, who has served as the guiding light of the project, allowing me to be a part of her own wedding to Paul Weir and putting together the best creative team I could have asked for: Lisa Ruffin Harrison—a truly gifted writer who was able to turn my notes, interviews, and ideas into flowing prose—and Fran Brennan, who, with assistant Janet Lentzen, spent countless, tireless hours turning each wedding into a spectacular visual presentation. All were a pleasure to work with and have become true friends.

To my New Orleans support team: Beverly Lamb, my priceless assistant; my best friends, Lynne White and Elizabeth Swanson; Pixie and Jimmy Reiss, who provided their home as a setting for the cover of the book, and who allowed son Crutcher and niece Samantha McAshan to pose with lovely Lessley Baldwin for the cover shot; Pat Kerr of Memphis for providing the exquisite wedding dress and children's clothes and accessories; John Jay and Joan Cazaubon of John Jay Beauty Salon for keeping everyone in the cover shot looking beautiful; Dathel and Tommy Coleman, Dathel and John Georges, Lindsey and Scott Biaggi, and Dottie and Jimmy Coleman, who shared two memorable weddings with us; and Lisa Newsom and *Veranda* magazine for being so generous with their spectacular photography.

To my creative team at Abbeville Press: editor Jackie Decter and designer Molly Shields, who worked diligently and patiently with me to make my book a reality. At Abbeville, I would also like to thank Bob Abrams, Josh Abrams, Dana Cole, Amy Handy, Robin James, Hope Koturo, Mark Magowan, Alan Mirken, and Rozelle Shaw for all their help and sage advice.

And of course, special thanks to all of the brides and grooms and their families, who allowed us to share with them a very happy and personal occasion: Cindy Brennan and Eddie Davis and their parents, Claire and John Brennan and Mary and Edward Davis; Player Butler and Mark Michelsen and their parents, Noel Sengel and Donald Butler and Mr. and Mrs. Bruce Michelsen; Lee Rutherford and Sumner Adams and their parents, Laura and Schley Rutherford and Ann and Marion Adams; Leslie Daubenberger and Bobby Lorton and their parents, Sharon and Charles Daubenberger and Roxana and Bob Lorton; Courtney Banks and George Pappas and their parents, Nancy and Dan Kingsley and Helen and Dino Pappas; Janet Mosely and Tom McMahan and her parents, Mr. and Mrs. Norman Mosely; Kathy Levenson and David Rubenstein and their parents, Renay and Alan Levenson and Judy and Arnold Rubenstein; Kelly Howell and Matt Strange and their parents, Billie and Jack Howell and Don and Frances Strange; and Gail Satterwhite and Thomas Hawkins; as well as those who prefer to remain anonymous. I will always appreciate their Southern hospitality, graciousness, and warmth. Our book is a tribute to them.

I would also like to extend my gratitude to the following people: Bunny and Les Adams, Betsy Agelasto, Charlotte Jones Anderson, Shy Anderson, Janet and Gene Aschaffenburg, Jane Avinger, Jan Bacon, Courtney Banks, Dr. and Mrs. Dennis Barek, Barbara Barton, Thomas Bates, Ann Beason, Marie Berry, Laura Beyer, The Bombay Club, Judith Bonner, Dr. and Mrs. Jack Borden Taylor, Tattie Bos, Laura Bowen, Mimi and John Bowen, Colleen and Harold "Pup" Born, Patricia and Vernon Brinson, Mr. and Mrs. Jack Brittain and family, Alice V. Brown, Ann Brown, the Very Reverend Charles A. Bryan, Bethany Ewald Bultman, Dr. and Mrs. Pete Bunting and their daughters, Allen and Mary, William Henry Byrd, Jr., Mr. and Mrs. Benjamin Caldwell, Trudy Caldwell, Alma Campbell, Liz Carpenter, Meg Garretson Carter, Ned Carter, Carl Casidy, Emery Clark, Ethel Clay, Mrs. Beau Clinton, Pat Cloar, Susan and Butch Cochran, Peter Coffman, Gary Coley, Luan and Al Copeland, Kathleen and Laurence Cowart, Molly Craven, Denise Chenel and David Daughtry, Doug Deckard, Tim Draper, Linda and Jean-Baptiste Ducruet, Emily Egan, Mrs. Edwin Ellinghausen, Rabbi Harry H. Epstein, Lee Epting, Edwin Eubanks, Evelynton Plantation, Karl and Bette Ewald, Karl and Margaret Ewald, Kate Ezell, James and Ev Feagin, Judy Feagin, Scott and Sarah Fletcher, Edna Forsythe, Donn Franklin, Kendra Lee Fuller, Mary Lynn and Gavin Garrett, Fritz Gitschner, Paddy Gordon, Kevin Graham, Carol Gross, Gigi and Martha Gunther, Mary Benton Gyess, Miles Hamley, Pat Hammond, Jenny Hampton, Jimmy Harrison, Margaret Haughton, Heidi Hayne, Bob Henderson, Eleanor Hermann, Hermann-Grima Historic House, Richard Hernandez, Irabelle and Harold Herring, Cricket Heumann, Mr. and Mrs. Donald Heumann, Historic New Orleans Collection, Frank Hoadley, Ann Holton, Deborah Hughes, Marcie Hughes, Hunter "T. J." Hull, Teak Hull, LuAn Hunter, Sallye and George Irvine, Alice Jackson, Mr. and Mrs. Coles Jackson, Jeff Jackson, Marley and Gary Jones, Kay and Bobby Kerrigan, Marlene Kreinin, Tamara Kreinin, Libby and Jim Landis, Louise Kraak Lay, Cindy Lee, Linda Lee, Valerie Leven, Stephanie Logan, Longue Vue House and Gardens, Robert Lupo, Maline McCalla, Irene McDonald, Eve McGrath, Courtney Cowart McHale, Charlie Mackie, Chica Manhart, Marsha Manhart, Maple Street Garden District Bookshop, Maple Street Uptown Square Bookshop , Alice Mathews, Kay and John Maybank, Maury Meekins, Marley Rose Meyer, Caroline Rennolds Milbank, Crystal Moffett, Louise and Jim Bob Moffett, Rose Monroe, Suzanne Morriss, National Museum of Women in the Arts, Betty and Bernard Neal, Lisa Neal, Patricia Neal, Sunny Norman, James O'Brien, Mr. and Mrs. J. Roby Penn III, Mr. and Mrs. Richard Perry, Philbrook Museum, Nancy Powell, Nancy and John Poynor, Jean Marie Randolph, Maddie Joe Ratcliff, Elise Bynum Reeves, Emily Gray Reeves, Cissy and Gus Reynoir, Martha Richardson, John Rivington IV, Nita and "Mac" Robinson, Robin Robinson, Betty Ruffin, Saunders Ruffin, Scoot and Charles Rutherford, "Toots" Rutherford, William Ryan, Kelly Miller Sanders, Richard Sanders, Nancy Schenecker, William A. Schultz, Karen Sherman, Jill and Jan Shoffner, Mary Singleton, Nancy Slaughter, Deborah Sloan, Jane and Robert Allen Smith, Donna Sorrell, Stanton Hall (Natchez, Miss.), Cyndy Storer, Bonnie Strathmann, Michael Sudbury, Swan House (Atlanta), Father Tim Thomas, Flo Treadway, Britton Trice, Kathleen Turner, Marilyn Van Eynde, Ruby Velasquez, Eric Voll, "Neetsy" Walker, Ambassador and Mrs. John G. Weinmann, Mary Virginia Weinmann, Cynthia Howsman and Robert Weinmann, Callie Williams, Susan Williams, Ann Wilson, Martha Woodham, Woodruff-Fontaine House, Phyllis Woodward, Judy Worthen, Christina Wysocki, Dr. and Mrs. Leopoldo Zorrilla.

Finally, to the following wonderful, creative people who graced me with the contribution of inspiring ideas and time:

Cakes & Catering

Affairs of the Heart, Atlanta, Ga. (Lori Bonsma)
Bella Luna Restaurant, New Orleans, La.
Evelyn Blair, Nashville, Tenn.
Bud & Alley's Restaurant, Seaside, Fla. (Dave Rauschkolb and Scott Witcoski)
Cakes by Debbie, Highlands, N.C.
Cakes by Jan, Fort Walton, Fla. (Jan Funk)
Sandra Carling, Atlanta, Ga.
Catered Occasions, Williamsburg, Va. (Jordan Westenhaver)
The Cherry Blossom, Potomac Riverboat Company, Alexandria, Va.
Commander's Palace, New Orleans, La. (Ella Brennan)
Criollo Chocolates, Washington, D.C. (Marilyn Mueller)
Croissant d'Or, Inc., New Orleans, La.

Crystaflower, Atlanta, Ga. (Anne Hodges)

Ellen Divers, Richmond, Va.

French Gourmet Bakery, Houston, Tex. (Patrice Ramain)

Susan Gage Catering, Washington, D.C. (Susan Gage and Jay Watkins)

Philippe Garmay, Tulsa, Okla.

Highlands Inn, Highlands, N.C. (Bryant Withers)

Ida Mae's Cakes of Distinction, Jacksboro, Tex. (Becky Sikes)

Kathleen's Short and Sweet, Tulsa, Okla. (Kathleen Short)

La Marquise, New Orleans, La. (Maurice Delechelle)

Michael's Catering, New Orleans, La.

Mr. B's Restaurant, New Orleans, La. (Ralph and Cindy Brennan)

Napoleon House, New Orleans, La. (Sal Impastato)

New Swiss Hôtel, Atlanta, Ga.

Oak Alley Plantation, Vacherie, La. (Zeb Mayhew)

The Old Edward's Inn, Highlands, N.C. (Pat and Rip Benton)

Ritz-Carlton-Buckhead, Atlanta, Ga. (Helene Adler Popowski)

The Silver Ladle, Mobile, Ala. (Homer McClure)

Soigné Sweets, Tulsa, Okla. (Suzan Schatz)

Southern Hospitality Systems, New Orleans, La. (John Rowland)

Don Strange Catering, San Antonio, Tex.

A Taste of Europe by Gisela, Fort Worth, Tex. (Gisela Techt)

Ruth Varisco, New Orleans, La.

Jody Walls and Company, Tulsa, Okla.

Sylvia Weinstock, New York, N.Y.

Flower Shops & Designers

Alamo Plants and Petals, San Antonio, Tex. (Sue Paciocco)

Anything Grows, New Orleans, La. (Tim Trapolin, Pam Hayne, and Louisette Brown)

Anne Bristow, Richmond, Va.

Casa Maia, New York, N.Y. (Ronaldo Maia)

The Cottage Garden, Atlanta, Ga. (Tom Woodham and Ryan Gainey)

Price Davis, Winston-Salem, N.C.

Betty Drennen/Dorothy Naughton, Birmingham, Ala.

Evelynton Plantation, Charles City, Va. (Annie Black)

Flowers Unlimited (by Jesse), New Orleans, La.

Forget-Me-Not Flowers, Atlanta, Ga. (Darva Stapleton)

Rusty Glenn Flowers, Dallas, Tex.

Haertel's, Mobile, Ala. (Tom Bailey)

In Bloom, Inc., Houston, Tex. (Bobb Wirfel and Scott McCool)

LaVoy Flowers, Atlanta, Ga. (David LaVoy)

Magazine Flowers, New Orleans, La. (Gordon Morey)

Michael's Florist of N.W. Florida, Inc., San Destin, Fla. (Michael Redman)

Mitch's Flowers, New Orleans, La. (Mitch Hebert)

Mary Murray Flowers, Tulsa, Okla.

Occasions/Flowers by Bob, Hampton, Va. (Bob Derr)

Petals/Colonial Herbs, Fortson, Ga.

Rohm's Floral Designs, New Orleans, La. (Cricket, Shirley, and Don Hermann)

Barbara and Mark Rudolph, Bethesda, Md.

Snapdragon, Washington, D.C., (Lou Dragon)

Tulip Tree, Nashville, Tenn. (Mark O'Bryan)

Zimlich Brothers, Mobile, Ala. (Ron Barrett)

Invitations/Stationery

Betty Hunley Designs, New Orleans, La.

Pacer's Papers, Atlanta, Ga. (Jackie Slutzky)

PS The Letter, Ft. Worth, Tex. (Carter Bowden)

The Stationer, New Orleans, La. (Mary Rose and Martha Wailes)

Jewelry, Department, Antique, and Wedding Specialty Stores

Coleman E. Adler & Sons, New Orleans, La.

Bromberg's, Birmingham, Ala. (Frank Bromberg III)

Country French Connection, Atlanta, Ga. (Jan Shoffner)

Estella's, New Orleans, La. (Kent Ozborn)

Legacy, Fort Worth, Tex. (Rhonda Aguillard)

T. A. Lorton, Tulsa, Okla. (Tracie Lorton)

Lucullus, New Orleans, La. (Patrick Dunne)

Mignon Faget Ltd., New Orleans, La.

Neiman-Marcus Bridal Salon, Dallas, Tex.

Petit Jardin, New Orleans, La. (Ann Lee Carrere)

Rich's, Atlanta, Ga. (Pam Parker)

Saks Fifth Avenue Bridal Salon, New Orleans, La.

Simply Gold, New Orleans, La.

Les Rubans, New Orleans, La. (Pam Ryan)

The Wedding Fantastic, San Francisco, Calif. (Kathleen Mahoney)

Other Wedding Professionals

Candlelight Linens, Richmond, Va. (Carolyn Bigler)
Chattanooga Tent Company, Chattanooga, Tenn. (Andy Nolan)
Creative Stenciling, Washington, D.C. (Molly Pritchett)
Presentations, Atlanta, Ga. (Lou Winship and Katie Jackson)
Table Toppers, New Orleans, La.

Orchestras/Musicians

Ned Battista and Orchestra, Houston, Tex.
Earl Clarke and Spectrum, Tulsa, Okla.
Peter Duchin and His Orchestra, New York, N.Y.
Al Hirt, New Orleans, La.
Kings of Swing, Richmond, Va.
Jimmy Maxwell and His Orchestra, New Orleans, La.
The William Noll Orchestra, Ritz-Carlton-Buckhead, Atlanta, Ga.
Richard Raphael, Seaside, Fla.
Stereo Strings, Washington, D.C. (Louis F. Coppola)

Party/Wedding Consultants

Cache Pot, New Orleans, La. (Frances Rodgers)
Creative Parties, Washington, D.C. (Marylin Bradley)
Design Consultants, Inc., New Orleans, La. (Andre de La Barre)
Matilda Dobbs, Atlanta, Ga.
Festivists, Fort Worth, Tex. (Brice Evans)
Michelene Gary, Virginia Beach, Va.
Jerri Glass, Tulsa, Okla.
Glorious Events, Atlanta, Ga. (Jim White)
Griggs Van Horn and Associates, Atlanta, Ga. (Tony Brewer)
Brooke Lively, Fort Worth, Tex.
W. Lawrence Morse, Inc., Little Rock, Ark. (Larry Morse)
M. I. Scoggin Designs, New Orleans, La.
Temi Silver, Atlanta, Ga.
Simply Perfect Parties, Nashville, Tenn. (Teenie Buchtel)
Gale Sliger Productions, Dallas, Tex.

Wedding Dress & Veil Designers/Shops

Alice Designs, New Orleans, La. (Judy Cobb and Alice DePass)
Anne Barge for Brides, Atlanta, Ga. (Anne Barge and Matilda Dobbs)
Helen Benton, Helena, Ark.
Beshara's, Tulsa, Okla.
Bill Blass, New York, N.Y.
Chris Endemetry, Atlanta, Ga.
Gentle Arts, Inc., New Orleans, La. (Bryce Reveley)
Richard Glasgow, New York, N.Y.
Annie Heckler, Atlanta, Ga.
Carolina Herrera, New York, N.Y.
Jim Hjelm, New York, N.Y.
House of Broel, New Orleans, La.
Pat Kerr, Memphis, Tenn., and New York, N.Y.
Yvonne LaFleur, New Orleans, La.
Arnold Scassi, New York, N.Y.
Vera Wang, New York, N.Y.
Watters & Watters, Dallas, Tex.

Wedding Photographers

Caston's at Regency Square, Richmond, Va.
Rita Chiesa, Birmingham, Ala.
Bea Daily Photographer, Ft. Walton Beach, Fla.
Claire Flanders, Washington, D.C.
Catherine Strauss Galloway, Seaside, Fla.
Brian Gibbons, New Orleans, La.
Grevy Photography, New Orleans, La.
John Haynesworth Photography, Dallas, Tex.
Jennifer Jennings, San Antonio, Tex.
John McCormick Photography, Tulsa, Okla.
Denis Reggie, Atlanta, Ga.
Wittmayer Photography, Atlanta, Ga.

Index

Photography Credits

Unless otherwise indicated, all color photographs are by Fran Brennan. Other photographers and sources of photographic material are as follows:

Courtesy Charlotte Anderson/Haynesworth Photography: 163.

Courtesy Atlanta Historical Society: 48, 51, 116, 161.

Courtesy of Biltmore Estate, Asheville, N.C.: 118, 187.

Courtesy Bill Blass: 52.

Courtesy Mimi and John Bowen: Grevy Photography, 54.

Courtesy Jack and Ann Brittain and their children: 11.

Courtesy Chattanooga Tent Company, Chattanooga, Tenn.: David Schilling, 166 (right), 173.

Rita Chiesa, Birmingham, Ala.: 59, 133 (right).

Courtesy Colonial Williamsburg: 12.

Russell Cross, Richmond, Va.: 6, 38, 39, 41 (right), 199 (left), 207, 221

Culver Pictures, Inc., New York, N.Y.: 27.

Courtesy Betty Drennen: 58.

David Durham, Birmingham, Ala.: 146.

Tom Eckerle, New York, N.Y.: 82 (right).

Claire Flanders, Washington, D.C.: 108 (left), 110 (right), 111 (right), 113.

Brian Gibbons, New Orleans, La.: 28 (right), 29 (bottom), 60 (right), 64 (right), 86 (left), 128, 147, 164, 177.

Grevy Photography, New Orleans, La.: 20 (right), 22 (right), 37, 64 (left), 140.

Courtesy Lisa Ruffin Harrison: 10, 50.

Courtesy Lisa Ruffin Harrison/Dementi-Foster Photography: 179 (right).

Courtesy Carolina Herrera: 53.

Courtesy Historic New Orleans Collection: 15.

Courtesy Jim Hjelm: 53.

Courtesy Ida Mae's Cakes of Distinction, Jacksboro, Tex.: 199 (right).

Image Bank South, Atlanta, Ga.: Garry Gay, 24; Michael Skott, 30.

Courtesy Alice Jackson: 28 (left).

Jennifer Jennings, San Antonio, Tex.: 205.

Courtesy Library of Congress: 14, 138 (left).

Sylvia Martin, Birmingham, Ala.: 145, 165.

Courtesy Player Butler Michelsen: Caston's at Regency Square, 40, 41 (left), 178 (right), 179 (left).

Courtesy Crystal Moffett: Mike Posey Photography, 55.

Narinder Sall, Jupiter, Fla.: 9, 46.

Rowland Scherman, Birmingham, Ala.: 2, 20 (left), 21, 22 (left), 23, 34 (left), 178 (left).

David Schilling, Atlanta, Ga.: 45, 61, 74, 120, 121, 142, 153, 162, 185, 194, 198.

Stock South/Atlanta, Ga.: Stephen R. Brown, 26 (left); William Schemmel, 8; Pete Winkel, 26 (right).

Courtesy *Veranda* magazine, Atlanta, Ga.: Murray Riss, Memphis, Tenn., 189 (right); David Schilling, 123, 166 (left), 174.

Courtesy Vera Wang: 53.

Courtesy Winterthur Museum and Gardens, Winterthur, Del.: 13, 49.

Courtesy Woodruff-Fontaine House, Memphis, Tenn.: 95.